D0146824

Donald L. Boisvert
Robert E. Goss
Editors

Gay Catholic Priests and Clerical Sexual Misconduct
Breaking the Silence

Pre-publication
REVIEW . . .

"The shrewdness and brilliance of the Holy Spirit are at work in the heart of the world and the church. This series of essays chronicles and diagnoses the series of steps the Roman Church has taken to silence criticism and escape the consequences of the sexual abuse crisis in the priesthood.

The essays in this book analyze how the hierarchy of the Roman Catholic Church has responded to the sexual abuse crisis in a series of moves that have as their primary motive to preserve the institution and bolster its power and authority. The hierarchy are desperately trying to hang on to a celibate, exclusively male clergy, adamantly refusing to ordain married men or women, and will try to eliminate all gay candidates for priesthood.

In the shrewdness of the Holy Spirit, these moves will guarantee the disappearance of cultic celibate priesthood. It will bring about the reform of the Church begun by Vatican II, which renamed the Church "the People of God"! The Church will become the Church that Jesus intended: a Church of equals; a Church where the Holy Spirit can designate anyone—whether straight or gay, male or female, celibate or partnered—to be the presider and leader in the community; a Church where authority will lie in the spiritual power to discern spirits, to listen and hear what the Spirit is saying through the People of God. This collection of essays will make a powerful contribution to bringing about that desperately needed reform. For that I am profoundly grateful to its authors."

John J. McNeill, PhD
Former Jesuit; Author,
The Church and The Homosexual,
Taking a Chance on God,
Freedom, Glorious Freedom,
and *Both Feet Firmly Planted in Midair;*
Co-founder, Dignity, New York City

Gay Catholic Priests and Clerical Sexual Misconduct
Breaking the Silence

HARRINGTON PARK PRESS®
Gay and Lesbian Studies
John P. De Cecco, PhD
Editor in Chief

From Drags to Riches: The Untold Story of Charles Pierce by John Wallraff

Lytton Strachey and the Search for Modern Sexual Identity: The Last Eminent Victorian by Julie Anne Taddeo

Before Stonewall: Activists for Gay and Lesbian Rights in Historical Context edited by Vern L. Bullough

Sons Talk About Their Gay Fathers: Life Curves by Andrew R. Gottlieb

Restoried Selves: Autobiographies of Queer Asian/Pacific American Activists edited by Kevin K. Kumashiro

Queer Crips: Disabled Gay Men and Their Stories by Bob Guter and John R. Killacky

Dirty Young Men and Other Gay Stories by Joseph Itiel

Queering Creole Spiritual Traditions: Lesbian, Gay, Bisexual, and Transgender Participation in African-Inspired Traditions in the Americas by Randy P. Conner with David Hatfield Sparks

How It Feels to Have a Gay or Lesbian Parent: A Book by Kids for Kids of All Ages by Judith E. Snow

Getting It On Online: Cyberspace, Gay Male Sexuality, and Embodied Identity by John Edward Campbell

Pederasts and Others: Urban Culture and Sexual Identity in Nineteenth-Century Paris by William A. Peniston

Men, Homosexuality, and the Gods: An Exploration into the Religious Significance of Male Homosexuality in World Perspective by Ronald E. Long

Mucho Macho: Seduction, Desire, and the Homoerotic Lives of Latin Men by Chris Girman

Side by Side: On Having a Gay or Lesbian Sibling edited by Andrew R. Gottlieb

Gay Catholic Priests and Clerical Sexual Misconduct: Breaking the Silence edited by Donald L. Boisvert and Robert E. Goss

Straight Talk About Gays in the Workplace: Creating an Inclusive, Productive Environment for Everyone in Your Organization, Third Edition by Liz Winfeld

Gendered Outcasts and Sexual Outlaws: Sexual Oppression and Gender Hierarchies in Queer Men's Lives edited by Christopher Kendall and Wayne Martino

Suffer the Children: A Prescription for the Ills of American Youth Sexuality by Richard Osborne

Gay Catholic Priests and Clerical Sexual Misconduct

Breaking the Silence

Donald L. Boisvert
Robert E. Goss
Editors

HPP

Harrington Park Press®
An Imprint of The Haworth Press, Inc.
New York • London • Oxford

For more information on this book or to order, visit
http://www.haworthpress.com/store/product.asp?sku=5331

or call 1-800-HAWORTH (800-429-6784) in the United States
and Canada or (607) 722-5857 outside the United States and Canada

or contact orders@HaworthPress.com

Published by

Harrington Park Press®, an imprint of The Haworth Press, Inc., 10 Alice Street, Binghamton, NY 13904-1580.

Cover design by Lora Wiggins.

Library of Congress Cataloging-in-Publication Data

Gay Catholic priests and clerical sexual misconduct : breaking the silence / Donald L. Boisvert, Robert E. Goss, editors.
    p. cm.
  Includes bibliographical references.
  ISBN 1-56023-536-5 (hardcover : alk. paper)—ISBN 1-56023-537-3 (pbk. : alk. paper)
  1. Catholic Church—Clergy—Sexual behavior. 2. Child sexual abuse by clergy. 3. Clergy—Sexual behavior. I. Boisvert, Donald L. 1951- II. Goss, Robert.

BX1912.9.G39 2005
282'.086'642—dc22

                                                                        2004021934

CONTENTS

ABOUT THE EDITORS

Donald L. Boisvert, PhD, teaches in the Department of Religion at Concordia University in Montreal, where he is also involved with the sexuality studies program. His research interests cover religion and sexuality—more specifically gay male spirituality—and Catholic popular culture, and he serves as co-chair of the Gay Men's Issues in Religion Group of the American Academy of Religion. His publications include *Out on Holy Ground: Meditations on Gay Men's Spirituality* and *Sanctity and Male Desire: A Gay Reading of Saints.*

Robert E. Goss, ThD, is Pastor of the MCC Church in the Valley and author of *Queering Christ: Beyond Jesus ACTED UP,* a Lambda Literary Awards finalist. He is former co-chair of the Gay Men's Issues in Religion Group of the American Academy of Religion and serves on the National Advisory Board of the Center for Lesbian and Gay Studies in Religion and Ministry of the Pacific School of Religion.

CONTRIBUTORS

Marie Cartier, Catholic feminist and activist. She is currently a doctoral student in theology at the Claremont School of Religion.

Chuck Colbert, gay Catholic columnist and a student at the Jesuit Weston School of Theology.

Lorine M. Getz, PhD, author of *Flannery O'Connor: Her Life, Library, and Book Reviews* and co-editor of *The Rite of Redemption: An Interpretation of the Films of Ingmar Bergman* and *Voices That Matter.*

William Glenn, former Jesuit and an activist in San Francisco. He serves on the local board of the Center for Lesbian and Gay Studies at the Pacific School of Religion.

Mary E. Hunt, PhD, co-director of the Women's Alliance for Theology, Ethics, and Ritual (WATER) and author of *Fierce Tenderness: A Feminist Theology of Friendship* and co-editor of *Good Sex: Feminist Perspective from the World's Religions.*

Edward J. Ingebretsen, PhD, director of American studies at Georgetown University. He is author of *Maps of Hell: Religious Terror as Memory from the Puritans to Stephen King* and *At Stake: Monsters and the Rhetoric of Fear in Public Culture.*

Jay Emerson Johnson, PhD, Episcopal priest and co-chair of the Gay Men's Issues in Religion of the American Academy of Religion and program director for the Center of Gay and Lesbian Studies at the Pacific School of Religion.

Mark D. Jordan, PhD, professor in the Department of Religion at Emory University. He is author of *The Silence of Sodom: Homosexuality in Modern Catholicism, The Invention of Sodomy in Christian Theology,* and *The Ethics of Sex.*

Michael Kelly, former Franciscan and founder of the Rainbow Sash Movement in Australia, a group that challenges the Roman Catholic bishops on their position regarding homosexuality.

Karen Lebacqz, PhD, professor of ethics at the Pacific School of Religion and author/co-editor of six books, including *Justice in an Unjust World* and *Ethics of Spiritual Care.*

David M. Mellott, PhD candidate in the sociology of religion at Emory University, and a former Roman Catholic priest and seminary professor.

Bernard Schlager, PhD, former program director of the Center for Lesbian and Gay Studies at the Pacific School of Religion and now serves as a consultant to the center.

Mary Ann Tolbert, PhD, a professor of Biblical studies at the Pacific School of Religion and executive director of the Center for Lesbian and Gay Studies. She is the author of *Sowing the Gospel: Mark's World in Literary-Historical Perspective* and co-editor of *Reading from This Place: Social Location and Biblical Interpretation from a Global Perspective* and *Teaching the Bible: The Discourses and Politics of Biblical Pedagogy.*

Introduction

This is a timely book. The current hysteria of the general Catholic populace, American bishops, and the Vatican has sadly tended to link the issue of clerical pedophilia with homosexuality. Much of the current crisis surrounding clergy sexual abuse is due to a church culture that for centuries has failed to develop and advocate a healthy sexual ethic and has kept secrets to prevent Catholics and outsiders from becoming aware of how important male-to-male desire has been to the development of its clergy. The Roman Catholic Church has long been fiercely homophobic, yet it is an intensely homoerotic culture. Men attracted to men have formed the ranks of its priests, male religious, bishops, cardinals, and popes. Some have been icons of sanctity and even raised to the level of saints. The Catholic Church has used a wide range of homophobic strategies to mask a homoerotic clerical culture. This has resulted in institutional secrecy, keeping scandals and the true nature of its priesthood hidden from public view.

Until recently, the Catholic hierarchy has chosen circumlocution to silence the issue of clerical sexual abuse. When evidence of a priest's homosexual behavior with a sexual minor was discovered, the priest was often moved to a new parish without the benefit of long-term psychotherapy to deal with sexual abuse and immaturity. Parishioners were seldom warned about clerical sexual predators. This has left a trail of human debris, with young people trying to cope with sexual abuse by moral and religious figures. One of the co-editors recently witnessed a one-man performance addressing clerical sexual abuse at a retreat for queer individuals. The performer portrayed nonverbally the loss of innocence and trust resulting from the sexual acts of violation. Afterward, in private conversation, he talked about how it impacted his faith and how as an adult he confronted his abuser, but the priest refused to acknowledge it ever happened. The rage of the victims and of American Catholics is truly unparalleled in American Catholic history.

Many American Catholics support the removal of bishops for their complicity in protecting clerical predators. In Dallas, the U.S. bishops listened to victims of clerical sexual abuse and adopted a policy of zero tolerance for any allegations against a priest. The slightest allegation of sexual abuse has led to automatic suspension of priests without any ecclesial due process. Victims of clerical abuse have asked, "Why did it take thirty years for the American bishops to listen to the victims?" Members of the Catholic laity have demanded the right to speak and have used the media and litigation to make their concerns heard. The fear of financial payoffs from impending lawsuits has motivated bishops to an extreme, almost hysterical, position of overreaction, while the protection of Catholic children apparently did not warrant sufficient motivation and reason in past years. The American bishops in Dallas still fell short of admitting their responsibility and complicity with the current scandal. They just could bring themselves to a public admission of their wrongdoing. Thus the laity perceives that there is one set of rules for those clergy in positions of power and another set for the rest.

In 2000, Judy Thomas, a reporter for the *Kansas City Star,* wrote a wonderfully sensitive story of Catholic priests who had died of AIDS. The numbers of priests dying from HIV-related illness was four times the numbers of the general gay male population. Catholics responded to the story with either denial or charges of Catholic bashing. When the *Kansas City Star* was able to document nearly 400 deaths of priests to HIV (though the number of deaths is perhaps ten times the documented cases among gay men), the Catholic hierarchy ignored the story. Its silence attempted to discredit the story, but most candidates entering Catholic seminaries and religious communities are now required to undergo HIV testing.

Later that year, two books were published addressing the priesthood as a gay profession. In *Papal Sin,* Garry Wills (2000) noted that Pope John Paul II exaggerated the doctrine of papal infallibility to create a "structure of deceit." Wills claims that John Paul II's real legacy to his church is a gay priesthood. Many priests, Wills claims, leave to marry women, thus leaving a gay clerical culture. In his book, *The Changing Face of the Catholic Priesthood,* Reverend Donald Cozzens (2000), a respected rector of the Cleveland seminary, argues that the Catholic priesthood has become a gay profession. Cozzens cites studies from 1989 which estimate that 48.5 percent of Catholic priests and 55.1 percent of seminarians are gay. He observes that this gay profession will prevent heterosexual men from becoming priests. Bishops have discussed this issue behind closed doors for decades.

The current sex panic of the Catholic Church which wrongly conflates homosexuality with pedophilia may lead to witch-hunts that will weed out many good gay priests and seminarians. No rational evidence suggests that homosexuals are more prone to child molestation than heterosexuals, but conservative Catholic bishops, in response to the general hysteria surrounding this sensitive issue, have still argued that homosexuality leads to child molestation. Significant numbers of gay priests work honorably in a wide range of ministries, but many of them are angry and fearful at the Vatican's preparation of a document to impose a sexual inquisition and weed out gay candidates for religious life and the priesthood.

It is an old strategy of scapegoating homosexuals for the failure of bishops to address the sexual abuse problem decades ago. The Vatican and the American Catholic hierarchy are playing on cultural homophobia to deflect the rage directed against themselves. The current scandal is about dishonesty and maintaining pastoral power at the expense of abused children or even gay priests. The hierarchy refuses to be honest about the dynamics of this homoerotic clerical caste and even their participation within a homoerotic subculture. The post-Vatican II church had developed a policy of "don't ask, don't tell, don't become public," much like that of the American military. This policy made an accommodation for the gay priesthood, ranging from closeted conservative priests and bishops to priests and their lovers to celibate gay priests. This accommodation was reached to preserve ecclesial power at the expense of honest and open discussion about gay men in ministry or the larger issue of the failure of celibacy, as many other denominations have engaged in for the past two decades.

The Vatican spokesman, Joaquin Navarro-Valls, told *The New York Times* that homosexual men cannot be ordained. He further compared the situation of a gay man who becomes a priest to a gay man who marries a woman (Henneberger, 2002). Such a marriage can be annulled and considered invalid from the start. This would mean that the ordinations of many, perhaps more than half, of the Catholic bishops and clergy in the United States should be invalid. This is an incredible statement that goes against centuries of sacramental theology. Many responsible and good gay priests are serving the church. For instance, Father Mychal Judge, a New York fire department chaplain, gave his life as a hero of September 11, 2001. Yet if the Vatican has its way, Father Mychal, who was openly gay, could be judged an invalid priest along with thousands of others. This response by the Vatican is another telling example of cultural and religious hysteria in response to the perennial human fact of same-sex male desire. It reveals a church that is unable to deal honestly and forthrightly with the adult sexuality of its ministers.

The American bishops have blamed the current crisis of clerical abuse on American pansexual culture, the gay liberation movement, and most insidiously on gay priests. This is no different from the wild and irresponsible accusations made by other religious leaders such as Jerry Falwell or Pat Robertson with respect to what they see as a secularized, Godless culture. The president of the American Conference of Bishops, Bishop Wilton Gregory, has stated that it would be wise not to admit gay men to seminaries in light of the recent scandals. Although social scientific research has demonstrated that heterosexuals are the predominant perpetrators of sexual abuse of minors, the Catholic bishops ignore the scientific research in much the same way as they ignored clerical predators in the past. They zero in on sexual abuse of young boys and fail to pay much attention to the abuse of young girls or vulnerable women.

The Catholic hierarchy is scapegoating gay priests for the sexual abuse and arguing, rather naively, that gay men cannot be priests. Cardinal Anthony Bevilacqua of Philadelphia stated the following in a news conference:

> There is a difference between a heterosexual and homosexual candidate for the priesthood. A heterosexual candidate is taking on a good thing, becoming a priest, and giving up a good thing, the desire to have a family. A gay seminarian, even a chaste one, by his orientation is not a suitable candidate for the priesthood, even if he did not commit an act of [gay sex]. He is giving up what the church considers an abomination. (Talbot, 2002, p. 18)

Many insiders and outsiders are wondering if an inquisition will be launched within the Catholic Church against its gay members. Archbishop Tracisio Bertone, secretary of the Vatican's Doctrinal Congregational, stated that "persons with a homosexual inclination should not be admitted to the seminary" (Tavis, 2002). All the institutional signs are there. The Vatican is preparing a document against the admission of gay seminarians; it has sent out inspectors to seminaries to weed out homosexual subcultures and ensure proper moral Catholic doctrine is being taught. A U.S. Vatican official at the Congregation for Bishops, Andrew R. Baker stated that homosexuality is a "disordered attraction" and that it can "never 'image' God and never contribute to the good of the person or society" (Tavis, 2002).

The media patterns of scapegoating and inquisition are in place, and the princes of the church are willing to sacrifice their priests and seminarians for their beautiful "queer" robes, personal prestige, and power rather than to take personal responsibility for their involvement in clerical sexual misconduct, just as some are unwilling to admit their homoerotic desires to themselves or to others. The problem is with a church structure and hierarchy that fosters evasion, dishonesty, silencing, scapegoating, misogyny, internalized homophobia, and hypocrisy.

THE SILENCE OF SODOM

This book evolved from the publication of Mark Jordan's *The Silence of Sodom: Homosexuality in Modern Catholicism* in 2000. Jordan is a gay theologian and medievalist, holding the chair of Catholic studies at Emory University. In *Silence of Sodom,* Jordan delineates how the Catholic hierarchy has used various rhetorical strategies for centuries to silence the fact that male-to-male desire has been vital to the development of the Catholic priesthood. The hierarchy's denunciations of homosexuals mask the issue of homosexuality within the priesthood and religious orders. Jordan's eloquent and thought-provoking book has been attacked by neoconservative Catholic groups and generally ignored by the Catholic hierarchy.

In November 2000, as a way of marking the book's importance and honoring Jordan for his work, the Gay Men's Issues in Religion group of the American Academy of Religion organized a panel of scholars on *Silence of Sodom* from the United States and Canada. The panel consisted of papers from Donald Boisvert, Mary Hunt, Robert Goss, and Edward Ingebretsen, with Mark Jordan responding to the individual presentations. The session was well attended by a number of Catholic scholars and priests. The papers were very well received, and a number of the attendees encouraged us to publish them.

This book expands the group of contributors to include a number of other men and women from a variety of social locations and, in one case, faiths. From the male voices, there are three former Jesuits, a Dominican, a Franciscan, and a former seminarian with the Congregation of the Blessed Sacrament. Three were ordained as priests. They provide gay insider experience to explain the closeted dynamics of the Roman Catholic clerical system. This Catholic system is an all-male caste, and such homosociality also breeds a deeply ingrained misogyny. It needs the voice of feminists to provide a critique of the misogyny and its interrelationship with homophobia. Several women contributors were invited to look at the issue of homoerotic clerical culture steeped in misogyny and homophobia. We are glad to have their feminist voices as correctives to the gay-insider voices.

The volume has been divided into four sections: different perspectives on gay priests, ecclesial misogyny, power games and abuse, and Mark Jordan's response to various issues raised by the contributors. We want to honor the men and women who speak in this volume. It has been the failure of the Roman Catholic Church to appreciate their gifts, talents, and contributions in keeping a Catholic spirituality alive, albeit a queer spirituality. Moreover, these are individuals who care deeply and passionately about their faith and who see same-sex desire as very much a blessing and a gift to their fellow believers. In all cases, they speak with eloquence and pain, yet also with a great deal of pride and a tinge of justifiable divine righteousness. The Catholic Church, after all, continues to deny and undermine the value of their queer experience.

DIFFERENT PERSPECTIVES ON GAY PRIESTS

The text opens with a contribution by sociologist of religion Donald Boisvert. Boisvert delineates his discovery of his own attractions to men within the "clerical hothouse that was the seminary." Catholic seminary culture glorifies the male saint, fostering an ever-shifting and murky boundary between desiring sainthood and the saint's body itself. How many gay seminarians have lusted after the beautiful Saint Sebastian as he was depicted in erotic martyrdom, or Saint Dominic Savio, or any number of other robust ideals of sanctity and beautiful male bodies! Boisvert speaks about how Dominic Savio, a saintly Italian youth, became his boyfriend and how he struggled to be like him, thereby graduating from religious devotion to erotic desire. He recovers Catholic saints as queer icons, archetypes that affirm sexuality as a gift to humanity and homosexuality as a legitimate site of human holiness. There is much potential to a recovery of queer Catholicism within a sex-positive spirituality. A queer hagiography could undermine Catholic theological discourse on homosexuality and plumb the depths of a positive homoerotic clerical culture. It can begin to pioneer a queer Catholic discourse, full of a history of pain and erotic delight.

David Mellott speaks as a seminary professor and Catholic priest involved in the training and formation of students. He describes how seminary administrators told him and other faculty that under no circumstances were seminary students allowed to raise or explore issues of sexual orientation. Such issues were to be discussed only in spiritual direction and in confidence. Being gay was not grounds for dismissal as long as a gay seminarian was celibate.

Seminarians were incorporated into a culture in which open discussion of sexuality did not occur. They were formed into a culture of secrecy. Mellott has raised questions about the dissonance between students' lives and public silence about homosexuality, between what they actually believe and what the church officially teaches about homosexuality. Tragically, Mellot's essay details the mechanisms of self-deception that have led many priests to maladjusted behaviors such as excessive drinking, double lives, anonymous sex in bathhouses, and the development of a false public persona.

Gay historian Allen Berube has observed that sex panics have occurred during politically conservative times. A sex panic is a "moral crusade that leads to crackdowns on sexual outsiders" (Berube, 1997, p. 4). Former Jesuit priest Edward Ingebretsen articulates a sex panic that is occurring within the Roman Catholic hierarchy, not directed merely at outside laypersons but at priests themselves. He points out the contradictions between Catholic theological statements about homosexuality and how they form a textual sex panic, addressing the growing visibility of the gay and lesbian movement and its supposed threat to Catholic moral teachings. Cardinal Ratzinger's infamous letter demonizes gays and lesbians as "intrinsically evil, objectively disordered." The church document announces that gays and lesbians are graced with a pathological condition. It designates a class of human beings created in the image of God as "intrinsically evil." John

Paul II echoed the sentiments of the Ratzinger document when he declared homosexuality to be an offense against Christian values. The Vatican's textual violence is terrorist; it attempts to exact silence, but at what cost? Both priests and gay and lesbian Catholics are caught in this cycle of violence and pastoral abuse.

Edward Ingebretsen asks what happens when a gay or lesbian person seeks pastoral care under the conflicting conditions of "speaking and silence, visibility and invisibility." What happens to the gay priest who attempts to administer pastoral care? Or the closeted priest who carries out the directives of the Vatican letters? The church performs the sacraments as a means of grace but uses them to violently exclude gays and lesbians. Ingebretsen tells the story of a twenty-one-year-old student at Georgetown University, a daily communicant who came out and was refused Communion. The priest turned a sacrament of grace into a sacrament of exclusion. Perhaps this story narrates what behavior Jesus meant as the sin against the Holy Spirit in Luke 12:10. It denies and regulates the unconditional grace of God. Limiting God's grace is unforgivable.

With Protestants from mainline and fundamentalist traditions, it is often necessary to deconstruct the so-called biblical texts of terror that are applied to homosexuality. The biblical text has less authority for the Catholic laity than the hierarchy and clergy. Chuck Colbert, a gay Catholic and student at the Jesuit Weston School of Theology, responds to Jordan's *Silence of Sodom* with enthusiasm. Jordan deconstructs Catholic ecclesial authority by unmasking the contradictions between the theological rhetoric against homosexuals and the gay homosexual clerical culture. Homosexual cardinals and bishops, gay priests, lavender rectories of queer camp, and aestheticism provide a cultural context for deconstructing the authority of Catholic homo-hatred. Naturally, closeted prelates in power are often the most violent and pernicious persecutors of the queer community. Homoeroticism is thoroughly interwoven with Catholic ritual and spirituality. Can there be Catholicism without homoeroticism? The gay Catholic comes to deconstruct Catholic theological hatred and understands that at the heart of hierarchical power is a bunch of closeted and scared queens in their ornate red dresses.

Jay Johnson's chapter may stand out because he writes as an Anglican. He notes that many Anglicans read Jordan's book with sympathy and some measure of condescension. Queer Catholics have not the courage to flee institutional violence to join their "liminal first cousins across the Thames." Not all is well within the Anglican institution, however, even though there are dioceses that celebrate same-sex unions and ordain noncelibate gay and lesbian clergy. Johnson points out that religious institutions, both Catholic and Anglican, have made a fundamental compromise of the Incarnation for the sake of maintaining power. Johnson's essay is a good transitional essay to the next two sections of the anthology that look at institutional misogyny, homophobia, and the abuse of power. Institutional silence threatens the revitalization of a textual tradition, and Johnson points to heretics who refused to adopt the church's disavowal of its own tradition of liminality. Queer Catholics and Anglicans are both necessary to a recovery of Jesus' message to outsiders.

ECCLESIAL MISOGYNY AND HOMOPHOBIA

The center of the collection is a critique of misogyny. Throughout most of Catholic history, maleness has been asserted as superior to femaleness in a complex of anti-body ideologies, interwoven with misogyny and homophobia. There is no way of dealing with contemporary Catholic institutional homophobia without dismantling its misogyny, for homophobia is embedded in a deep misogyny. Ordained males are the primary power holders in the Catholic Church. This section examines the interrelationship between misogyny and homophobia and between sexism and heterosexism within the Catholic Church.

Catholic lesbian feminist Mary Hunt opens the section on institutional misogyny by tackling three areas of concern: (1) the Catholic gay structures of duplicity, (2) the economics of ecclesial injustice, and (3) their implications for women. Hunt verifies the duplicity of gay clergy, professing celibacy yet remaining sexually active. Bishops have been aware of noncelibate clergy for some time but have maintained the secret to keep the hierarchical, clerical caste in power. Hunt's second exploration unmasks gay clerical privilege and raises the issue of economic injustice. Catholic employees within churches and schools are grossly underpaid while clergy reside in luxury in rectories. She claims that the Catholic priesthood is a "large system of gay male prostitution." Women priests would disrupt this homoerotic clerical culture, based upon the nuptial imagery of Jesus as bridegroom and church as bride.

Where Hunt leaves off in her exploration, former Jesuit priest Robert Goss picks up the question of the Catholic priesthood as expressing a female masculinity. Goss describes how he and his Jesuit lover Frank began the process of leaving the Jesuits and how friends threw a wedding shower for them. The event was magnified to epic proportions in the minds and imaginations of other Jesuits, construing it as a Jesuit wedding performed by the rector of the seminary. Goss explores the gender-bending nature of seminarians and clergy. The terrible secret of closeted, clerical culture is not its homoeroticism but its misogyny. Women must be kept outside because they would reveal that the Catholic Church already has (fe)male priests, who enjoy dressing up in ornate vestments.

Goss picks up an insight from Ingebretsen on how priests occupy a cultural space of social femininity. The priest functions similarly to a battered wife. The hierarchy psychologically batters the priest, coercing him to remain silent and keeping silent the secret of abuse. When a priest comes out as gay, he is stigmatized as a fallen woman. For Goss, priestly (fe)masculinity has not threatened the rigid binary gender system, for it lacks the prophetic transgressions such as dyke masculinity or gay effeminacy because it is so wedded to a deeply ingrained misogyny and a culture of secrecy. It lacks the parodic critique of out queer individuals while it supports the subordination of women to an all-male clerical caste.

Marie Cartier wanted to be ordained a Catholic priest early on but was denied so because she was a woman. She describes her life as a Catholic dissident who finds sexism just as upsetting as homophobia. Both are interconnected issues. Why do priests have the privilege and freedom of leading double lives while the lives of lesbian nuns are tightly regulated and some are even separated because they are seen as "particular friends"? Cartier also asks why gay activists fight for their rights within the church but fail to commit themselves to women's ordination. Sexism crosses over gay boundaries, and often gay Catholics will make excuses for the heinous behaviors of the Catholic Church in allocating monies to support the ballot initiative Proposition 22 in California to deny the recognition of same-sex unions. They are driven by nostalgia for a church that has never been their home and that has never accepted them as fully legitimate members.

Lorine Getz explores the relationship between ecclesial homophobia and misogyny that creates a *"dis*ease" and a *"dis*honesty" among church leaders. Getz notes the widespread illegal and immoral practices of clergy sexual abuse, long ignored by the Catholic hierarchy. She challenges the recent Vatican strategy to obfuscate the issue by shifting blame for clerical sexual abuse on homosexuality. Getz narrates two stories of a heterosexual male graduate student pulled into a homoerotic relationship with his clergy adviser and the student's subsequent suicide. No social sanctions were levied against the priest for abusing his authority. Getz contrasts the unhealthy behavior of the clergy faculty with her brother who came out and established one of the most effective statewide HIV-prevention efforts. It is sad that the church protected the priest and ignored his homoerotic abuse of power over students while her own brother who was saving lives could not find a home within the Catholic Church.

Mary Ann Tolbert raises a significant question in the current atmosphere of clerical sexual misconduct: "Where have all the young girls gone?" She cites the statistics from Sipes's study that for the past twenty-five years, twice as many Catholic priests have been sexually involved with females as with males. Cardinal Francis George distinguishes between a moral monster such as the Boston priest John Geoghan who molested some ninety boys and a cleric who gets drunk and engages in sex with a sixteen- or seventeen-year-old girl. Although both are crimes, the focus on same-sex crimes reveals the heterosexism that the church is using in protecting itself during the current climate of sexual scandal. Tolbert notes that heterosexism trivializes the victimization of females by clergy abusers. Heterosexism makes the story of sexual abuse of male youths more dramatic and more heinous.

GAMES OF POWER AND ABUSE

Michael Kelly analyzes an article he wrote: "'Father I am Troubled': The Secret Life of Gay Priests." It was published in the *Sydney Morning Herald* and precipitated a letter to all the Catholic churches from Australian Archbishop George Pell. For Kelly, Archbishop Pell's response is an example of hysterical speech, attempting to keep the lid on the secrecy of gay priests. Pell asserts the Catholic teaching on human sexuality in heterosexual marriage only. It stops the discussion of gay priests and their need for sexual intimacy. Kelly notes that Australian media sources did not pick up the story. Pell may have intimidated the media, but he did not fool the Catholic laity who had begun to accept the fact of gay priests. Michael Kelly offers some reflections on breaking the silence about gay priests. It is necessary to break the silence on the secrecy of the Catholic closet. Because of the publicity generated by clerical sexual abuse scandals, Catholic hierarchs are scapegoating gay priests and threatening witch-hunts to weed out gay seminarians. Gay priests must have no illusion that the system is benign, and it is now time for queer Catholics to defend gay priests.

Bernard Schalger recounts his entrance into minor seminary and the Dominican order. Many of his Dominican classmates found the church's teaching on homosexuality and sexuality unhealthy but could not voice their misgivings within the current climate of enforced silence. Schlager realized that he could live as gay within religious life only if he agreed to enforce the codes of silence about gay priests. It is no secret that bishops and religious orders have admitted gay men into seminaries for years. The current crisis of clerical sexual abuse of minors has provided the hierarchy with an opportunity not only to discuss the issue of gay priests but also to lay blame upon gay priests for sexual abuse rather than take responsibility for their decades of complicity in protecting sexual predators and failing to protect minors. Bernard Schlager follows Jordan in calling for queer people to break the silence of Sodom, which thoroughly informs official Catholic teaching on homosexuality.

William Glenn picks up the question of scapegoating raised by both Kelly and Schlager. He makes it evident in a meditative reflection that this scapegoating is related to many larger issues: the silencing of priests and laity, misogyny, the church's dogmatic heritage, secrecy, and institutional power. Glenn relates the story of a meeting at the White House with First Lady Hillary Clinton. He was the only male in attendance, but the women were intuitively aware that at the heart of homophobia was the fear of the feminine. Glenn looks to the story of the woman caught in adultery in chapter 8 of John's Gospel. Like the mob of men, the encircled hierarchy looks at its victim but fails to hear the voice of Jesus. We are called to speak as Jesus did in defense of the victims of mob actions.

Ethicist Karen Lebacqz notes that gay Roman Catholics may be attracted to the priesthood because gay alternative roles are not respected whereas the priesthood has been a respectable and powerful role within the Catholic community. The assumption during the current sex-abuse scandals is that the clerical abusers are gay. Lebacqz cites the findings of a Canadian commission which discovered that only one-third of the abusers of young boys were homosexual. She challenges Jordan and current queer theory that argues for sexual fluidity and sexual identity as invented. For her, such a position opens the ground to ethical relativism. Lebacqz takes the view of studies stressing that there is a personal core damaged in victims of sexual abuse. She emphatically takes the position of the Canadian commission whose findings assert that the sexual use of children is wrong and that both social and church structures have contributed to the culture of clerical abuse of children.

Edward Ingebretsen ends the series of essays with a literary history of the genre of priest as sexual abuser. The current fury of clerical sexual abuse is fueled by the fact that priests are forbidden sex while children are ideologically perceived as pure and innocent. Ingebretsen underscores what others in this volume have noted about the hierarchical conflation of clerical sexual abuse of minors with homosexuality despite the availability of research to the contrary. He points out an inherent contradiction in the long-standing willingness of bishops to ordain gay men and to profit from their good labors while now using them as scapegoats in the current scandal. Priests are under either promises or vows of obedience. Under the all-male managerial system that has produced submissive priests, the bishops can easily offer gay priests as media fodder. Ingebretsen explores the institutional and spiritual abuse of priests who, in turn, become tormentors of pain and torture. He notes that torturers are not born but are produced. He indicts the ecclesial system of tyranny that produces abusive priests who perpetuate a cycle of abuse.

AFTER SILENCE

Mark Jordan responds to the essays by noting how the multiple sexual scandals of child abuse in Boston and the nightly television coverage retrieved *Silence of Sodom* from a host of negative Catholic reviews and made it required reading. However, the silence machines of the Catholic hierarchy have mounted an effort to do damage control with the Catholic populace, the victims of sexual abuse, and the American public.

Jordan talks about how *Silence* is a personal book, born from his conversion from a liberal Unitarian family to a queer Catholic identity with "testimony of old loves that couldn't be spoken." His queer passions were aroused to stimulate faith and discover his identity while the church pounded them into a deformed homoerotic submission. In such a violent culture, Jordan observes that most queer Catholic theology has been written at the margins of Catholic institutions. He admits that the best Catholic sexual theology will be produced outside of Catholic institutions because the church can tolerate neither public dissent nor the ambiguities requisite for such honest theological explorations. With apodictic force, he writes, "The assembly of Jesus the Messiah has always been in diaspora. Diaspora is the original and final form of the church, the mark of its burning desire for an eschaton." Queer Catholics and queer Catholic theology are stigmatized as sexual deviants in the heritage of branding heretics as such. Jordan grieves for many queer Catholics and women, the squandering of vocations, and the need to enter into exile to be queer Catholics. The diaspora is where the gospel can be authentically preached in a mire of bureaucratic concerns to preserve silence and power at the expense of lives. Catholic bureaucrats, he observes, use the current pedophilia crisis to "expand the homophobic regime they have been building since the 1980s."

Mark Jordan and the contributors in this volume have given us a compelling indictment of Roman Catholic teaching on homosexuality and sexuality. The problem is not homosexual clergy or their right to serve as priests, as the Catholic institutional response to the current crisis would have us believe. The problem is age-old Catholic hypocrisy and silence; it has attempted to regulate human sexuality without ever discovering its original blessings. The Catholic Church condemns same-sex desire in unequivocal terms, just as it marginalizes female sexuality. It keeps alive a clerical camp culture of amazing proportions and influence while simultaneously expanding a violent homophobic regime of power. Along with Jordan's final comments on the diaspora, this volume asks whether the church can survive without acknowledging and embracing this culture of sexual difference. It is time for homoerotic clerical culture to come out of the scarlet ecclesiastical closet. The time has also come for women to claim their full status as equal citizens of the church and for gay clerics to make room for them as partners. If a Catholic Stonewall cannot change the bureaucratic necrophilia, then it is time to shake the dust from our shoes and to journey into diaspora to find an authentic gospel preached with compassion and respect for the sexual lives of many faithful Catholics. This is what this timely and courageous collection of essays aims, in part, to do.

REFERENCES

Berube, Allen (1997). History of sex panics. In Proceedings of the Sex Panic Summit, November 13, San Diego, California.

Cozzens, Donald (2000). *The changing face of the Catholic priesthood.* Collegeville, MN: Liturgical Press.

Henneberger, Melinda (2002). Vatican weighs reaction to accusations of molesting clergy. *The New York Times,* March 3.

Jordan, Mark D. (2000). *The silence of Sodom: Homosexuality in modern Catholicism.* Chicago: University of Chicago Press.

Talbot, Jack (2002). Calling all gay priests. *The Gay and Lesbian Review* 9(4): 18-19.

Tavis, John (2002). Vatican prepares draft directives against admitting gays as priests. *Catholic News Service,* October 8. Available at <http://www.catholicherald.com/cns/draft-gays.htm>.

Thomas, Judy L. (2000). AIDS in the priesthood: Concern grows over AIDS rate among priests. *Kansas City Star,* November 4. Available at <www.kcstar.com/projects/priests/folo1.htm>.

Wills, Garry (2000). *Papal sin: Structures of deceit.* New York: Doubleday.

PART I:
SPEAKING IN NEW
AND DIFFERENT TONGUES

Chapter 1

Celibate Men, Ambivalent Saints, and Games of Desire

Donald L. Boisvert

Four summers ago, while vacationing in Provincetown, I went into one of those classy antique stores that are so common in the gay resort. This one was a bit special. It sold, among other items, a variety of religious artifacts, and I was struck by its selection of Catholic holy cards. As a child, I used to collect, with much reverence, these tacky yet strangely moving images of pastel saints and powder-blue Virgin Marys. In the store, one in particular struck my fancy, more by what was handwritten on it than by anything else. In shades of green, it shows the image of a rather effeminate Christ putting an old-fashioned Roman chasuble on a very young, bright-eyed priest, while a golden chalice hovers seductively in the background. Obviously, it is an ordination portrait. In fact, the card, dated 1948, marks the silver jubilee of ordination of a parish priest from Huntington, West Virginia, a certain Father Jerome Hoepf. What enthralled me most was what the priest (I assume) had written on the card in red ink. It reads: "I hope you look like this some day." Perhaps it was destined as a special keepsake for a favorite nephew or a particularly pious and promising teenage boy from the priest's parish. Or perhaps some nun in the local Catholic school had given it to a slightly bookish, withdrawn youth, thinking that she had discerned in his queerness some mark of a priestly vocation. Perhaps a proud mother engraved it in her own hand for her favorite son, the one who was so smart at school and who was such a good altar boy.

This holy card brought me back, in one sentimental flash, to my childhood, to that time in my life when I yearned to be a priest and moreover, as all good Catholic boys should, a saint. It was a time when the angelic and ethereal Pius XII and the robust and earthy John XXIII in turn ruled a Catholic Church still uncertain and insecure as to her exact place in a rapidly shifting world. As the eldest male child of a French-Canadian family, I was heir to a universal Catholicism imprinted with its sense of divine election and theological righteousness. It was a church high in color and rich in its rituals and clerical privilege, a place where I felt comfortable and secure, and which imparted to me a sense of religious yearning and awe. It was a church that took itself and its privileges for granted, and certainly expected the same from others. It was the church triumphant, the best possible spiritual and material haven for a little queer boy—which is why, in fact, I so desperately wanted to be one of its acolytes, part of its chosen elite.

Perfect, I thought, my academic mind salivating profusely at the magnificent subtext hidden in those few precious words on the card. *What a wonderful introduction to a paper on the work of Mark Jordan,* I told myself in a rare fit of scholarly rapture. *What an excellent way to begin talking about the pedagogy of clerical desire, or the anointing of young, attractive men by older celibates, or the homoeroticism, so terribly loud and brash in its tightly locked closets of Catholic theological discourse about homosexuality!* I do think that this gaudy holy card has a great deal to say, in one simple but powerful sentence, about what Mark Jordan (2000) so eloquently and defiantly writes in *Silence of Sodom.* If Mark is anything like me, I suspect he would have jumped on that card, just like I did when I first saw it. It confirms what we have always known instinctively about our Catholic roots. More than anything else, I saw myself in that card. When I was growing up, my parish priests, grammar school nuns, aunts, and mother told me the same thing as what was written there. I knew, almost by osmosis, that I was chosen to be a priest, one of God's special men. Of course, the fact that I was bookish, nonathletic, an altar boy, or even unusually pious had everything to do with it. Some would have said I was odd, a sissy, queer. Others called it "having a vocation." *I* wanted to look like *that* some *day.*

Reading and rereading *Silence of Sodom* has veritably been for me one of those "Aha!" experiences that fail to happen often enough in our lives. The most basic reason has to do with the recognition factor. Its sharp observations about Catholic clerical culture ring so true with my own experience and that of so many other men my age, several of whom I knew when I was in the seminary, that I cannot help but identify strongly and even passionately with what Mark Jordan is saying. To make sense of my reaction, one needs to know something about my story. I spent five-and-a-half years in the seminary: four in minor seminary, from the ages of thirteen to seventeen, and a year-and-a-half in the novitiate, until the age of eighteen. I was with a group called the Congregation of the Most Blessed Sacrament, whose unique charisma at that time was perpetual, round-the-clock adoration of the exposed host. I have written elsewhere that these years in religious formation were for me some of the happiest of my life; they were not for me the trauma of religious discipline, or the supposed abuse, sexual or otherwise, so often claimed by others. Seminary life has forged my intellectual, spiritual, and sexual self as an adult in some very positive and enriching ways, and it still continues to do so (Boisvert, 2000).

In retrospect, however, I do recall the campiness of the whole affair, and the subtle homoeroticism simmering just beneath the surface of all the rules and rituals, ever ready to burst forth at any moment. I think that is why I felt so at home. Here I was, a gay boy (though I was not fully aware of it back then) being allowed to play priest in the company of other pubescent boys, who themselves were struggling to discover why they were where they were. And we were watched over, on a daily basis, by celibate men in skirts who would encourage us to be like them: men called to the service of an asexual, though terribly erotic and desirable, half-naked god-man. Moreover, and most significantly, our unique calling as a religious community was to service the body and blood of this god and to stand guard over him on a twenty-four-hour basis. Our lives as Blessed Sacrament religious were to be spent in adoration and contemplation of this god's publicly exposed body, encouraging others to do the same. There was a dose of both exhibitionism and voyeurism in our calling. It was almost a form of religious cruising. Though I do not recall the word *homosexual* being uttered once in all that time, what better environment than this in which to discover that one is one, or, at least, potentially so? In other words, what better place than the seminary to make your uncertain and confusing wet dreams come true? I do not mean this disrespectfully; on the contrary. I do not, for one moment, deny the beneficial impact of my seminary experience on the hopefully well-adjusted gay man I am today. It was clerical culture that formed, and continues to nourish and deepen, my gay culture. It was also clerical culture, I profoundly believe, that fashioned my nature as a man who desires other men. Though very much a taboo, the seminary nonetheless made loving men possible.

Roman Catholic clerical culture is what Mark Jordan writes about. He analyzes and condemns it, not because it does not make genuine expressions of spirituality or religious life possible, but because it is ultimately so secretive. It is composed of secrets, within secrets, within secrets. The most amazing thing of all is that this eminently fragile edifice of concealment is constructed around one major and undeniable secret, a secret which, while being vociferously condemned for everyone else, remains very much alive within the institutional confines of the church. That dirty little secret is the erotic desire of men for other men, the homoerotic longings of supposedly celibate men for others like them. Yet it continues to be denied and ostracized from the very highest levels of Roman theological authority. It fuels the vitality and the colorfulness of Catholic clerical culture, yet it remains closeted, disdained, and viciously denied. Not only does it account, in part, for traditional clerical patriarchal and misogynist thinking (see Chapter 6), it also gives rise to remarkable forms of self-hating homophobia. The open secret of homoerotic desire in the Catholic Church does what all such open secrets do so beautifully in society at large: it makes living with them possible. It also gives permission for indulgence, while paying lip service to moral incongruity and panic. What it allows for oneself, it denies to others.

Apart from naming what needs to be named, Jordan also does something else in *Silence of Sodom.* He challenges and he celebrates. The challenge is, of course, a double-edged one: addressed, in the first instance, to the church's magisterium, it also summons the believer to an engagement with his God and with his conscience. It is actually a call to honesty and to rebellion, and his last few chapters—his "schools for new speech"—ring with the vision of a man *and* a theologian who has loved much but who must move on. I like that. It bespeaks integrity, and that is the one virtue I admire most not only about *Silence of Sodom* but also that other masterful work, *The Invention of Sodomy in Christian Theology* (Jordan, 1997). I feel like yelling from the sidelines, "You go, Mark!" I also know, however, that those words of encouragement and victory can and do come back to haunt me, as indeed they should for all of us. It is one thing to admire, quite another to take up the gauntlet. Cheering is easy; engaging in the indispensable work of subversion is far more daunting. Mark Jordan, I am convinced, is a hopeful man. Why else would he celebrate so gloriously who and what we are? Why else, indeed, would he dare us to create a new language for ourselves, one not fixed by the church-defined categories of "sodomite" or "homosexual"? It is difficult for us to think beyond these labels, but think we must, and boldly.

As a way of engaging myself with his book—and of honoring it—I propose to attempt to grapple, humbly and uncertainly, with Jordan's challenge for what he calls a "queer Catholicism." Early in his text, when describing the tedium of the church's rhetorical program of teaching on homosexuality, he states: "I consider pleasure an important sign of success in moral teaching" (Jordan, 2000, p. 56). Pleasure is also significant, I strongly believe, in any discussion of what it means to be fully religious, as is desire. As a pleasure-seeking, desiring gay man formed in the clerical hothouse that was the seminary, I therefore offer these reflections, these "notes," on a queer Catholicism. I take my cue from Jordan, who summons us to a state of permanent questioning, a precious moment of intellectual engagement and discovery.

I should like to linger—for that too is a mode of pleasure—on two aspects of Jordan's sketchy though certainly highly suggestive exploration of what a queer Catholicism might look like. The first has to do with holiness, what he so rightly calls "human fullness" (2000, p. 257); the second, with language and writing, the vital and necessary tasks for the invention of new ways of seeing and being. About the latter, Jordan has this to say: "[T]he quarrel over homosexuality is not a quarrel to be settled by arguments, because the passions it provokes are not amenable to rational persuasion. Other means are necessary" (2000, p. 259). What are these "other means," and how can they be actualized? Jordan asks us to repent for having assumed the Church-imposed mantles of "sodomite" and "homosexual." Yet what leaps of the imagination are necessary in order for us to speak in a new tongue that is neither of these but something yet unspoken? Are any of us, gay theologians included, really that creative? I will set aside the question for now, but it is one that has been with me throughout my reading of *Silence of Sodom*. It still lingers on the margins of my consciousness, unsettling yet persistent in its urgency. If the task is daunting for the gay theologian, how much more so for the gay sociologist of religion, who cannot afford to fall back on the normative comforts of faith?

QUEER BOYS AND QUEER SAINTS

At the 2000 American Academy of Religion panel on Carolyn Dinshaw's (1999) brilliant book *Getting Medieval,* I recall Jordan's (2001) eloquent and elegant phrase about how touching the body of the modern homosexual really means touching a theological artifact. I have touched many artifacts in my day, some more theological—and certainly much holier—than others. As a young boy growing up in an intensely Catholic culture, however, it was the male saint in all his glorious and pious virility who was my religious object of desire, my gateway to the underlying homoeroticism lingering within myself and the institution of which I felt so much a part. When I touched, in my mind's eye, the idealized body or image of a Sebastian, a Tarcisius, a Michael, or even a Joseph, I was touching the perfect masculine body, the holy body at once sensual and spiritual. The saint was, for me, friend and icon, both holy personage and daily (and nightly) companion. It was quite irrelevant, and the thought highly suspect, whether he may have been homosexual. In wanting to be like him, in aspiring to the same heights, I was touching, through him, a normative Catholicism which, while concealing and condemning male-male desire, still encouraged me to hanker for it in the guise of the distant, sensual saint. The Catholic Church made it possible and necessary for me to want to be with other men, to love them, to model myself on them, to touch them, and, of course, to touch myself, though that was the source of much lingering and soul-deadening guilt. What the Catholic Church gives with one hand, it somehow manages to take away with the other.

The body of the male Catholic saint, so desirable in his glorified and transfigured state, not only taught me the meaning and attractiveness of holiness. It also gave me a sense of the ever-shifting boundaries between holiness and desire, between the spiritual and the erotic. This was an important life lesson, for it inculcated in me an ability to see the sacred in the sensuous, and vice versa. As a young boy, I was obsessed with Saint Dominic Savio, a fifteen-year-old Italian saint. In thinking back upon it, I can see that he was my boyfriend. My desperation in wanting to be like him (to the point of taking a self-imposed "vow" of chastity) was a way of declaring my love for him, of claiming him for myself. His very unattainability was the source of his attraction and power over me. In my relation with Dominic Savio, I learned the virtue of religious heroism. Equally important, I learned that I could fall in love with boys, even though they may have been saintly and quite beyond my reach. In fact, their incorruptibility only augmented their desirability. It was precisely in their holiness that they were most desirable, and hence most malleable and susceptible to my emerging feelings of same-sex attraction and need. The saint-as-model became the saint-as-lover. From religious devotion, I graduated to erotic desire.

Mark Jordan cautions us, however, about assuming uncritically and too readily the sinful identities—or the erotic object choice—that Roman Catholic theology has invented for us. In doing so, we continue to play the wily game of the oppressor, engaging him on terrain long since mined to cripple us.

> The position of queer abjection seems to me still to exist within theological theatre. A sodomitic sin-identity, medicalized or camped, turned therapeutic or ironic, is still in many ways a sin-identity. So, too, abjection made into the solicitation to community may also solicit us for damaging roles. (Jordan, 2001, p. 184)

These are strong words of warning. On the other hand, they could also be read as words of encouragement. If we are able to move beyond the theologically normative onto the considerably more rocky landscape of the theologically unorthodox and subversive, then perhaps we stand a chance at redemption. Such redemption is not only our own; it necessarily includes that of others like us.

Catholic culture has always had a great deal to say about human holiness, some of it quite profound and grandiose, and some of it sadly vacuous in its sentimentality. Mark Jordan's (2000) first challenge for a queer Catholicism is that it "must show an intimate relation between 'homosexuality' and holiness [but only] so that we can be queerer than 'homosexuals' were ever supposed to be" (pp. 257-258). In other words, we need to "queer" two things: sanctity *and* the understanding of the homosexual as this term is constructed by theology. The latter, as Jordan states, assuredly entails the creative calling into question and ultimate rejection of traditional categories of thought and action and, perhaps more important, the exploration of novel modes of speech emerging from the centers of new spiritual communities. We "queer" sanctity, I would argue, by the use of three interrelated strategies: first, we *do* make a case for the existence of holy homosexuals, though Jordan warns us about limiting ourselves only to this; second, we need to decipher saints in terms of their strategic possibilities as queer archetypes; and third, we must reaffirm human sexuality—homoerotic, nonprocreative, and diffused—as a legitimate site of human holiness. Saints can and should be erotic creatures, if not outrightly promiscuous ones. In fact, their very holiness, as nonnormative and outrageous as it may have been (and some of it certainly was), calls into question established paradigms of virtue and sanctity. No longer is it possible simply to assume that their saintliness was primarily a function of standard hagiographic models or material. The saint stands, on the contrary, as the epitome of human wholeness, and there is nothing theologically suspicious or murky about a perspective that also sees him or her as sensual.

I will not try to argue here that there were, and are, homosexual saints. I take this as a given, and I leave it to our historians and theologians to provide the proof for the skeptical. This scholarly work, however, is both necessary and compelling. As gay men, we desperately need to see ourselves included in "the army of God's chosen ones," for reasons of visibility but also for ones of pride and self-worth. If you are not seen to be there, then the assumption is that you simply do not exist. My concern is much more with what sanctity or sainthood can represent for gay men, the kind of fully human models it makes possible for us. For me, this becomes genuinely feasible only if we take desire itself as our starting point. I understand desire fundamentally as a mode of religiosity, a way of being religious. Desire can and certainly should include the erotic. We desire to be with our gods and goddesses, to adore them, because they touch something profoundly sensual in us. The same dynamic, I would argue, applies to saints, and perhaps even more to Catholic saints as these have been traditionally portrayed. Saints, after all, once were human—all the more reason why they could and should be a source of desire for us. The "touch" of which Dinshaw and Jordan speak is the touch of others like us, summoning us across the centuries to the mutual encounter of ostracized yet proud humans. It is the secret, exalting touch of desire: a fluttering sense of human solidarity and connection.

A queer Catholicism will consider saints not only in their lived sexuality but also in their symbolic worth as objects and embodiments of erotic feeling. Actually, this is not very different from the kind of official hagiography which the Catholic Church itself has endorsed down through the centuries. Reading these "lives of the saints," there is always a slight whiff of repressed sexuality, bodily cravings, and the struggle with attractive, if perhaps slightly obsessive, demons. The act of martyrdom lends itself particularly well to a discourse of the erotic. Descriptions of torture and death, vivid and unsettling in their scripts of unspoken desire, play upon the classic theme of the intimate connection between *eros* and *thanatos,* and how these become embodied in *religio.*

We need to reinterpret male saints from our lived experience as gay men—the better to sound our own humanity, or rather its impoverishment. We need to see Michael not only as the Prince of Angels (though that might be fun) but also as the brother-protector; Francis not only as a charming rebel ecologist but also as a founder and lover of communities of men; and Joseph not only as father but also as the Daddy with all that this implies in terms of the attractiveness and ambiguities of paternal power. I won't even begin to talk about Sebastian or any of those other hunky and brave martyrs and how they tap into the language and imagery of physical ache. I am calling for a subversively queer Catholic hagiography, one that takes these male saints as perfect models—for that is what saints are—of that to which we can and should aspire.

Such a queer hagiography will help undermine Catholic theological discourse on homosexuality by pointing to richly diverse alternate modes, or, at least, alternate interpretations of traditional modes, of holiness. More important, it will place human sexuality—in this case, same-sex desire of the nonprocreative kind—at the very heart of sanctity, of what it means for humans to be holy. Jordan (2000, pp. 259-260) writes:

> It would indeed be nice to have a standard moral theology in which we were not being attacked, but our aim should be higher. We should see the theological controversy over homosexuality for what it is: a privileged opportunity to rethink the genres of moral theology altogether. Our lives can challenge not just the principle that sex has to be procreative, but the assumption that moral theology has to be founded upon such principles.

If saints can be seen and revered as sexual beings, and moreover ones not necessarily heterosexual or procreative, then moral theology would indeed be hard-pressed to continue demonizing us. Jordan is quite right in pointing out that our special challenge to moral theology, from our unique perspective as gay men, must move well beyond our own self-interest. Ours is primarily a pedagogical task but one that is universal in its implications. We must teach the Catholic Church (and perhaps all churches) that human sexuality need not always be a means, but that it can very legitimately and morally be an end in itself, that pleasure is not always suspect and sinful. It is in sum our lives as proud and out gay men that will provide the stuff of holiness, to the point where we just might subvert the entire edifice of traditional moral theology *and* sanctity.

SPEAKING AND WRITING QUEER

Now to language and writing, the necessary tasks of the revolution and of the "schools for new speech." I was struck by two of Jordan's comments: first, how so much of our recent writing about homosexuality and Christianity—or perhaps religion generally—has become circular, as though we kept rediscovering the same truths about ourselves and our condition; second, how we desperately need a new language for both our erotic and our sacramental lives, one not tinged by the old categories of "sodomite" and "homosexual," which were created for us by a controlling and deadening Catholic bureaucracy. The first is a well-placed critique, though perhaps a bit premature in its implied severity. The second calls for a staggering leap of the imagination, yet one which remains intensely and profoundly exciting. I can attempt a reply only through the lens of experience, so I put myself on the line as both a writer and a believer.

About five years ago, I came out with my first book. Titled *Out on Holy Ground: Meditations on Gay Men's Spirituality* (Boisvert, 2000), it argues that much of our lives can be understood and appreciated in religious terms. Yet when I was writing it—and even more so after taking note of Jordan's implied criticism—the thought did cross my mind that I was simply doing more of the same, that, in fact, I was echoing, perhaps all too readily, the ideas and words which colleagues had already put out there. Jordan speaks of this being caused partly by the excitement of each author rediscovering some important truths for himself or herself. Fair enough. On the other hand, "doing more of the same" is, I would submit, precisely what needs to happen. It is how great edifices, be they brick-and-mortar or theological, are brought down: by the slow and repeated eating away of the foundations. Perhaps patience is no longer possible or desirable. Perhaps we need to be bolder and far more direct in our subversion. Perhaps Catholic theological discourse is already too tainted, too mined with their homophobic categories and idioms. Or perhaps we are doing exactly what we should be doing: tearing at the structure piece by piece. I would think that we must first learn to talk before we can challenge the parent. Part of this "talking of new speech" includes the necessary yet dangerous task of reappropriation: mimicry in order to better undermine and surpass.

Moreover, if everyone is doing "more of the same," then that very fact may point to the slow emergence of certain truths and to a possible consensus with respect to their relevance and applicability. The harsh yet hopeful reality is that traditional religion as we have known it garners less and less support and appears more and more problematic. This unusual phenomenon that we call "gay spirituality" is therefore surely more than a passing phase. Though perhaps a bit freaky at its edges, it might be forging a totally novel religious path for us. The gamble is certainly worth the effort. On the other hand, do we really have a choice? If one no longer hears one's name coming from the lips of the Catholic hierarchy, what is "a poor homosexual" to do? Jordan reminds us that, in fact, our name is very much on their lips, though it is a whispered, dirty little secret. What gay religious writing does, as Jordan himself demonstrates so superbly, is amplify these sullen and scandalous whispers. With enough amplification comes the beat of angry queers dancing on the grave of a dead theological edifice.

The writing of new discourses requires a dramatic shift away from existing ones, and I wish we would break, as Jordan invites us to do, with this compulsive need that we seem to have to keep justifying ourselves on *their* theological terms, to keep responding over and over again to *their* scriptures, and to insist on being a part of *their* sacramental lives. I include myself in this critique. All of us working in this offbeat field, whether as activists or scholars (and the two are by no means mutually exclusive), need to think through and to propose original ways of being homoerotically religious. The striking thing about Mark Jordan's *Silence of Sodom,* of course, is his argument that one can be precisely that in the very midst of the most homophobic of all religious institutions, an institution which would not really exist in quite the same way were it not for repressed male same-sex desire. The writing therefore needs to be bold and daring, and for a long while it may indeed be repetitious. But it must ultimately—and no doubt regretfully—turn its back on what is, on what *they* have chosen as the field of engagement. It must move to new and higher ground. Indeed, it may even necessitate the discovery of a totally new place for us, one where homoerotic energy and power are the norm.

I cannot even begin imagining, and neither can Mark Jordan, what it might mean to create "a new language" expressive and respectful of our persons. I know only that there are a thousand possibilities emerging boldly out there. The simple fact is that Roman Catholic teaching on sexuality, let alone homosexuality, is fighting a losing battle. Loving and caring human beings can no longer bring themselves to live their lives by its repressive, puritanical standards. In this shifting context, the creation of new erotic and sacramental languages for ourselves is not only a task of the utmost seriousness but also one over which we should dally with much pleasure and delight. One of the truly wonderful things about changing an antiquated world is that there is no need to rush. It sometimes takes care of itself, eating away at its own foundations and vitality from the inside.

In his response to Carolyn Dinshaw's book, Mark Jordan (2001, p. 181) offered the following observation:

> When I am called a "gay Catholic"—or so call myself—I am placed within at least two communities that make claims for touch across time. . . . Not a Catholic touch, but a Catholic grip. One traditional Catholic claim is that I can not only touch, but eat the body of Jesus. Another is that there is only one time for God—and that we anticipate our entry into this eternal moment by liturgy and vision.

These are words of hope for gay Catholics. In Jordan's "schools for new speech," we must remind ourselves of two important facts. First, that the man-god Jesus is a tactile, sensuous being, and that our communion with his body is an act of erotic affirmation. Second, that the Godhead is encountered in the here-and-now, and that there is no disjunction between eternity and the present. The liturgical moment therefore stands at the very epicenter of where the gay Catholic—any Catholic, for that matter—comes to terms with the challenges and all-too-human drawbacks of the faith. I should like to push Jordan even further, if I may. If there is to be a "new school," I would suggest that it should emerge, first and foremost, from the very center of secular gay culture. In fact, it should be as irreligious as possible. The liturgical life should be none other than the life of full erotic affirmation and excess. Sodomites through the centuries may have little in common, but at least they "touch" through the continued assertion of their deviant desires. Roman Catholic moral theology certainly understood that, if nothing else.

Speaking and writing a queer Catholicism is dangerous and disorienting business. It is more about loss than gain, more about sorrow than celebration, more about not belonging than feeling part of a wider whole. Yet this is exactly where and how the new language will be forged. If we learn to wait and see, speaking and acting uncertainly, we will slowly find our way. If we continuously challenge the very raison d'être of the theological house of cards, we will discover new ways of speaking of ourselves and our burning desires. If we stand upon the Lord, we will begin to hear the voice of inclusion. And if, in response to Jordan's challenge, we call ourselves neither sodomite, nor homosexual, nor pervert, nor sinful, perhaps then—and only then—shall we glimpse a new beginning. In the process, let us also hope that we inflict serious and lasting damage on a moribund theology which has, for far too long, chosen to dehumanize us for its own secret gain.

When I was a boy, I used to love playing priest. I would make my own vestments from rags, turn my bedroom bureau into an altar, and force my younger brother and sisters to attend my improvised masses in strict silence. When I entered the seminary, I was still playing, though now I could play with other boys my age who were also playing at the same thing, and there were even adults around me who were playing a life-long game. The wonder, beauty, and delight of Mark Jordan's book is how he lays bare the rules of this game. It is a game I and others know so very well, and from which we never fully opt out. It is at heart the game of desire. But it is equally a game of darkness, full of oppressive and dangerous language: a game in which the odds are stacked against us from the start. We can still play the game, and we should. It is great fun. But we must desperately rewrite the rules on our own terms.

REFERENCES

Boisvert, Donald L. (2000). *Out on holy ground: Meditations on gay men's spirituality.* Cleveland, OH: The Pilgrim Press.

Dinshaw, Carolyn (1999). *Getting medieval: Sexualities and communities, pre- and postmodern.* Durham, NC: Duke University Press.

Jordan, Mark D. (1997). *The invention of sodomy in Christian theology.* Chicago: The University of Chicago Press.

Jordan, Mark D. (2000). *The silence of Sodom: Homosexuality in modern Catholicism.* Chicago: The University of Chicago Press.

Jordan, Mark D. (2001). Touching and acting, or the closet of abjection. In "History's queer touch: A forum on Carolyn Dinshaw's *Getting medieval: Sexualities and communities, pre- and postmodern." Journal of the History of Sexuality* 10(2): 180-184.

Chapter 2

Naming the Mechanisms of Self-Deception: A Call to Liberation for Gay Roman Catholic Clergy

David M. Mellott

From my experience, there are moments (what I like to call *inter-ruptions*) in the life of Roman Catholic seminary communities when both the seminarians and the formation faculty are confronted with discrepancies between the rhetoric of the formation program and the way in which the program policies are actually administered. This confrontation often happens when seminarians become aware that the seminary's policy of forbidding any discussion in formation sessions of their sexual identity or sexual development completely contradicts the faculty's long-held philosophy that self-knowledge and self-acceptance are necessary for psychological health and spiritual growth. Once this disparity is recognized and named the faculty can either change its practices to better embody its philosophy or it can ignore the disparity. When the disparity is ignored, the strained silence surrounding sexuality and sexual development is interpreted by the seminarians as a cue either to ignore their sexuality or to pursue their sexual development in secret. In either case, a fragmentation within the seminarian occurs. For many gay seminarians, living among fragments is nothing new. They have considerable experience with keeping their sexuality and their sexual experiences secret from their families, their friends, and themselves. For these seminarians, the seminary only reinforces the development of a fragmented self.

The seminary program of fragmenting the self is equally problematic for the seminary faculty. In particular, gay faculty members put themselves into the position of perpetuating a self-destructive system that poses as a program of spiritual formation. For gay priests who wish to keep their sexual identity secret, the seminary can be an ideal hiding place, albeit a complicated one. I share my experience of discovering and naming the mechanisms of self-deception that I helped perpetuate in the seminary in order to subvert this deadly system of secrecy. This essay is also about my experience of resisting these mechanisms and my journey toward liberation and spiritual wholeness. I share these experiences with the hope that they will inspire others to explore their own experiences and to seek liberation for themselves and others.

PERSONAL TESTIMONY

In 1994, after two years of parish ministry, I joined a Roman Catholic religious community dedicated to the formation of Roman Catholic clergy. I joined for two reasons. First, I was interested in doing spiritual formation in the context of teaching theology. I remember speaking passionately about my desire to accompany people in their process of spiritual growth. I believed that this religious community would be an ideal place where I could help others become healthy priests.

Second, I wanted to belong to a community that would support me in my own growth process. My experience of priesthood within the diocese was difficult. When the bishop addressed the faithful, he spoke solely about raising money and the importance of official church teaching. Many of my fellow priests were angry with the lack of substantive dialogue about spirituality, sexuality, and ministry but reluctant to initiate any conversations among themselves. Their unhappiness led many of them to participate in a variety of self-destructive behaviors, including sexual misconduct, binge eating, and alcohol abuse. I knew that I needed to get out of that situation or else I, too, would become angry, alone, and very unhealthy.

Leaving the diocese and joining the religious community opened up a whole new way of being a priest for me. I was assigned to a seminary faculty in the summer of 1994. I was very nervous about my new ministries of teaching, mentoring, doing spiritual direction, and being a faculty member, but the transition went very well. Both the faculty and I agreed that I was gifted at doing seminary formation. Student and faculty evaluations of my contributions were extremely positive. I felt at home.

I did have a few problems, however, in the transition. During my first seminary formation training session, a high-ranking member of the community told the group of new members that we were not to speak openly at faculty meetings and that we were not allowed to request where we wanted to be assigned until we had "more money in the bank." He interpreted his own expression by saying that until we had paid our dues or did what we were told, we were not to speak freely about what we thought or what we wanted to do. Through these experiences and others, I quickly learned the importance of remaining silent.

Less than a year after I joined the seminary faculty, I was asked to take on more mentees and spiritual directees, as well as the position of coordinator of liturgy. To the surprise of many on the faculty, including myself, I was able to develop a working relationship with the seminary administrators, including people who were perceived to be homophobic and difficult. By the time I left the faculty in 1997 to pursue my PhD, there was a growing conversation about my future leadership role as rector and possibly provincial.

During my second year on the faculty of a Roman Catholic seminary, some of the students in the pretheology program expressed to me their confusion about whether they were allowed to talk about being gay with other students or with faculty members. They said that they were confused because they thought the formation team was giving them a double message. On the one hand they were being told that in order to be spiritually and psychologically healthy they needed to know themselves better and accept who they are. They understood the formation sessions to be opportunities where they could learn more about themselves through their sharing with fellow students and the formation team. On the other hand, I and the other team members had told them that certain topics, which we didn't identify, were off-limits. So, the students were wondering whether discussions surrounding sexual orientation were off-limits.

I raised the question at one of our pretheology team meetings, and we discussed the dilemma at length. We agreed that we were giving the students mixed messages. Our team raised the question to the administrators of the seminary. We were told that under no circumstances were students allowed to discuss or explore issues of sexual orientation during formation sessions. Given their public nature, formation sessions were not the appropriate places in which to discuss such issues. Questions about sexuality and sexual orientation could be discussed only in spiritual direction, which was held in complete confidence. We were also reassured that being a homosexual was not grounds for being dismissed from the seminary. Celibacy was required of all seminarians and priests. So, whether one was gay or straight didn't matter. Although I was unsure about the policy, I joined the team in repeating the seminary's policy to the pretheology students at their next session.

Realizing that I couldn't facilitate formation sessions around questions of sexual orientation, I began to initiate those discussions with students in spiritual direction sessions. Even in these confidential relationships, however, many students were reluctant to talk with me about their sexuality. A few students did respond to my invitations. Although most of those students identified themselves as gay, they didn't have any experience with gay relationships, they hadn't read much literature on homosexuality, and they didn't know any gay couples. Without hesitation, I suggested that they needed to meet other gay people, especially couples, and to read about the experiences of other gay people.

As a new member of the faculty I had my own mentor, and I reported to him what I was suggesting to the gay seminarians. He responded by telling me that the year before I arrived, a faculty member was fired because he had been introducing gay seminarians to gay couples who were friends of his. He also said that another faculty member was fired because as a spiritual director he knew that a student was in a sexual relationship but didn't pressure the student to tell the rector about that relationship. My mentor warned me that if the rector found out what I was recommending to students I, too, would be fired.

Although I was afraid that some of the seminarians might tell the rector about my suggestions, I continued to think of ways in which I could encourage students to explore their questions about sexuality without revealing my own homosexuality. I would read books on homosexuality but recommend them to students by saying, "I heard that this book, x, is a good one to read." I worked hard to support students in their process of growth without revealing anything about myself. I remember telling several of the seminarians that I didn't want them to come back to me ten years after ordination and ask me why I never told them there were other ways of living as a gay man.

Through informal conversations over dinner or at our regular cocktail hour I heard from other members of my community about how the seminary was associated with homosexuality in recent history. One member told me that the seminary parking lot, according to a popular gay magazine, was one of the top ten places to pick up men. Another member told me that the seminary had been dubbed "the pink palace" and that the seminary was having a difficult time losing its tag. Periodically a senior administrator would report to the faculty on how well the seminary was doing at cleaning up its reputation. On one occasion he announced that "we have solved the homosexual problem" at our seminary.

In an informal conversation with students, a seminary administrator explained why he had spent so much money to change the maroon-colored carpet in the main hall, when it was only a few years old. He said that shortly after the carpet was installed, he came home late one evening and the lights were on in the hall. From the street, the large, lit hall looked pink, and he vowed to himself that he would remove that carpet as soon as he could.

Beginning in my second year on the seminary faculty I began actively dating men and seriously exploring the possibility of being in a gay relationship and remaining a priest. All of my attempts at having a gay relationship failed, in part because I could not withstand the anxiety that came with leading a double life. There were times when I would leave my boyfriend's apartment, return to the seminary, change into my clerical collar, and then go to chapel for mass. I struggled under my guilt because I knew that I was not following the church's rule of celibacy for all clergy and because I was being hypocritical with the students. When the tension from my feelings of guilt got too intense I would break up with my boyfriend. After several weeks had passed and my tension had eased, I began looking for a new companion.

In 1998, I entered the PhD program of the Graduate Division of Religion at Emory University and embarked on what became a path of transformation. To my surprise, my graduate seminars were the context where I began to discover my voice. Week after week I was asked to articulate and share my response to the assigned readings, as well as the extent to which the ideas in the readings conversed with my own worldview and projects. As simple as this practice sounds, it changed my life. When I had studied theology in the seminary, professors did not invite us to engage the materials in this way. We were expected to listen, memorize, and repeat the information presented to us. What we thought or felt in response to the ideas presented was neither important nor essential to the learning process. In fact, during my first three years of theology we were strongly discouraged from asking any questions in class.

My Emory professors' simple practice of organizing student learning around the students' input was truly liberating to me because it allowed me to claim my voice. I was given the permission to explore what I was thinking and feeling. Furthermore, my own struggles with the ideas presented were considered not only helpful but also essential to doing theology. This new way of learning and doing theology was also painful, because I realized that for years I had been denied the opportunity to learn about myself while taking courses in college and theology.

At the end of my first semester at Emory, a classmate hosted a small dinner party and invited her friend Lance to join us. At the time Lance was attending Columbia Theological Seminary in Decatur and was a candidate for ordination in the Universal Fellowship of Metropolitan Community Churches. The following month we began dating and developing a mutually loving relationship. Lance and I were not only attracted to each other but also united in our Christian commitment to bring about justice and peace. In one of our earliest conversations, Lance asked me why I was dating when I was not allowed to be in a committed intimate relationship. I told him that I didn't agree with mandatory celibacy and that many of the priests I knew were in a committed relationship or were seeking such a relationship. He then asked, what was I thinking, then, when I committed myself to celibacy? I repeated to him a comment, a mantra I used to say regularly when I was in the seminary. When I would see a handsome man I would say to myself, and sometimes to others, that if I looked like that handsome guy, I would have never considered the priesthood. At the moment I repeated that comment to Lance I realized that the reason that I didn't hesitate in committing myself to celibacy was because I never thought that I would ever meet someone who would love me as much as I loved him. For the first time I saw the connection between my self-hatred and my commitment to celibacy.

Thanks, then, to Lance, Emory University, and the Metropolitan Community Church that I began attending, my true self, the gay self

—the one who supported women's ordination, partnered clergy, and equal rights for all people, regardless of gender, sexual orientation, or ethnicity—emerged from behind my institutional self, the one who spoke the party line, who expected students to memorize the church's theological positions without regard for the ways in which it might harm their spiritual development, who turned a deaf ear to the fear and confusion of gay seminarians while secretly seeking out a life partner of my own.

So, in the spring of 2000, when the provincial of my religious community made his canonical visit with me in Atlanta, I was hoping to share with him my insights into the layers of sexism and heterosexism that pervaded our ministry of priestly formation. During our official visit I suggested that our religious community needed to open up communal conversations about our church's policies on the ordination of women, mandatory celibacy, and homosexuality, as well as how these policies were affecting us personally and our ministry of formation. My sense was that many of the members were suffering because of the dissonances we experienced between what we believed and what the church officially teaches. These dissonances, I suggested, were leading the members to engage in maladaptive behaviors: secret sexual partners, excessive food and alcohol consumption, and ultimately the development of false selves.

My argument was that we could either ignore these dissonances and their symptoms or we could see them as life interruptions that have the power to lead us into healthier and holier living. This is what we tell our students, I posed: "If you want to know God more deeply, you must seek to know yourself and be honest with yourself and others." To me, that means dealing honestly with the dissonances and interruptions we experience in our lives. I continued by reminding the provincial that our programs insist that Christian formation includes all aspects of ourselves: the emotional, the psychological, the physical, the spiritual, and the academic. Only then, when we are dealing with our true selves, will we encounter the living God. I ended by saying that if this is true for our students, how much more true it is for us, who are called by God to be ministers of formation. Unfortunately, the provincial dismissed my concerns as those of a young graduate student. Also, he indicated that my expectation that the members of our community be able to engage in an open and honest conversation about who we are and what we believe was "unrealistic."

I decided that to initiate the difficult but life-giving conversation that I was calling for, I needed to begin by being more open and honest with my family, friends, and community about who I was and what I believed. I decided that voicing my concerns about our lack of significant conversation was not enough; if I believed God was calling us to this conversation, then I must initiate the revelatory process myself. So, over the course of the next year, I began sharing more openly about my relationship with Lance and my concerns about critical issues in the Roman Catholic Church. Encouraged by the support I had received from family and friends, I shared with the provincial that I was living in a committed relationship with a man and that I believed that God was calling me both to ordained ministry and to this relationship.

With this revelation, the provincial moved to dismiss me from the community. When I requested to meet with the council of the province to discuss these matters and to present my perspective on the situation, the provincial replied that such a meeting would be inappropriate. After the council's deliberations, one member responded to my call to greater authenticity by saying, "I think it is important to translate carefully what it means to be 'prophetic.' You raise obviously critical questions in terms of the church's stance on difficult issues, e.g., women's ordination and gay sex between committed partners. . . . I believe that it would be harmful for the leadership of [our community] to take a public stance on these or any other critical issues, and thus jeopardize the personal beliefs of many or most of the membership." This suggestion that prophesy should not address "any critical issue" absolutely confirmed for me how powerful the mechanisms of self-deception can be.

I appealed the provincial decision to the general council with the following letter:

22 November 2001

Dear Brothers of the General Council,

I am writing to you to appeal the decision of the [Council] to terminate my membership. On 13 November 2001, I received from . . . a Decree of Dismissal, accompanied by a letter which failed to articulate any specific reasons for my dismissal. In addition, he proceeded to notify the bishop of my home diocese before allowing me the opportunity to appeal the decision, thereby undermining the authority of the General Council and committing a breach of confidence. The Council's decision to dismiss me from . . . because I have requested that our members be given the opportunity to enter into open and honest conversations about important teachings of our church, as well as our own disagreements with them, is exceedingly punitive, unfair, and unjust.

As the enclosed correspondence records, I have been voicing to . . . my concerns about certain unjust policies of our church with which many of our members disagree: the ordination of women, mandatory celibacy, and homosexuality. Our silence about and refusal to grapple honestly with these significant *moral* and *theological* issues undermine the integrity of our ministry of seminary formation. In addition, I have expressed deep concern with the church's abuse of power used to suppress any significant conversation of these issues.

During [his] visit in Spring 2000, I shared with him that we need more communal conversations about our church's policies on the issues mentioned above, as well as how these policies are affecting us personally and our ministry of formation. My sense is that many of our members are suffering because of the dissonances they experience between what they believe and what the church officially teaches. These dissonances lead to maladaptive behaviors: secret sexual partners (including seminarians in some cases), excessive eating, excessive drinking of alcohol, and ultimately the development of false selves.

My argument has been that we can either ignore these dissonances or we can see them as life-interruptions, which have the power to lead us into healthier and holier living. This is what we tell our students: if you want to know God more deeply, you must seek to know yourself and be honest with yourself and others. That means dealing honestly with the dissonances and interruptions we experience in our lives. That is why our programs insist that Christian formation includes all aspects of ourselves: the emotional, the psychological, the physical, the spiritual, and the academic. Only then, when we are dealing with our true selves, will we encounter the living God. If this is true for our students, how much more true it is for us, who are called by God to be ministers of formation.

In order to initiate this difficult, but life-giving conversation, I decided that I needed to begin by challenging myself to be more open and honest about who I am and what I believe with my friends, family, and, church. I have learned that voicing my concerns about our lack of significant conversation is not enough; if I believe God is calling us to this conversation, then I must initiate the revelatory process myself. I began this conversation with . . . and had hoped to include the Provincial Council. I have enclosed copies of my letters to [him] and the Council in order to share with you, at least in part, what I have shared with them.

Unfortunately, during our initial conversation concerning these issues [he] dismissed my concerns as those of a "young graduate student." Since then he has clearly indicated that my expectation that the members of our community be able to engage in an open and honest conversation about who we are and what we believe is "unrealistic." In addition, he has falsely accused me of being the *only* member of the American Province who has a life partner. When I requested to meet with the Provincial Council to discuss these matters and to present my perspective on the situation, [he] replied that such a meeting would be inappropriate.

The truth is that I am being unjustly punished because I have chosen to be *open and honest* with my brothers about what I really believe, not because I disagree with church teaching on these matters. The Council's decision to dismiss me because of my honesty only serves to highlight and reinforce the mechanisms of self-deception which are so pervasive in our church and community. To demand that our members be secretive about how the Spirit of God is working through them not only conflicts with the formation process we propose for our seminarians, but also prohibits us from being disciples of Jesus.

I am well aware that what I am suggesting is difficult. Healing and liberation always are. But, I believe, that if we wish to be faithful to our call to form ministers of Jesus Christ . . . we must learn how to be authentic with one another. God demands no less from us.

The members of the [Council] have responded to my requests out of fear. Their fear of the truth has been so strong that they have decided to dismiss me from . . . . Additionally, they have broken confidence by communicating this decision to my bishop before I had had the opportunity to appeal the decision.

The decision before you is an important opportunity for all of us to move our community and church in the direction of greater authenticity and healing. We have the chance to initiate a reform by beginning with ourselves. I can only hope that you will respond out of faith, not faith in me, but in the Spirit of God, who is calling all of us to more abundant life.

In the Spirit,
David M. Mellott

The general council ruled in favor of my dismissal and found the actions of the provincial council to comply with the constitutions of the community and the code of canon law. My dismissal from the community became official on January 9, 2002, and I returned to the jurisdiction of my home diocese and was suspended by my bishop.

THE MECHANISMS OF SELF-DECEPTION

By writing about my own struggle for greater integrity, I am neither suggesting that all priests have had the same experience nor asking the reader to feel sorry for the ways I have been treated by the Roman Catholic Church. My intention has been, and continues to be, to find ways to minister to those priests who are suffering and who have been disempowered in their becoming the kind of compassionate, loving, wise, and spiritual ministers they wish to be. The clergy must take responsibility for articulating and seeking out what they need in order to be psychologically and spiritually healthy. We cannot wait for the institutional church to bring about liberation and healing. We must become liberators ourselves.

Reflecting upon my experiences of teaching in the seminary has led me to discover how Roman Catholic seminarians and priests are subtly, but deeply, shaped by mechanisms of self-deception, which the church and seminary perpetuate in order to disempower Roman Catholic clergy from speaking the truth about who they are and what they truly believe. These mechanisms of self-deception have become institutionalized in the Roman Catholic seminary system and have a particular impact upon gay seminarians and priests.

As my personal testimony suggests, both students and faculty members in Roman Catholic seminaries participate in a formation process in which they must learn to double. The seminary and the church require us to disavow or at least quarantine parts of ourselves, namely, our sexual identities and any theological perspectives that contradict or challenge church policies. As seminary faculty we commit ourselves to the spiritual and mental well-being of our students, and we publicly proclaim that this kind of healthiness demands self-knowledge. At the same time, we prohibit significant conversation among seminarians in supervised formation groups because any discussion of sexuality is thought to increase genital activity, especially among the gay students.

As a seminary formator I became painfully aware that I was participating in a formation process that was teaching seminarians how to hide, how to deceive themselves. I, too, learned how to double, how to keep my personal life (my true self) separate from my institutional self (my false self). As a gay priest working with mostly gay seminarians, I became a minister of spiritual disease, not spiritual health.

In many U.S. Roman Catholic seminaries today, seminarians are not permitted to discuss their sexual orientation with anyone in the seminary except within the confidentiality of spiritual direction. Furthermore, seminarians are increasingly encouraged to talk about issues of sexuality and sexual identity only in therapeutic relationships outside the seminary. As a way to deny the importance of sexual identity and sexual development, seminary officials state that celibacy is required of all seminarians and priests, regardless of orientation. This strictly enforced code of silence surrounding issues of sexuality effectively teaches seminarians that if they wish to survive in the church they must learn how either to deny their sexual identity or to hide their attempts to pursue sexual development and maturity. Because the code of silence refuses to acknowledge the possibility of sexual activity of seminarians, it also serves to camouflage the reality of sexual activity. In each of these cases seminarians are taught that doubling and self-deception are important aspects of their spiritual development and their progress in the church. Successful self-deception is rewarded by ordination.

Seminarians and priests can experience all sorts of "interruptions" in their self-deception. While teaching in the seminary I frequently experienced interruptions when dealing with gay seminarians who were afraid of being "outed" but were desperate to connect with other gay men. I also experienced interruptions in my personal life in the form of guilt and anxiety over my own desire to pursue gay companionship. The seminary system and my religious community were well equipped to numb the pain that came with the dissonance of living a fragmented life and teaching seminarians how to do the same. Every night before dinner we had cocktail hour where alcohol flowed freely and faculty members were permitted to vocalize how insidious the system was (as long as no guests were present, of course). When one of us felt particularly oppressed or frustrated, a member of the administration would remind us that we were not responsible for making the rules. Our role was to enforce them. Those with the real power to change the system were the bishops. We refused to acknowledge *our* complicity with the bishops in administering such a program of self-destruction.

At one point I asked one of our more articulate faculty members why he was willing to live with such dissonance. He replied by saying that he was well taken care of and that he had a good life with many opportunities to travel and meet people; these compensations eased his discomfort. At first I was stunned by his response. Although I was appreciative of his honesty, I was expecting him to propose some deeper reason of why he remained. In the days that followed, my shock from the conversation eventually wore off and I had to admit to myself that my colleague had articulated the reasons why I was having such difficulty thinking about leaving the community. I was just as attached to this life of privilege as he was. I have since realized that what began as a numbing process had escalated into a reward system.

In this case the rewards were very attractive: job security, meaningful work, significant retirement benefits, complete health care, fine dining, and world travel.

I was greatly rewarded for doubling, that is, for ignoring my true self in support of developing a loyal institutional self. In fact, I had grown so accustomed to doubling that I was afraid I would never be able to completely recover my true self. Furthermore, I had grown accustomed, if not addicted, to the privileges I had received as payment for disregarding my true self. After discovering the liberation that comes with finding one's voice, I am no longer willing to quarantine my true self to support an institutional self.

Gay seminarians and priests are particularly vulnerable to the mechanisms of self-deception because they often come to the seminary having a great deal of experience with hiding their true selves from themselves and others. The seminary, then, becomes a perfect place where they can continue to hide and be affirmed in their denial. The practices of denying and numbing the pain that comes from living this kind of fragmented life considerably limit seminarians' and priests' capacity to have compassion for other victims of the institutional church. This partially explains why gay seminarians and clergy have been slow, and even stridently resistant, to seeing connections between their own oppression and the oppression of women in the Roman Catholic Church. In fact, the institutional selves that are created and sustained by these mechanisms of self-destruction are so vulnerable to, and concerned with, being exposed that the clergy expend their energy defending the church's present policies and authority structures in order to keep their positions stable and their rewards ongoing.

My analysis of how Roman Catholic seminaries mentor seminarians in learning self-deception and in developing institutional selves also exposes the spiritual damage done to seminarians and priests. By offering seminarians and priests rewards and benefits as a way to numb the pain and discomfort that comes from the required fragmentation of their selves or by ignoring their compensatory practices, the church *subverts* their spiritual growth. In essence, the church is abandoning the ancient spiritual discipline of detachment by promoting unhealthy attachments for the sake of creating loyal institutional selves among its clergy. Many well-intentioned men enter the seminary with the understanding that they are going to be mentored in a process of spiritual development. All of the promotional literature and formation guidelines speak about the importance of self-knowledge and psychological health, but seminarians learn very quickly that the way "to get through the system" is to hide what they really think and believe.

Roman Catholic gay seminarians and priests are being systematically silenced and controlled through the inculcation of self-deception. I have named here the mechanisms that I have encountered in my own life and that I have perpetuated as a seminary formator. I encourage other gay seminarians and priests to name the mechanisms of self-deception in their own lives that seek to disempower them and keep them silent.

We can break our silence. We have the power to liberate ourselves from these deadly mechanisms and to initiate our own healing process. But we need alternative communities of support where we can help one another rediscover who we are. Situations similar to the ones I described occur in communities where self-deception is not only supported but also nourished and rewarded. By rekindling our desires for spiritual and psychological wholeness, we can find the strength to withdraw our dependency upon the institutional rewards we have received for our participation in the self-deception. We can rediscover our true selves. But the work of naming and resisting the mechanisms of self-deception requires solid community support and cannot be entered into without considerable discernment. We need to begin a movement—a "Clergy Come Out!" movement—in which both clergy and laypeople can learn how to create safe spaces for clergy and others to rediscover who they are and to join forces with those committed to the liberation of all people. Striving for greater authenticity has the power not only to liberate and transform gay Roman Catholic clergy but also to liberate, transform, and heal a church in desperate need of rediscovering its true self.

Chapter 3

Speaking Loud or Shutting Up: The Homosexual-Type Problem

Edward J. Ingebretsen

"I'm not Gay, I'm normal . . . in case you are wondering."

A priest, speaking to a Sunday school class[1]

In *The Invention of Sodomy in Christian Theology* (1997), Mark Jordan traces the process by which a geographical location, Sodom, is transmuted into a symbolic site of perfect metaphysical evil. In his more recent book, *The Silence of Sodom: Homosexuality in Modern Catholicism* (2000), Jordan details some of the ways in which that projective fantasy of the sodomite homosexual—unnatural, unmanly, disordered—must constantly be produced in order to sustain the systemic homosociality undergirding Roman Catholic authority. Although this point is not precisely his issue, I argue that the "silence" to which his title refers points toward the larger paradox of Christian discourse, on which the "ideological sexism" (Sipe, 1995 p. xiii) of a rigidly hierarchical system depends, for its effect, upon the near association of the thing it most fears: homosexual intimacy. In its severe gender phobia, ecclesiastical governance parallels that of the military, and much more can be said on that point.[2] For now, however, I wish to observe that discipline in each is constructed around, and policed through, a complex sexual discourse whose articulation consists, in large part, of taboo, repression, and—in Jordan's word—silence. In short, the gendered obedience on which the male-male system depends must be guaranteed by foreclosing, through anticipatory panic, its own logical consequence. These consequences—homosexual intimacy and the apocalyptic trauma associated with the homosexual body—must, at all costs, be eliminated. Yet it is the energy needed to police the taboo and enforce the silence that, paradoxically, "produces" the abject body of the homosexual, making it available for the various purposes of pity, moral example, demonization, and other public dramas it usefully serves.

In Chapter 15, I examine the dynamics of a "celibate/sexual structure" (Sipe, 1995, p. 6) in which a cult of obedience and subjection is rewarded with dramatic social power. In this chapter, I wish to explore how the symbolic homosexual body underwrites the authority of church doctrine at the same time that its social abjection—often colluded in by homosexual persons themselves—is used to guarantee that authority. If the crisis in the modern Catholic Church is, as Jordan and others observe, a sense that the homosexual has been speaking *too* loudly during the past twenty or thirty years, one should not thereby conclude that homosexuality has ever been very silent in church. Indeed, Jonathan Dollimore (1991) anticipates Jordan's examination of Catholic culture when he argues that the development of Christian theology along the binary of natural/unnatural *required* the homosexual body as an object of scorn, moral example, and symbolic repudiation. Augustine of Hippo was a chief architect of the Christian subjectivity, and his biographer notes the "intensity with which he had driven the problem of evil into the heart of Christianity" (Brown, in Dollimore, 1991, p. 138). To this point, Dollimore (1991) observes, laconically, that Augustinian theodicy was crucially responsible in Christian thought for the "happy consequences of making God rather than Satan the ultimate or original pervert" (p. 146).

As Jordan explores in *Invention of Sodomy* (1997), the homosexual body satisfied the centralizing authority of the medieval church with great economy, serving theological needs and narrative pleasure simultaneously; as the locus of grave and unnatural sin, grand and lurid fantasies could be yoked to it, and the more extravagant, the more successful their preacherly effect. One could preach, condemn, pity, and profit from this taboo topic—in the peculiar way that unspeakable horrors produce the pleasures of endless speech. This essay explores such an apparatus of naming and silence, devised of rhetoric and policy, and underwritten in large measure by those most at risk.

I wish to use as a place of entry Cardinal Joseph Ratzinger's 1986 "Letter to the Bishops of the Catholic Church on the Pastoral Care of Homosexual Persons." I begin with this document because, in a general way, it symbolizes most clearly the fantasies of violence that often disrupt rhetorics of altruism. Second, this letter is crucially important to the history of the homosexual body "in modern Catholicism"—Jordan's subject. Third, this "pastoral letter"—issued by the Congregation for the Doctrine of the Faith, traditionally given the task of policing doctrinal purity—must be placed within the expansion of homosexual visibility in America that occurred (coincidentally) during the years following Vatican II. That is, the letter distills in virulent ways a revision of earlier ad hoc, local, and scattershot policies around the place of the homosexual in Catholic pews. By this I mean actual persons in actual pews, for the crisis of homosexual visibility was a perception that indeed there seemed to be many more *of* them, in seminaries, rectories, even in the pews. Many factors can account for this perception; whether accurate or not it would have consequences. In *Sex and the Church,* Kathy Rudy (1997, p. xi) observes matter-of-factly that the "issue of homosexuality threatens to divide Christian churches today in much the way that slavery did 150 years ago." It is within this fissured, ecclesiastical scene and cultural context that Mark Jordan and others place the homosexual body. The crisis of Sodom in Catholicism is not, in fact, its silence, but a continually loud speaking, historically ancient, which even today goes willfully unheard.

Ratzinger's 1986 document provides a fascinating contour to the ecclesiastical panic of the time, which to this day continues to drive Roman response—among other things—to American politics and media. What had for so long gone without saying, or even needing to be said, in church—the "inordinate disorder" of the homosexual—needed increasingly, and loudly, to be spoken since fewer and fewer people apparently believed it. This is the firewalling context of Ratzinger's "pastoral" letter, whose pinched altruism at times barely masks other motives as well. Given its ostensible aim—"the pastoral care of homosexual persons"—the letter may not be perceived as having an extortive edge to it. Nonetheless, the text's superficially benign pastorality exactly demonstrates the collusion of power, pain, and abjection that I am arguing lies at the heart of Jordan's "silence." This may seem an outlandish claim, but one has only to turn to the document itself, where circulating just below a surface rhetoric of compassion are implications of far darker sorts—including, among others, fantasies of exclusion, titillation, and sexual voyeurism. Such subtextual energies are not unique to this text, of course. They, or similar ones, have propped up the deviant homosexual body for view in Catholic discourse since the Middle Ages; it is axiomatic that the energy needed to hold a body under taboo means, paradoxically, that it must be attentively held.

In the first place, the document title misleads, although I would argue that it does so with full intent. That is, the document is a directive rather than a pastoral document, as indicated by its issuance by the Vatican Congregation for the Doctrine of the Faith. A further disciplinary indication is evident in that the signatory, Joseph Cardinal Ratzinger, explicitly directs his remarks toward Catholic bishops, addressing them in their roles as "ordinary authority" rather than as "shepherds" or pastors. The document's purpose is to outline and support the exclusionary actions and disciplinary reprisals discreetly slipped into the last lines of the document. In its final two paragraphs the author's tone shifts from the dry explication of theological and scriptural texts that makes up the greater portion of the document. Instead, the text speaks intimately and, it seems, with liberal compassion: "It is deplorable that homosexual persons have been and are the object of violent malice in speech or in action. Such treatment deserves condemnation from the Church's pastors wherever it occurs" (Ratzinger, [1986] 1994, p. 43). Nonetheless, shortly afterward Ratzinger exonerates those same pastors while deftly restating the governing prejudice that Church and society should not be surprised at irrational responses and violent social reactions when homosexuality is affirmed as a positive lifestyle.[3]

Here the text's "panic" is most evident—akin, if you will, to the colonial overseer who suddenly finds the docile house servant "turned." In the United States, the Gay Pride movement gathered force through the 1970s. A combination of religious freedom and secular liberalism gave a new range of expression and public confidence to a previously stigmatized "minority." The Vatican document, as noted earlier, seeks to firewall—and if possible, reverse—this liberalizing secular trend in American Catholicism, and the text is accordingly direct. It reasserts in particularly ugly language the "objectively disordered" nature of homosexual actions.[4] Further, the document explicitly burdens homosexuals with the problem; they are responsible for the distress and pain that befall them as a result of their becoming "visible" by acting in a manner that suggests them to be "not disordered." In Article 10 two things happen simultaneously. The text exonerates the perpetrators of violence (physical actions are intended), first by a passive grammar which mystifies violence—refusing to ground it in any one place or affix it to any one person. From this follows a further consequence. By making violence rhetorically disappear, the author thereby prepares the reader to accept the text's spiritual, even emotional violence, by which institutional responsibility is evacuated ("neither Church nor society at large"). Tacit violence becomes the underside of the text's ostensibly benign pastoral moment.

"Letter to the Bishops of the Catholic Church" intends, on the face of things, to give care to the homosexual who might face such violence. However, the care proffered is rather bleak. In fact, it is neither more nor less than a push into spiritual and social silence. The remainder of Article 10 underscores this conclusion. Since homosexuals are "inordinately disordered," the text argues explicitly that they have no right to any discourse that might suggest otherwise. Translated into the terms of daily life, homosexual persons are to take no practical means by which to talk about, or safeguard, their own lives. Nor can it be said that the document simply refers to the possibility of someone else's violence, in some distant place far removed from the sanctuary of the church. To the contrary, the words of the document itself *enact* violence, enforcing it with the ecclesiastical sanction outlined in the penultimate Article 17 that encourages ecclesial withdrawal of support organizations undermining church moral teaching. Thus, while decrying violence against homosexuals, in the name of the church, the document authorizes violence—here, in the form of silence, exclusion, expulsion. Not without reason was the ancient punishment of excommunication so widely feared. To be cut off from one's community was to be shorn of all material and theological supports of personhood—spiritual death, in other words. In terms of church canons—and, therefore, within the "Catholic community"— one concludes that homosexual persons exist without spiritual safeguard and that this, too, is with church warrant. Analogies with the early years of the Nazi regime come to mind, when laws codified the incremental erasure of Jewish legal existence and finally made possible their physical elimination.[5]

During the decade and a half following this 1986 publication, local and national church authorities worked in concert to support Ratzinger's ban of Dignity, a community of dissenting gay and lesbian Catholics that had been founded in the early 1970s.[6] Some authorities acted on their own volition, but others acted reluctantly, under relentless pressure from the Vatican. Indeed, although there may not have been much popular (or even administrative) sympathy for Ratzinger's movements, individuals had few organized ways to resist. As a consequence, recalcitrant clerics, prelates, and laypersons found themselves isolated and alone. Individuals were targeted for failure to comply and, by their compliance, found themselves in situations where they in turn passed on the coercion. Priests, particularly, but bishops and others in authority as well, were silenced; advocacy groups eliminated; ministries to homosexual persons closed down.[7] Encouraged, perhaps emboldened by a general apathy of response, the Vatican even took to making pronouncements about homosexuality and American civil law: "There are areas in which it is not unjust discrimination to take sexual orientation into account" (Catholic News Service, 1992, p. 1). Capping a decade of such maneuvers, at the turn of the century, the pontiff, speaking from his piazza at the Vatican, called homosexuals "an offense to Christianity" (Hughes, 2000).[8] This was an extraordinary moment for many reasons. Homosexuality, once a sin, and then in the heady days immediately following Vatican II, a psychological condition, had now received the ultimate demonization—achieving a symbolic recognition seldom accorded other sins or conditions.[9] Sodom, as Jordan put it, was no longer just a geographical place; it was now a recognizable metaphysical site, easily recognized as the locus of all evil. There is no question but that, in keeping with the military imagery noted previously, the 1986 document from the Congregation for the Doctrine of the Faith took its place as one more step in a campaign whose goal seemed nothing less than symbolic genocide.

Such pastoral treatment is, as Robert Goss (1993) argues in *Jesus Acted Up*, "far from liberating; it is restrictive, oppressive, and even terrorist" (p. 120). Nonetheless, it is also evident that as the 1990s advanced toward the millennium, many persons (homosexual as well as heterosexual, lay as well as cleric) went to great lengths to disguise the significance of these concerted church reprisals from themselves. If they were observed at all, the actions were dismissed as something other than reprisals.[10] The question is, why were such actions not more widely recognized for the violence they intended? In addition, even when one keeps in mind the history of its subsequent use, the pastoral letter issued under the authority of Cardinal Ratzinger is not, as observed earlier, immediately perceived to be extortive. Nonetheless, its origins in the Vatican's disciplinary Congregation for the Doctrine of the Faith reflect that it is not exactly "pastoral," either.

A text published two years before Ratzinger's letter may help shed light upon some of these points. According to the norms set out in the United Nations' 1984 Document Against Torture, the Vatican document issued by the Congregation for the Doctrine of the Faith is exactly to the point, in that it extorts a "confession" and does so coercively. Nor does it make a difference that in the ecclesiastical, rather than military, context the "confession" extorted by the document *silences* words, rather than speaks them. Yet silenced words are as consequential as speech. The legal adage suggests *Qui Tacuit Consentit:* silence gives consent. As Eve Sedgwick (1990) argues, however, rarely is silence an *absence* of opinion. To the contrary, silence is a very powerful speech and evidence of a very persuasive opinion. When one considers the effects of the Vatican document as well as the implications of its violent language, it is arguably the case that isolation imposed by such pastorality is tantamount to solitary confinement and thus punitive. The Vatican condemns all pastoral programs and homosexual organizations that do not explicitly state that homosexual activity is immoral (Ratzinger, [1986] 1994). Blunt, banal, commonplace, but exquisitely effective, Ratzinger's sought-for "confession" takes the form of a self-silencing that is, for the gay Catholic, a radical self-denial—a disavowal of spiritual life as well as a repudiation of social ties more generally.

Nor are priests the only ones caught in the cycle. Take, for example, the gay-identified person (female or male) whose place in the pews of a Catholic church is rhetorically always under siege. Even the most laconic gay person must continue to manage anxiety about his or her place in this church. Minimally, they are at risk of being individually shamed and treated poorly by its ministers; collectively, gay persons are dependent upon the good will of strategic "gay-friendly" structures or authorities who afford them protection or "opportunity." As will become clear, it is important to note that distinct parallels can be drawn to women, who, in similar ways, find they must don a symbolic burka when they enter the Catholic Church.

What happens to the gay man or woman who seeks pastoral care under these conflicted conditions of speaking and silence, visibility and invisibility? Assuming that he or she is eager to remain "in communion" with the Roman Church, and that he or she accepts the Sacred Congregation's "On the Pastoral Care of Homosexual Persons" (1986), the homosexual person must still come to terms with its pragmatic consequences—first with its institutional proscriptions (dismissal of Dignity from Catholic property), and second with its personal implications (theological as well as social). Two consequences can follow. Fully aware of the stigma, the gay person can announce himself or herself to be gay and demonstrate that identity by some "obvious" sign—say, walking arm-in-arm with a lover into church, wearing a rainbow sash, etc. On the other hand, realizing the stigma that attaches to "talking about it," the gay person can be pressured into silence, drop the lover's arm, and make no visible sign of social self-possession. In the first case the self-naming brings with it a complicated set of social responses, including stigma, refusal, and, in some cases, liberal "compassion"—which is, as I argue later, only a different face of stigma. The self-silencing required by the second option is, arguably, an act of spiritual anorexia.[11] In any case, the effort required either to admit an identity or to erase its public effects takes considerable mental agility. In other words, the violence done to the homosexual need not be *physical,* nor do threats to gay persons exist only in the rural countryside of Wyoming or urban streets of eastern cities. Even the church can be a place of hazard, reflected by this Vatican document and almost two decades of sustained public interventions. Sometimes sanctuary is no sanctuary at all. The violence mandated by this example of Vatican pastoring (text and consequent action) is, perhaps, a "more sophisticated form"; such pastoring rarely leave marks, yet the erasures it demands makes physical violence possible, even likely.

Let's return for a moment to the case in which a gay-identified person decides, despite the costs, to "talk about it" in church. Such a declaration would be a "confession" very different from the "confession" of silence demanded by the Vatican's pastoral/disciplinary care. In addition, however, the gay person's resistance here also exposes something about the pastoral encounter that compliance ensures would remain hidden. That is, resisting the priest effectively raises the stakes, since the church's moral authority likewise comes into question. What does the priest have at stake? As I shall explore, the gendered authority implicit in the very role of "Father" comes under question.

The clerical structure outlined by Jordan (2000) in *Silence of Sodom* underwrites its obedience by offering a variety of rewards for compliance. Any priest loyal to Rome (and, in addition, not indifferent to his own advancement within the clerical ranks) will take exquisite care to follow church directives. In the case of "Letter to the Bishops of the Catholic Church," this means a priest who counsels a homosexual person can advise him or her only to accept or, in the horrible phrase, "come to terms" with an unfortunate fate—as if life ever responded to negotiation. Beyond this severely minimal response, the priest can offer no substantive help, at least publicly. Garry Wills (2000, p. 190) tartly observes that "silence covers many kindnesses—departures from the official line that serve the pastoral needs of perplexed Catholics." If he hews to the doctrine, he will tell the gay or lesbian person that he or she has a pathological "condition," one that the Vatican text emphasizes is "intrinsically disordered." Not all priests are this thoughtless or this direct. Perhaps few are. Realizing how little comfort he can actually *give* the gay person, and thus, perhaps, acting with "well-meaning" intention, a sympathetic priest might offer as a palliative an economy of suffering in which pain itself becomes something else. He might use language such as, "You are *graced* with a pathological condition," or "*gifted* with." Realizing how little help he can give, at some point the priest will encourage the man or woman to pray for grace to accept this "gift" from God. In this case pain is *not* pain but a form of spiritual nourishment. [Mis]using the example of the cross is also common. The priest may extol the example of Jesus, telling the homosexual person to endure the pain that is part of his or her (ironically) "natural" state. Now, even "natural" is used *against* them. Priests from a slightly older generation can invite the person to "offer up" suffering for the poor souls in purgatory. Thus, when viewed from the gay person's perspective, all options are bleak, binding him or her or him into a pattern of spiritual anorexia. Endurance and diminishment are, perversely, extolled as grace and spiritual nourishment. From the point of view of the priest, in whatever manner he cooks or juggles the spiritual accounting books, he, the pastoral agent, becomes complicit in underwriting pain. Participating in its use, by degrees, the priest enters a realm entirely removed from pastoring, one in which compassion is exchanged for power. From either perspective, what may have begun as a moment of potential spiritual care becomes a contest of will and power, words and silence. Altruism gives way to an S/M-edged encounter, with all the mixed motives prompted by such exchanges.

Let's consider these mixed motives for a moment, because they are shared equally by counselee and priest. The gay person who seeks the comfort of counsel or church can be threatened into silence by the bleak prospects facing him or her; these include, at a most obvious level, overt expulsion from church property and being banned from full sacramental participation. The more private discourses of shame, guilt, and gradual moral ossification that must be managed are hardly ever apparent. Nonetheless, these, too, are steep prices to be paid for a place in the pew. On the other hand, the priest can also be coerced, although in different ways and for different rewards. A priest attentive to clerical prerogative (in church as well as sedimented in Catholic societies) will be acutely sensitive to the calculus of power as it is held or withheld within the church's administration. Thus he will take care not to give offense to his superiors. For reasons of his own job security, among other motives, he will be cautious not to seem to be too "gay friendly." On occasion, he will also lie, defer to, and protect his superiors by looking the other way at evident illegality.[12] The current scene of clerical misconduct in the United States is noteworthy in this regard, since it demonstrates how priests (gay or straight) are hardly in a position to defend themselves—not necessarily from charges of personal sexual irregularity but from the rank prejudice exhibited against them by their own superiors. Why? As Robert Goss (1993) observes, "Silencing, exclusion, expulsion, condemnation, and other forms of ecclesial terrorism are the rewards for . . . solidarity with the oppressed" (p. 120). Thus, whatever his personal feelings about the matter, the loyal priest will support Roman doctrine in public, even if in private he tries to act "pastorally"—that is, with sensitivity and compassion. Often this tension becomes the chief dynamic of the pastoral encounter—perhaps even the *point* of it, especially if the priest is gay himself.

Priests and other agents of authority—indeed, even corporate salespersons, for that matter—find themselves having to follow procedures with which they might disagree. Homosexuality has no privilege here. Unlike corporations, however, the discursive energies taken to manage homosexuality distill in particular ways the tensions by which authority is structured, and kept authoritative, in the Roman Church. Consider the gay priest, for example. Caught between harsh doctrine and his personal conflicts, the priest may seek a counselee's collusion in his struggle. Through a shrug, a wink, or other sign, the priest makes it clear to the counselee that, in a telling phrase, his hands are tied. He offers doctrine ironically, or apologetically; he may actually *say* that although he speaks in the name of the church, he wishes to distance himself from—even deny responsibility for— what he must say. In whatever way the priest signals his "personal" discomfort with the doctrine or his implication in—whether by words unspoken or body movements (a shrug, a wink, a roll of the eyes)— nonetheless the priest will make it clear that he cannot contravene the Magisterium. Often such conversations end, or sometimes begin, with a linguistic maneuver by which the priest exonerates himself: "Surely, you understand that . . ." Such a rhetorical preemptive strike intends, in literal ways, to disarm the counselee and to bolster the priest's tainted authority. This verbal coercion, leveraged by the priest upon the counselee, signifies the larger network of rhetorical and institutional forces that bind both persons together in a web of du- plicity and constraint (Kelman, 1995). This is why Amnesty Interna- tional refuses to isolate the individual agents of state violence from the "crimes of obedience" that make such action almost inevitable.[13]

The priest's shrug or wink, inviting the counselee's collusion, may make explicit a range of interlocking economic and social pressures. However, if the priest himself is gay, the shrug or wink may have even *more* meaning. Often in such cases the extra significance is evident to the counselee—indeed it is meant to be. The priest—perhaps known to be gay by the person sitting opposite him—must, because of that knowledge and in an odd reversal, appeal for sympathy *from* her or him. As a consequence the priest enacts, in his own person, the good cop/bad cop of formula TV melodrama. This is what the shrug or wink means: two persons share the same stigma, although in the counseling room or confessional they meet at radically different points. One has the power to extort and compel, and the other only the power to silence, deny, or be complicit. Either way, the one seeking pastoral care is put in the insupportable spiritual position of buttress- ing a lie. As we see, silence, differently leveraged from each side, works to different ends. Even straight priests find themselves pulled into the murk, as they must find ways to manage the illogic and the spiritual disassociation that obedience to the doctrine necessarily im- poses. As Garry Wills (2000, p. 5) remarks:

How can one aspire to a high calling and yet accept low standards for his own truthfulness about what he really believes?
How can one be in service to others, yet peddle to them "religious truths" whose truthfulness rings so obviously hollow?

How can one? The answer, too often, is that one *cannot*, but one does,
under duress to economic as well as ideological constraint.[14]

One could argue to a depressing conclusion: that under the existing
circumstances, the pastoral encounter does not actually pervert power;
it is, in itself, perversely, power of a distinctly gendered and sexist
kind. Although the priest—straight *or* gay—counsels the penitent
"for his or her own good," he must act cautiously for *his* own good.
He cannot do otherwise save at great personal risk. Even if he has no
wish for advancement, the feudal economic system under which ordinary priests live guarantees that they are under pressure to conform—
partly because they lack training to do anything else, and importantly
because traditionally the priest has little in the way of financial security.

Let me emphasize this. One can presume the liberal "goodwill" of
individual priests and applaud the rhetorical generosity contained in
such "forward-looking" church documents as the National Conference of Catholic Bishops' "Always Our Children" (1997). Nonetheless, even the most "gay-friendly" priest remains obliged to confirm
pathology in his gay counselee, and even bishops' laudable documents can be revoked by Rome—as was this one. Liberal feelings
cannot stand against retrenched policies, canons, and the power to enforce "pathology." Just what this pathology consists of, in, or means,
the mish-mash of traditions and revisions that constitute the doc-
trine(s) do not in fact clarify. Nor do they all agree. That is, many,
probably most, post-Vatican II documents admit that the condition of
homosexuality is not a personal choice. "Always Our Children," for
example, sympathetically calls sexual orientation a "fundamental di-
mension" of personality, one that is "experienced as a given." The
document likewise quotes what surely must be an ultimate authority,
the catechism of the Catholic Church, which says definitively that
"everyone . . . should acknowledge and accept his sexual identity"
(#2333). The statement issued from the highest level of the Vatican in
1986, under the signature of Joseph Cardinal Ratzinger ([1986]
1994), however, spins the text differently. This document emphasizes
that this condition is "inordinately disordered": it is a "more or less

strong tendency ordered toward an intrinsic moral evil; and thus the inclination itself must be seen as an objective disorder" (p. 40).[15]

But suppose a gay man or woman, aware of these contradictions, nonetheless challenges the priest, calling attention to the illogical quality of the theology which the priest must disseminate? After all, he or she might say, "To the extent that I am 'inordinately disordered' in my essence, to that extent I am (also by doctrinal definition), less morally responsible and thus less 'sinful.'" The point is an exact one, since grievously sinful acts are those that involve full consent of the will. Thus the illogical paradox at the heart of the tradition which Ratzinger cuts and pastes together: being homosexual is not the fault of the individual, and therefore the individual cannot claim full moral responsibility for any actions—this, according to the canonical equivalent of diminished capacity. On the other hand, with Vatican authority, conditions are put in place that must seem, to the homosexual, punitive. Rarely, however, does such a possible confrontation between gay layperson and priest ever get this far. In the first place, very few persons, straight or gay, *can* argue theology; this is just one consequence of the pervasive silence imposed upon public discussion—a point I will address next. Nonetheless, presuming a homosexual person uppity or outspoken enough to challenge the theology, the priest's pastoral demeanor can take on yet another aspect. Facing such resistance (colonial uprisings come to mind), the priest can—again, for "the counselee's own good"—refuse the sacrament or the spiritual service under petition. Institutions do have ways of making up the minds of their suppliants, and ensuring that they stay made up.

So, here is the bind—again to use a telling word—in which the homosexual person finds himself or herself. On one hand, even the harshest doctrine admits that the individual is not responsible for his or her condition, and thus by canon law, moral responsibility is, accordingly, diminished. Notwithstanding this, the "tendency" toward homosexuality, if at all publicized, apparently, becomes a visible and dramatic sign of original sin itself. Nor am I speaking euphemistically. John Paul II, speaking from the Vatican on July 7, 2000, decried homosexuality's "offense" against Christian values. Fourteen years previous Ratzinger distanced himself and his church against the social violence done to homosexuals, writing that such violence, while "regrettable," is, after all, "understandable." If ever one wondered why Ratzinger felt it necessary to make the apology in the first place, the pope's comments go a long way to clarify the point. Visible homosexuals are a threat, and however much we might not like it, social violence is the deplored although sanctioned response. Matthew Shepard and Brandon Teena might concur, if they could.

CONCLUSION: KILLING LANGUAGE

Stories abound of egregious treatment of gay and lesbian persons at the hands of clerics and church officials—even if most "liberal" Catholics wince when they hear them. Some examples include homosexuals being refused absolution; gay men and women being refused Communion; gay men, in confession, being advised to undergo exorcism, therapy, surgery; babies, inappropriately enough, being refused baptism because their adoptive parents are homosexuals; gay students being offered "ministry" at a Catholic university only under condition of secrecy. A priest at Georgetown University, for instance, refused a twenty-one-year-old student Communion because the young man (a daily mass-goer) announced himself to be, also, a homosexual. The pious student turned away from the altar reveals the fist in the Vatican's gloved rhetoric. So does the refusal of Communion to groups who will not renounce their homosexuality in public church meeting (Freiberg, 2001).

I once argued in favor of a Catholic Bill of Rights, the first point of which would guarantee equal access to sacraments for all Catholics.[16] We are far from that minimum spiritual right, however. What is often overlooked by many Catholics—indeed willfully unattended to—is the arcane system regulating sacramental access. That is to say, all sacraments are not uniformly available to all Catholics. Some are excluded by age, others by gender, others by legal edict. Add to this the social shame of "sin"—whether publicly known or privately endured—and one understands why, almost thirty years after the window opening of Vatican II, many Catholics still feel themselves to be looking through windows that are securely locked. Many find themselves neither invited to the table nor welcome to sacramental participation. Church teaching, as well as local practice, conspires to create a managerial system of exclusion.

Well-intended, loyal, and intelligent Catholics participate in this daily disconnect between a rhetoric of divine mercy and the actual practice in which too often sacraments are carefully calibrated, often by whim. The *Baltimore Catechism* insists that sacraments are "instituted by God to give grace"; despite this, sacraments are routinely denied those who seem most in need of them. Worse, access to the sacraments is further limited by custom and managerial policy sometimes far removed from doctrine. As a result, participation in the sacraments becomes tied to ambiguous factors of good will, indifferent knowledge of theology, perhaps the exercise of clerical whim—all excuses, of course, for controlling power and maintaining the status quo. Consider the example of two neighboring parishes on the surely nonthreatening issue of girl altar servers. Despite Vatican approval (some years ago), parish A permits altar girls; parish B denies them because, as the pastor says, he wishes to support male vocations to the priesthood.

Leaving sacramental access up to "good will" merely ensures that informal blackmail will continue to be the norm. Indeed, no one who has attempted marriage (the canonical phrase) in the Roman Church or sought to have a child baptized or even asked for some lesser form of pastoral aid has any doubt as to the powerful means of coercion that can be extorted in exchange for the petitioner's spiritual "grace." Here, indeed, is the issue at stake—the threat made so eloquently clear in the demeaning encounter between the priest and the gay student refused Communion. To return to my question, why do homosexuals (in particular, although not exclusively) permit the subtle, and not so subtle, curtailing of their presence in Christian congregations? Why, specifically, do Catholic homosexual persons allow themselves to be blackmailed into creeping, unacknowledged and silently, into the pews of their own church? In this ecclesiastical equivalent to domestic violence, the answer, at least partially, lies in a subtle capitulation. Repeated beatings wear down one's soul as well as body; settling for what little one can get shows how little hope one has for anything better. To put it delicately, their place at the eucharistic table depends upon how well homosexual persons can straighten up in public, and so they do. Meanwhile, on the side, they take what means they can to nourish themselves spiritually.

Straightening up takes a variety of forms, incrementally measured. Like "coming out," however, "straightening up" is never completely accomplished. This is where documents such as "Letter to the Catholic Bishops on the Pastoral Care of Homosexuals" make themselves felt. The priest who withholds Communion from a gay student is no more remarkable than Rome's denying the sacrament of marriage to homosexual persons; both actions, private and public, are justified by explicit doctrinal sanction. Nor does this "pastoral care" differ materially from many other instances of sacramental regulation that could be mentioned. In all such cases the withholding or conforming priest, in effect, carries the enemy's weapons, whether he acts on principle or is coerced through fear of his own "exposure." Some might argue that there are differences between the refusal of Communion to a homosexual student and the blanket proscription against a blessing, private *or* public, of sacramental unions. The difference, however, is only one of degree; so accustomed are we to the latter *public* refusal that we fail to see it for the *personal* coercion it effects. The priest–student encounter over Communion dramatizes more directly the pressure the other intends less directly: forego your homosexual identity, give voice to the lie that you are straight, and the Sacraments will be open to you. Often, even liberal priests will encourage a duplicity breathtakingly at odds with spiritual integrity. They will argue that the "words" spoken by a person do not matter—that the public lie (that is, "straight acting," appearing as two "singles" rather than as a "couple") is a meaningless gesture, just a formality. The closeness of this formulation to the extortion of a confession under torture ("it's just words anyway") should be noted.

In exploring the symbolic use of the homosexual body in the Roman Catholic Church, Mark Jordan points toward mechanisms that link ministerial preoccupations to other issues. One concludes his study, and others like it, by taking a fresh look at the basic doctrines and language of Christian discourse. One is struck by the pervasive violence of the discourse, on the one hand (beginning with the Crucifixion, of course), and on the other, the use of language to mystify violence and to evacuate its responsibility (see Schwarz, 1997). In particular, homosexual presence within Catholic doctrine and practice, whether as a moral or demonic show, at whatever degree of explicit or implicit coercion, demonstrates the ceaseless ability of the scapegoating gaze to disguise itself as something benign. Ratzinger's bland rhetoric of moral uplift, and compassionate "care for," is an example. Scapegoating works by particularizing the deviant while keeping unaddressed aspects of the system most in need of change—aspects whose terms make necessary the deviancy in the first instance. It is in this context that one finally understands the hopelessness of the argument that one should stay in this or that church because one must "work from within for change." Such an argument ensures only that nothing changes. Why? The homosexual who stays, under the conditions laid out in the "Letter to the Bishops of the Catholic Church on the Pastoral Care of Homosexuals," guarantees that his or her presence will be used against him or her; silence will be accepted as consent, permission, acceptance—even while his or her symbolic body is compelled to do the various social works churches find useful and necessary for their deviants to do. Thus we are back where we began, asking, why should we do the enemy's work for them?

Homosexual Catholics are disarmed and seduced in church as much by the threat of pain as by an unrequited desire for kindness. Homosexual persons are cajoled into partial representation at the table of the Lord even at the expense of dignity and self-worth, ultimately even to the point of self-erasure. That we accept these terms is only one indication of the extent of our spiritual starvation.

Let me conclude by returning to the consequences of enforced silence. Article 10 in "Letter to the Bishops of the Catholic Church" makes evident they are permitted no speech or power of nomination save accepting those that demean, deny, and humiliate them.[17] At its most direct level, forbidding speech (including, of course, writing and thinking or chapters like this) means that no homosexual person is able, with any integrity, to arm, develop, deliberate, or nuance his or her conscience upon the very points under dispute: thus *dis*armed in concrete intellectual and material ways, they are rendered defenseless against the powerful words of a Ratzinger, or even John Paul. These leaders, having words—and the power to enforce them while silencing others—need be neither right nor accurate. They can misargue a tradition and patch together texts out of context with no one to say nay. The homosexual person, personally silenced, serves the status quo by being kept institutionally ignorant. In this way they remain at the whim and will of any interpreter of holy writ, however poorly it is interpreted. For this reason, the challenge a gay priest, who is also a writer, makes to the system concerns less what he might do (or be perceived as doing) as a practicing homosexual than in what he might write or say as a gay man. But this is true of the homosexual more generally. The organ on their body that church doctrine finds most offensive is not, in fact, a sexual one. The threat and their subversiveness comes via a more profoundly "disordered" tendency—the need to question, to think, and, in the end, to ask the church to do right by its God-given mandate to speak truths and to set captives free.[18]

NOTES

1. The chapter title is a reference to Cardinal Adam Maida of Detroit who, during a Vatican meeting called to discuss the events, referred to behavioral scientists who argued that the molestation scandal was "not truly a pedophilia-type problem but a homosexual-type problem" (Whittington, 2002).

2. In both systems advancement depends upon an unspoken but informally recognized cross-hatching of loyalties, tightly woven allegiances supported by feudal economic constraints.

3. Prompted by wide "distress and anger" caused by this and other documents released by the CDF concerning homosexual rights, Cardinal Basil Hume subsequently tried to offer "further clarification" upon the church's teaching. He cites Ratzinger's condemnation of violence but passes over the exculpation that shortly follows (see Hume, 1997, paragraph 14).

4. According to Hannah Rosin (1999, p. A1), "The highly publicized ruling [closing down New Ways Ministry] reflects the church's increased impatience with the growing number of Catholics who call for full acceptance of homosexuals by the church." Even Cardinal Hume notes lamely that the English translation of Ratzinger's language ("disordered") "is a harsh one in our English language. It immediately suggests a sinful situation, or at least implies a demeaning of the person or even a sickness. It should not be so interpreted" (Hume, 1997, paragraph 7). Hume's efforts to render Ratzinger benign are not convincing.

5. Herbert C. Kelman (1995, p. 28) argues that in

> the modern state, individual rights in effect derive from the state. Thus, to be excluded from the state—to be denied the rights of citizenship—is tantamount to becoming a non-person vulnerable to arbitrary treatment, to torture, and ultimately to extermination.

6. Many feel the Congregation for the Doctrine of the Faith's letter was aimed at this group, even if it went unmentioned in the text. Of all Catholic homophile groups, Dignity was, at its inception, the least willing to accommodate itself to older doctrine; even its name drew attention to the pervasive *indignity* of church doctrine toward the homosexual. The irony is that in many places Dignity has re-created some of the worst aspects of Roman patriarchy.

7. In July 1999, the Vatican Congregation for the Doctrine of the Faith, still under the leadership of Cardinal Joseph Ratzinger, summarily foreclosed the ministry of Father Robert Nugent and Sister Jeannine Gramick, founders of New Ways Ministry, an educational and pastoral outreach to homosexuals that was over twenty-five years old. In September 2001 it was reported that Gramick was leaving her religious order, the School Sisters of Notre Dame, when it bowed to pressure from the Vatican to forbid her working with homosexual persons. Gramick had been a member of the order for forty-one years. She joined a noncanonical group, the Sisters of Loretto (see "Well-known Nun to Leave Baltimore for Order in Colo.," 2001).

8. John Paul II expressed "bitterness for the insult" of having the festival "during the grand Jubilee of the year 2000 and for the offense to Christian values in a city that is so dear to the heart of Catholics all over the world" (Hughes, 2000).

9. Mark Jordan (1997, pp. 6-9) traces a similar rhetorical elevation in his wry commentary about the "invention" of sodomy, by which a geographic designation becomes, through a series of displacements, a measure of moral turpitude.

10. For examples of the work done by colonized persons, see *Voices of Hope* (Gramick and Nugent, 1995), a collection of "friendly" statements by church officials, although it is painful in places to note how systematically the editors must ignore, rewrite, even *unwrite* large portions of documents to get their "friendly" statement. In the essay by Ratzinger (who is not named in the text), the editors pick out less than a paragraph of the originally lengthy essay.

11. Remaining "in communion" with Rome is not just an expression. Further validation of this stigma against homosexual persons—despite a rhetoric of altruism to the contrary—can be found in the recent Rainbow Sash Movement, in which gay men and women, draped in rainbow-colored stoles, approach the altar for communion. An article in *The Washington Blade* recounts incidents in which these men and women were turned away without Communion (Freiberg, 2001).

12. Richard Sipe writes about one priest whose job to provide a "young male prostitute" to his bishop became a "regular part" of his duties. "The incongruity between the young priest's own moral standards and his personal devotion to his superior/boss forced him into a psychological corner. Depression was a substitute for death as the only passage out of his bind" (Sipe, 1995, p. 23).

13. The sympathetic priest can even turn to church pronouncement itself to support his position of altruistic care. He can acknowledge, with sympathy, as the NCCB does in its 1997 document, that homosexuals are "always our children." Yet even this image, as comforting as it initially seems, is problematic, since it suggests the limits of compassion and the reach of patriarchy: children are, after all, subjects, without agency over their own lives. It is their parents—in this case, the range of Fathers up the hierarchy—who "know better."

14. Scholar Frederic S. Roden (2001) cites the "obvious freedom of a lay scholar such as Wills or Mark Jordan" who points to "the amount of dissent that underlies forced clerical silence."

15. The National Conference of Catholic Bishops took an initially softer line. In "Always Our Children," the conference writes, "By itself, therefore, a homosexual orientation cannot be considered sinful, because morality presumes the freedom to choose." "Always Our Children," issued in October 1997, was recalled by Rome when it was reported to be too liberal; a Vatican review was responsible for its being rewritten, in a form much less "friendly" to gay and lesbian persons.

16. "Ingebretsen said he hopes New Ways Ministry helps draft a 'bill of rights' for Catholic Church-goers that would 'sanctify human experiences across gender, race, creed and across a range of sexual expression'" (Tandon, 1998).

17. In Ratzinger's (1986, p. 43) own words:

> But the proper reaction to crimes committed against homosexual persons should not be to claim that the homosexual condition is not disordered. When such a claim is made and when homosexual activity is consequently condoned, or when civil legislation is introduced to protect behavior to which no

one has any conceivable right, neither the Church nor society at large should be surprised when other distorted notions and practices gain ground and irrational and violent reactions increase.

18. Mark Jordan (2000, p. 82) pointedly notes that

Sodomy was and homosexuality is important in Catholic moral theology because it has been intimately connected to the exercise of power in the construction of priestly lives. It was one of the sites where moral regulation could be exercised purely, with a minimum of resistance. In this inner realm of churchly power, regulation could be exercised for regulation's sake.

REFERENCES

Catholic News Service (1992). Responding to legislative proposals on discrimination against homosexuals. *Origins* 22(10)(August 6): 1.

Dollimore, Jonathan (1991). *Sexual dissidence: Augustine to Wilde, Freud to Foucault.* Oxford, UK: Clarendon Press.

Freiberg, Peter (2001). Rainbow Sash group works to gain acceptance. *The Washington Blade,* September 7, pp. 25, 27.

Goss, Robert (1993). *Jesus acted up: A gay and lesbian manifesto.* San Francisco: Harper.

Gramick, Jeannine and Nugent, Robert (Eds.) (1995). *Voices of hope: A collection of positive Catholic writings on gay and lesbian issues.* New York: Center for Homophobia Education.

Hughes, Candice (2000). Pope denounces gay pride parade. *AP Online,* July 7.

Hume, Cardinal Basil (1997). A note concerning the teaching of the Catholic Church concerning homosexual people. Accessed at <http://www.catholic-ew. org.uk/mi/homose01.htm>.

Jordan, Mark D. (1997). *The invention of sodomy in Christian theology.* Chicago: The University of Chicago Press.

Jordan, Mark D. (2000). *The silence of Sodom: Homosexuality in modern Catholicism.* Chicago: The University of Chicago Press.

Kelman, Herbert C. (1995). The social context of torture: Policy process and authority structure. In Ronald D. Crelinsten and Alex P. Smid (Eds.), *The politics of pain: Torturers and their masters* (pp. 19-34). Boulder, CO: Westview Press.

Ratzinger, Cardinal Joseph (Congregation of Defense of Faith) (1986). Letter to the bishops of the Catholic church on the pastoral care of homosexual persons. In Jeannine Gramick and Pat Furey (Eds.) (1988), *The Vatican and homosexuality: Reactions to the "Letter to the bishops of the Catholic church on the pastoral care of homosexual persons"* (pp. 1-10). New York: Crossroad.

Roden, Frederic S. (2001). Queer Christian: The Catholic homosexual apologia and lesbian/gay practice. *The International Journal of Gay and Lesbian Identity* 6(4): 251-265.

Rosin, Hannah (1999). Vatican intervenes against gay ministry. *The Washington Post,* July 14, p. A1.

Rudy, Kathy (1997). *Sex and the church: Gender, homosexuality, and the transformation of Christian ethics.* Boston: Beacon Press.

Schwarz, Regina M. (1997). *The curse of Cain: The violent legacy of monotheism.* Chicago: University of Chicago Press.

Sedgwick, Eve Kosofsky (1990). *Epistemology of the closet.* Berkeley: University of California Press.

Sipe, A.W. Richard (1995). *Sex, priests and power: Anatomy of a crisis.* New York: Brunner/Mazel.

Tandon, Shawn (1998). Bridge of the gay and the Catholic. *The Georgetown Voice,* February 12.

"Well-known nun to leave Baltimore for order in Colo" (2001). *The Washington Blade,* September 7, p. 35.

Whittington, Lewis (2002). Holy gay purge. *Philadelphia Citypaper.net,* May 2. Available at <http://citypaper.net/articles/2002-05-02/slant.shtml>.

Wills, Garry (2000). *Papal sin: Structures of deceit.* New York: Doubleday.

Chapter 4

Silencing Sodom

Chuck Colbert

The following review of Mark Jordan's fine book is a longer version of the one that I wrote for *The National Catholic Reporter* (*NCR*), published on February 16, 2001. It was a little less than a year before the scandal of clerical misconduct with minors and vulnerable adults exploded in the Boston archdiocese, with newfound and heightened awareness—along with shock, horror, and disgust—spreading rapidly across the U.S. Catholic Church, and indeed the Church universal.

Shortly after the *Boston Globe* and *Boston Herald* broke the story here, I became the lead reporter for *NCR* on the local scandal, following its developments and reporting on them for a national audience of Catholic readers. Quickly on I realized that this scandal would have a profound effect on the lives of gay men in the seminaries and priesthood. I also feared a similarly adverse effect on gay-positive and -affirming lay ministers with lesbian and gay Catholics, our families and friends, not to mention the ripple effect on the lesbian and gay community writ large.

For example, the disproportionately high numbers of gay men in the priesthood suddenly became general knowledge to the American public. But as the allegations of clerical sexual abuse increased, it also became clear that the vast majority of cases—at least those so far reported and under the media spotlight—involve sexual misconduct with boys, young men, and vulnerable adult males. Some people seized upon this phenomenon, rushing to a judgment that gays in the priesthood, and indeed homosexuality, lay at the heart of the matter. These people had an easy scapegoat, something and someone to blame. Far too often rhetoric from Vatican officials, including members of the hierarchy here and abroad, perpetuated this blame game. Gay priests, gay subculture, homosexual atmosphere—get rid of the queers and all will be well—that seems to be the politics of an ugly game plan.

What I propose to do in this chapter is twofold. First, I include the longer version of my review of *The Silence of Sodom* (Jordan, 2000). The book is significant and profound for reasons that I discuss—and hope readers come to appreciate by reading this long version. Second, I offer some postreview reflection, nearly one year out from scandal and crisis, its Boston explosion, and nationwide aftershocks. I write as a layman and out gay Catholic in a committed same-sex relationship, a journalist, and a graduate student of theology at the Weston Jesuit School of Theology, where I have found both academic encouragement and spiritual nourishment. I have no intention of leaving the Catholic Church, which is a place I call home. Nor do I have any intention to deny the truth, beauty, and joy of a gay male sexual identity and spirituality, God-given gifts for which I am now deeply grateful. So here is what I would write about the book:

> Insightful and provocative non-fiction about homosexuality and the church—written by openly gay Catholic men—does not come along often. While the works of John Boswell, John McNeill, and Andrew Sullivan come to mind, they don't quite cut through institutional church denial about homosexuality the way Mark Jordan does in *The Silence of Sodom: Homosexuality in Modern Catholicism.*[1]

"You will not understand modern homosexuality unless you understand Catholic homosexuality, and you cannot understand Catholic homosexuality unless you begin with the clergy," Mark Jordan (2000, p. 5) writes. That statement is the main thesis the author develops. What Jordan accomplishes is nothing less than brilliant, giving readers with open minds a better appreciation of the intrinsic homosexual fixation, as well as homoerotic imagination, of the Roman Catholic Church. His scholarship deserves serious consideration by faithful Catholics in America.

Silence of Sodom begins with a hopeful, if not fanciful, vision. Jordan asks us to indulge in a Monday-morning-after, Pentecostal epiphany. Imagine, he writes, a majority of Vatican officials experiencing a conversion—a complete change of heart regarding homosexuality.

The inspiration of the Holy Spirit has even touched the pope: "The Holy Father asks, What is required for the thorough correction of the teachings?" (Jordan, 2000, p. 2).

Such a correction, or change, Jordan argues, cannot come about simply as the result of theological argument. It will happen only when the real lives of gay believers become visible. Jordan is onto something significant when he argues that the silence of Sodom is more than just a fact. It is an actively pursued strategy to prevent a correction in church understanding and teaching from happening.

In other words, theological arguments are going nowhere because those adhering to the teaching of the Congregation for the Doctrine of the Faith simply repeat, repeat, and *repeat* old doctrinal lines—intrinsic evil, objective disorder, to name just a few. Their aim, Jordan suggests, is to wear people out with fruitless theological argumentation. Counterstrategies are what need to be developed, Jordan insists. Then perhaps the church in larger circles will be able to experience the conversion that families often do when a member comes out.

Still, as the author soberly reminds us, a correction of change of church teaching about homosexuality remains for some—the resolutely orthodox and rigidly conservative—incomprehensible, unimaginable. Even some liberals will have their share of mind stretching to do. Nonetheless, Jordan remains optimistic. What he advocates is not impossible: the people of God—the church, including courageous lesbian and gay Catholics—asserting ourselves and shouldering responsibility for freedom and liberation, honesty and courage. For Jordan there is no turning back. Theological and ecclesial truth telling must be proclaimed out loud:

> The Church, in some broader sense, will have to encourage homosexual Catholics to live openly and proudly. Serious moral theology cannot be principally the framing and manipulation of quasi-legal propositions. It must begin and end in the discovery of particular lives under grace. Lesbian and gay lives will have to become audible to the church, readable within it, before their graces can be discerned and described. (Jordan, 2000, p. 3)

According to Jordan, the church's problematic teaching about homosexuality, gay people, our love, and its sexual expression persists in no small measure because of the large numbers of homosexual priests among the ranks of the clergy. These men are gay—out in

varying degrees to themselves, friends, family, and even parishioners—but not *fully* out of the closet, certainly, not out to the public, at
least in any significant numbers.

Estimates of homosexual priests in the U.S. Catholic church range
anywhere from 10 to 25, to 50, and as high as 75 percent.[2] This pervasive clerical closeting truly bothers Jordan. Underlying the tone and
tenor of the book run strong feelings of anger, if not outrage. The title
of the book, *The Silence of Sodom,* in fact points to the Catholic
clergy, to those in the past who, over hundreds of years, invented the
"Catholic science of sodomy," and those in the present, the heirs of
this legacy, who refuse—or are unable—to bear witness to a truth
about their own fundamental sexual orientation. Clerical closeting is
a problem, Jordan maintains, because of the chilling silence it im-
poses on any open—and really honest—conversation about homosexuality and the church.

"There is indeed a silent Sodom," Jordan (2000, p. 6) writes. "It is
housed in the structures of churchly power. Its silence must be disturbed before there can be mature Catholic teaching on 'homosexuality'—or mature criticism of how 'homosexuality' itself fails to describe gay Catholic lives." Jordan's book continues to disturb status
quo theological and spiritual complacency, bringing to more conscious awareness a heretofore churchly unmentionable. Yet it would
be a mistake to misread this book as an exposé of scandal and secrets.
Jordan honestly attempts to flesh out just how clerical closeting
within the church's power structure affects—indeed compromises—
its teaching, preaching, and ministering.

In the book's first part, "Church Words," for instance, Jordan puts a
much less benign spin on doctrine and other official documents such
as the recent Catechism, the 1975 "Declaration Regarding Certain
Questions of Sexual Ethics," the 1986 "Letter to the Bishops of the
Catholic Church on the Pastoral Care of Homosexual Persons," and
the 1997 American bishops' letter, "Always Our Children." Jordan
(2000, p. 11) argues that these documents are nothing more than
"theological rhetoric," unworthy of "counter argument" because "they
don't mean to authorize discussion."

A particularly insightful part of "Church Words" is Jordan's critique of "Always Our Children," released in 1997, revised, and released again in 1998. Reaction in the press and from the pews was
generally favorable, but Jordan has a more skeptical view. "Despite

its gentleness, 'Always Our Children' echoes the anti homosexual rhetoric of the 'Christian Right,' " he writes. "It emphasizes that it is 'not intended for advocacy purposes or to serve a particular agenda,' nor is it 'an endorsement of what some call a 'homosexual lifestyle.'" Nonsense, Jordan writes: "Of course the letter serves a 'particular agenda.' It serves the agenda of the American Catholic bishops, who are trying to figure out how to keep people in the church at a time when official condemnations of homosexuality are driving many from it" (Jordan, 2000, p. 46).

As Jordan's excellent rhetorical analysis points out, official documents are written as if the all-straight clergy are to welcome the hurting/Other homosexuals. One would never gather from the language of the documents, Jordan argues, just how many members of the clergy are homosexual themselves.

Moreover, the language of "Always Our Children" overlooks the fact that some parents might be gay themselves. Still others, when finding out their children are gay or lesbian, are in fact not destroyed or thrown into crisis—except insofar as they become enraged at church teaching and how it maligns their sons and daughters. These important subtleties are overlooked in the otherwise compassionate-sounding language of the bishops' letter. Yet, implicitly the language of "Always Our Children" hammers the point home: gays in question are pitiable and pathetic souls.

The author's insight and rhetorical analysis are well directed in light of several recent developments. A few years ago, for instance, the Vatican completely silenced Sister Jeannine Gramick and Father Robert Nugent, a pastoral duo who worked tirelessly to bridge the gap between gays and the church. The New England Catholic bishops issued a public statement decrying civil unions in Vermont. Shortly thereafter, the ecclesial and political bungling of Italian prelates and Vatican officials during World Pride Roma—and the very success and visibility of the event itself—prompted a papal scolding of gays, from the balcony of St. Peter's no less.

Before Thanksgiving, the Pontifical Council for the Family, a bureaucracy within the Vatican curia, issued a seventy-six-page document—"Family Marriage and 'De facto' Unions"—that decries same-sex unions as "a deplorable distortion of what should be a communion of love and life between a man and a woman in a reciprocal gift open to life." Although unmarried heterosexual couples pose a threat to the stability of society, "making homosexual relations equivalent to marriage is much more grave," according to Vatican bureaucrats. To put "de facto unions" on a "juridical level similar to marriage," they say, is tantamount to "publicly qualif[ying] this kind of cohabitation as a 'good,' elevating it to a condition similar to or equivalent to marriage, to the detriment of truth and justice."[3]

This style of hierarchical rhetoric still resounds—blocking respectful listening and sharing about the reality of gay and lesbian life in a postmodern world. Those who critique the church are dismissed as anti-Catholic. Scholars such as Jordan are labeled "gay activists" or worse—"militant homosexuals."

But as Jordan prods us to think, polemics have consequences in the form of painful aftershock. In the wake of the nasty swipes at gays— what some gay and lesbian Catholics experience as spiritual abuse— more of the gay faithful are leaving the church. Self-respecting gay Catholics can tolerate only so much abuse and neglect, experiencing disappointment and desolation, their faith becoming increasingly more irrelevant, if not toxic, to their spiritual lives.

Jordan hints here at a very real and lurking danger: secular atheism. This phenomenon is not so much a denial of God's existence or a repudiation of all things Catholic, both cultural and spiritual. Rather, it is the atheism of irrelevancy.

Jordan stirs us to ask: What on earth were these prelates and the pontiff thinking during the past nine months? For his part, the author has given the posturing, positioning, and power playing serious thought. He spares no punches when he writes:

> Many male homosexuals are in positions of power within the church. They are often the most violent persecutors of "out" homosexuals. We are here, among the oppressed, and also already there, among the oppressors. Indeed the machinery of church oppression may be in many important ways just what homosexual men use to oppress other homosexual men. (Jordan, 2000, p. 80)

That truthful insight rings loud and clear. It is an experience that more than a few gay men—and lesbians—know all too well, having been victimized by church politics and other hurtful dealings in which the truths of gay life, both its joys and pains, have been dismissed and diminished.

The second part of *Silence of Sodom,* the book's longest, shuttles the reader along major and minor highways of church living. Life within, the author argues, is where the institution's real knowledge of male homosexuality resides—in the "fragments of history" and "unspoken but widely known features of clerical culture" (p. 13).

To a certain extent, this part, "Church Lives," revisits some of the terrain covered in Jordan's 1997 book, *The Invention of Sodomy in Christian Theology,* which won the 1999 John Boswell Prize of the American Historical Association.[4]

In part two, the reader learns about the theological construction of sodomy, thanks in large part to Peter Damian, who wrote *Book of Gomorrah* or *Gomorran Book* (circa) 1050. This was "the first polemic against sodomy in Catholic theology" Jordan writes, "in order to stop the spread of 'sodomitic vice' in the priesthood" (Jordan, 2000, p. 85).

Readers also learn about charges of "papal sodomy." Here Jordan provides several historical examples, pontiffs such as John XII (reigned 955-964), Boniface VIII (reigned 1294-1303), Paul II (reigned 1464-1471), and Sixtus IV (reigned 1471-1484). Pope John XII, for instance, "was accused by one chronicler of various debaucheries, including sex with men and boys" (Jordan, 2000, p. 118). Paul II "was ridiculed with feminine epithets for his love of ecclesiastical costume and beautiful young men" (p. 188). And Sixtus IV "created his lover (and nephew) a cardinal at the age of seventeen. Perhaps for that reason he was reputed to have given permission to the College of Cardinals to practice sodomy in times of summer heat," Jordan writes (p. 118).

As a more modern example, Jordan offers the case of Paul VI (reigned 1963-1978). Here the author relies on the work of Roger Peyrefitte, a French writer, who in 1970 "began to hint at the homosexuality of Pope Paul VI" during his reign.

> Peyrefitte said, for example, that the Pope had taken the name "Paul" because it was the name of his former lover, a young movie actor; that this man was known in Milanese clerical circles and protected by them; that the pope, while a cardinal, would go to a "discreet house" to meet young men. (Jordan, 2000, pp. 92-93)

He also writes about Julius III (1550-1555), "who participated in and then reconvened the reforming Council of Trent, [and] is also reported to have elevated a favorite boy, one Innocent, to the College of Cardinals" (2000, p. 119).

Church historians have yet to weigh in fully on what Jordan reports about John XII, Boniface VIII, Paul II, Sixtus IV, and Paul VI. But one highly regarded historian, J. N. D. Kelly, wrote the following about Julius III in *The Oxford Dictionary of Popes*:

> Although an outstanding canonist, Julius was a typical Renaissance pontiff, generous to relatives, pleasure-loving, devoted to banquets, the theatre, hunting. Essentially weak, he created scandal by his infatuation with a fifteen-year old youth, Innocenzo, picked up in the streets of Parma, whom he made his brother adopt and named cardinal. (Kelly, 1989, p. 265)

No doubt some readers will find Jordan's historical reporting to be shocking, disturbing—if not scandalous. Judging from the reactions among certain U.S. Catholics, Jordan has hit raw nerves. One reviewer, Robert Lockwood, director of research for the Catholic League, lambasted Jordan's book as "opinion—outrageous opinion—based on little more than the author's own fantasy life." Yet Lockwood (2000) may reveal a little too much about his own biases when he writes, "Jordan's book will remind the reader of that sophomoric sex-obsessed boy."

Jordan does not attempt to make up history. His book is not a work of fiction. Although there are those who feel compelled to discredit him, a truth—the point Jordan drives home—persists: homosexuality or "sodomy," whatever the nomenclature, is no stranger in the Roman Catholic Church. Gay clergy, in disproportionate numbers, when compared to the general population of American males, fill the ranks of the U.S. church, and have done so churchwide throughout time, place, and history, everywhere from deacons to priests, prelates, and even, as Jordan describes, pontiffs.

Jordan (2000) deals with the various surveys and studies that attempt to count homosexual clergy members. These attempts encounter a fundamental problem, as Jordan explains, because

> [i]n the empire of closets that is the modern Catholic church, no one knows more than a few of the compartments. The church is not one big closet. It is a honeycomb of closets that no one can survey in its entirety. (p. 108)

This clerical honeycomb, moreover, is riddled with nuances and distinctions. For example, "Discussion of homosexual activity within the Catholic clergy often emphasize a distinction between 'homo-social' and 'homosexual' or 'homogenital' and 'homophilic,'" Jordan writes.

> The purpose of such distinctions is more than differentiating feelings or dispositions from acts. The intention is to divide an unacceptable realm of homosexuality from an acceptable realm of male bonding or comradely affection or buddies' slaps on the butt. (2000, p. 108)

Furthermore, Jordan writes, "No one can know the extent of homo-sexual acts or desires within the Catholic clergy" (2000, p. 88). But the author does underscore two significant and nuanced phenomena. The first is the rejection of self-identification as "homosexual" by clergy who regularly perform genital acts (pp. 176-177). The second is a correlation: priests who are the most closeted are more likely to be the most homophobic. Quoting from what one priest told a reporter, Jordan (2000) writes, "Some of the worst homophobes are guys in the clergy and hierarchy who are gay" (p. 89). These men, who would be the last to acknowledge their orientation, actively pursue the anti-gay strategy that is the silence of Sodom.

Moreover, a real tension exists within the ranks of the clergy, between those who would like to be more out and those who do everything for the silencing. The latter group, at least at this time, hold all the power.

Studies, surveys, honeycombs, distinctions, and nuances notwithstanding, for all their inherent dangers, insider anecdotal knowledge may offer more reliable sources of information, especially given the possibility—in fact likelihood—that people just do not self-report accurately. One of the major strengths of Jordan's book is his rather modest claims. He uses a stylistic method to convey just how limited, how fragmentary are the history and anecdotes. He writes: "Indeed, I have broken the text up into short sections, some no longer than an aphorism, precisely to remind the reader of how fragmentary are the speeches now available. But I do persist in trying to speak" (2000, p. 14).

Another important reality should be noted here. These days not just a few lay Catholics know a gay priest or two. More and more

Catholics are no longer in denial about homosexuality. "Gay priest," for an increasing number of beyond-denial Catholics, has become synonymous with sensitive pastoral care and counseling. This priestly professionalism includes everything from compassionate ministry to people living with AIDS, to consolation and words of encouragement in coming to terms with a gay or lesbian identity, to sensitive and insightful spiritual direction—not to mention the hundreds, if not thousands, of ordinary day-to-day pastoral duties that priests perform such as baptisms, confirmations, burials, weddings, and masses.

Increasing numbers of Catholics don't see much of a problem with acknowledging the reality of gay priests among the ranks of the clergy. Even more important, many laymen and -women don't understand why the hierarchy and other Catholics in denial have such a difficult time coping with such an obvious and long-standing reality.

To help readers understand this confounding phenomenon, Jordan's book is a godsend. He treats his readers in "Church Lives" to a sobering voyage. It's a journey, however, where lesbian and gay Catholics may have an advantage, especially those with highly refined gaydar: the ability of gay people to hone in on all cues gay—cultural, personal, and in this case liturgical. Nonetheless, with the eye-opening descriptions that Jordan provides, non-gay readers are sure to get a clear picture. At times, readers travel along tragic church boulevards, those littered with "spiritual fatherhood" and "sexual abuse," the scandals of pedophilia, and clerical celibacy—both the abstinence from sex and the lack thereof.

This section also includes one of his best insights concerning seminary students' surveillance of one another. "A seminary is a big Catholic family in which all the children are suspected of being gay—and watched accordingly," Jordan (2000, p. 169) writes. He quotes from Richard Rodriguez's 1992 book *Days of Obligation: An Argument with My Mexican Father*: "To grow up homosexual is to live with secrets and within secrets. In no other place are those secrets more closely guarded than within the family home" (Rodriguez, 1992, p. 30).

There are, however, better-maintained and more pleasant-to-travel streets and avenues. At these junctures, Jordan treats readers to colorful markers, those of clerical culture, its "gay tastes and gay fantasies." In Chapter 7, "Clerical Camp," for example, we meet the Liturgy Queen, whom Jordan defines as "a fierce fan of 'good liturgy'"—in other words those people "typically in the vicinity of the altar—or at least the choir loft" (p. 189) Not necessarily members of the clergy, liturgy queens may well serve the church as sacristans, Eucharistic ministers, lectors, choir members, and organists.

The author also showcases other campy church features, including its "clothes, furniture, all elements of the visual décor." One short section on the chasuble—the outermost garment, worn by a Latin-rite priest during mass—explains the sartorial features of liturgical drag (p. 191). In revealing these features of gay culture and sensibility within, Jordan's writing wields a double-edged sword: "Being a gay fan of liturgy offers a beautiful fantasy in a homophobic church" (p. 193).

Still, Jordan's observations on Catholic art are perhaps his most incisive, if not most confrontational. Here the author has in mind the representations of Jesus. "Jesus shouldn't be shown too explicitly as a man. Indeed naked representations of Christ crucified or raised from the dead are too much for modern Catholic sensibilities," Jordan writes, adding that "naked crucifixes," however, would be "historically accurate" (p. 202).

But a naked Jesus was not always verboten in Catholic art. In discussing Christ's depiction in earlier works and relying on Leo Steinberg's 1996 *The Sexuality of Christ in Renaissance Art and in Modern Oblivion,* for example, Jordan writes, "Steinberg must account not only for the prominence of Christ's genitals in Renaissance paintings, but for our own ability to study those paintings for centuries without noticing the genitals" (2000, p. 202).

Again, Jordan drives home a significant point. He presses us to reconsider the presentation of the sexuality of Jesus and any homoerotic connection it may have to an all-male priesthood:

> Gay men are brought into the priesthood with the understanding that they can live out their gayness in various ways. They are not permitted to copulate with other men, of course, but in exchange for renouncing sex they are given the power to make a man's body with their very own breath and hands. The gender of the priesthood is constructed around this tacit approval of the one Catholic way to be gay. If this explanation seems too bizarre, it is worth considering not just the implications of transubstantiation, but the vehement insistence that only men can perform it. (Jordan, 2000, p. 207)

Silence of Sodom identifies a rich male homoerotic sensibility within the church. What Jordan suggests is a natural homoeroticism is almost intrinsic to Catholicism itself. But with so much of homoeroticism abounding, yet denied, what is a good gay Catholic person to do? For that matter, what should the non-gay faithful make of the various homoerotic elements? Part three, "Church Dreams," tackles the dilemma of being a gay Catholic—to leave the church or not. Jordan approaches the matter head-on: "At the turn of the millennium, the Catholic church is in many respects a voluntary tyranny" (2000, p. 212). In one subsection titled "Ecclesiastical Bondage," Jordan quotes from the Congregation for the Doctrine of Faith's 1986 *Homosexualitatis problema*.

> Recall Cardinal Ratzinger's advice: What then should a homosexual person who wishes to follow the Lord do? To speak briefly, these persons are called to complete the will of God in their lives, joining all the pains [or punishments] and difficulties that they might experience because of their condition to our Lord's sacrifice of the cross. (p. 219)

Fewer and fewer gay Catholics find any sign of hope for salvation or God's love for them in that advice. Good conscience and gay liberation present tickets out of Vatican-imposed spiritual bondage and sinful identities. At the advent of a new century, gay men are no longer bound to the bars, baths, and beaches. Gay and lesbian life on the outside, moreover, is promising and diverse—complete with a well-constructed infrastructure of cultural, political, business, recreational, artistic, religious, and health care institutions, among others. More often than not, it is in the secular world—with little, if any, help from the dogma or the curia—where gay people find welcome and affirmation, where our voices are heard, our committed relationships, families, and children are respected. In that vein, Ratzinger's advice is largely irrelevant. By offering such "advice" he demeans the truth of gay life and dismisses it entirely.

So, the title of the book, *The Silence of Sodom,* is addressed not only to the gay clergy. The author also has in mind lay Catholics who are gay when he writes: "You must, in short, ask whether you shouldn't leave the Catholic church in order to live as a Catholic" (p. 227). Other "eucharistic tables are available" (p. 227) he writes, referring to Dignity, a several-thousand-member national faith community of gay

Catholics, and the predominantly gay Universal Fellowship of Metropolitan Community Churches, an international association of more than 300 congregations.

Jordan also holds out various "liberal" Catholic parishes or centers across the United States as viable options. But even there, he argues, gay Catholics are diminished and neglected. "They are most of all denied adequate words and rites, truthful preaching and sacraments, to articulate their faithful lives," he writes (p. 22).

Silence of Sodom is no ordinary book for these non-ordinary, unsettling times. Fortunately, Jordan is not alone in breaking silence. Garry Wills's best seller *Papal Sin* (2000) does its own share of truth telling about homosexuality within church ranks. Perhaps Jordan's book may be best read and understood along with *Papal Sin* and another brave and courageous book, *The Changing Face of the Priesthood*, by Donald Cozzens (2000).

Wills, for example, cites evidence suggesting that the priesthood today is between 40 to 80 percent gay. "If that's not true, it's trending that way," he said during a book reading in Cambridge, Massachusetts. Although Wills does not give a bibliographical listing of his works cited, he does reference many of the same studies, journalists, and authors—authorities in the field of clerical sexual abuse and homosexuality within the priesthood—that Jordan drew upon to make his observations of the numbers of gay priests.

In Chapter 13, "A Gay Priesthood," Wills also takes on the issue of celibacy or noncelibacy among members of the clergy. The numbers of gay priests—out of the closet or not out—is not so much a matter of concern for Wills. What rankles him are the gay "celibates"—those gay priests who are in reality sexually active. "They may claim they are 'celibate' by their own private definition of that word," he writes. But such gay "celibate" priests "are living a lie" and "people are fooled by them" (Wills, 2000, p. 200).

From my perspective and experience, gay Catholics are not so much fooled by them as much as we are frustrated and disappointed with these (mostly closeted) "celibates"—some of whom even have boyfriends on the side. There is also anger at the hypocrisy. The frustration arises in figuring out what to do, if anything, about their refusal or inability to come out and speak out about the truth of their own homosexuality, not to mention advocacy of civil rights for gays in the public arena. If a priest cannot be truthful about something as basic as his identity and integrity, how can he bear witness to the truth of the gospel and Jesus Christ? After all, the truth, we are told, is supposed to set us free. There seems to be a serious compromising here of basic gospel values—values that go to the heart not only of church teaching but also pastoral care and counseling. Imagine the difference in more authentic ministry if more gay priests were out.

Cozzens's book *Changing Face of the Priesthood* (2000) also deals with the phenomenon of a gay priesthood and its impact on modern Catholicism. Like Wills and Jordan, Cozzens acknowledges the higher and disproportionate numbers of gay priests and seminarians. In fact, all three authors are aware of the field of social science research on the topic. Cozzens uses the figure of 50 percent. One reviewer made note of Cozzens's concerns with this observation: "If this estimate is close to the truth, then half of our priests and seminarians are being recruited from roughly five to eight percent of the general population of American Catholic men. This is a very sobering statistic" (Eagan, 2000, p. 21).

While Wills is concerned with the noncelibate "celibates" and problems they present to modern Catholicism, Cozzens (2000) addresses the "significant difficulties substantial gay populations present for straight seminarians" (p. 102). It is the impact that priesthood as a gay profession will have on both vocations and straight priests and seminarians that concerns Cozzens. "Unaware that his [non-gay seminarian's] psyche senses a challenge to his own integration and identity—and therefore is standing on alert—he notices only a vague feeling of discomfort and a loss of psychic energy," Cozzens writes. Continuing, he adds, "A good deal of the seminarian's psychic energy, energy needed for study and prayer, is diverted into managing or coping with inner turmoil" (Cozzens, 2000, p. 102).

Despite a preponderance of evidence—numbers essentially agreed upon by Wills, Cozzens, and Jordan—and nearly 250 footnotes and more than 350 works cited in the bibliography[5]—some will remain unconvinced about the extent and effects of homosexual sensibilities within the ranks and culture of the church. One reviewer of Jordan's book wrote:

> What evidence does Jordan offer for the view that male homo-eroticism is endemic in the Catholic church? . . . Normal empirical evidence is not, it turns out, all that important. . . . To agree

with Jordan stretches the normal warrants that one applies for deciding truth and falsity. (O'Brien, 2000, pp. 33-34)

This reviewer's attitude reflects what I call that of an "in-denial Catholic," one who cannot fathom the truth and reality of homosexuality within the church. No matter what the "evidence," this sort of mind-set will remain opposed to any consideration of a topic considered unimaginable at worst, beyond the limits of polite conversation at best. If *Silence of Sodom* has a weakness, it is that it cannot speak convincingly to those who are firmly set against homosexuality in general and, most of all, boggled by even a hint of it within the ranks and history of the Catholic Church.

For his part, however, Jordan has done a great service for the Roman Catholic tradition of faith. He has told his own truth and many other truths, and in doing so he holds out the possibility of a better way, truth, and life for everyone. Beyond the deafening silence that Jordan shatters lies a truly Christian place where gay and lesbian life is acknowledged, welcomed, and fully affirmed among the people of God. Ultimately, that is where this book aims.

SOME CONCLUDING REFLECTIONS

My postreview reflections include three observations. First, my own personal experience with Catholic priests, men and women religious, brothers and nuns, has been nothing less than wonderful. During critical times—for instance, coming out to family and friends, healing from broken relationships, and speaking out in the public arena—nuns, brothers, and priests have offered professional pastoral care and witness of personal integrity. Any number of these ministers of the church—gay and straight alike—have thrown me critical lifelines at pivotal moments in my spiritual life. In hindsight, I consider them to be miracle workers, building a bridge between the challenge of God's call to authentic discipleship and God's creation of me as a gay man.

These gifted pastoral counselors did not throw me tired church teaching from the Catechism about the evil and disorder of homosexuality and same-sex loving expression. Rather, these ministers of the church listened and were present to my pain—my suffering as I broke the silence of an anguished struggle with homosexuality. Then I carried with me the heavy baggage of church teaching that pathologizes homosexuality and denies the reality, truth, and joy of healthy gay and lesbian identity and spirituality. Through respectful, nonjudgmental listening and spiritual guidance, and through richer encounters of God's grace in the sacraments, therapy, and prayer, I came to experience the unconditional love of God. I now feel, to the core of my being, that God loves me, embraces me, if you will—along with all my quirky postmodern American but very human strengths and vulnerabilities.

I realize that I have been fortunate in my positive experience of pastoral care and counseling within the Roman Catholic tradition. "There but for the grace of God go I" has taken on profound meaning as I have listened to the stories of abuse victims/survivors, both gay and non-gay. Like them, I was once a vulnerable young adult—well into my late twenties. I shudder at the thought of where I might be today if I had encountered the type of spiritual misdirection these men and women speak of in horrific detail. Thank God that was and is not my experience. Still, I suspect that I am not alone in finding gay-affirming, gay-positive—if not livesaving—gay-sensitive ministry. For this gift of God's good graces, I have only deep gratitude. We need to acknowledge this reality by spreading the word that good pastoral care and spiritual direction *is* available within our faith tradition.

My second reflection concerns gay men in the seminaries and priesthood—the celibates and the noncelibate celibates. I have had a change of heart, a change that has come to me in listening to the stories of gay priests and religious brothers. During the New Ways Ministry symposium held in Louisville, Kentucky, I heard a priest speak of the "turmoil inside of me for a long time" before coming to full self-acceptance of a gay identity. The priest told how he "retreated in silence," grasping onto the positive words he received from a spiritual director: "No matter what, God loves you," he was advised. "I always held onto that image of God, who comes to us as we are." During a workshop that he facilitated I learned how brothers and priests dealt with their loneliness and isolation, their need to connect with other gay priests and brothers. In this safe small-group setting, these men asked out loud, "How do people become mature [in their human sexuality] within a celibate context?" In addition, they wanted to learn how to speak honestly about the "sexual experience we do know about and occurs." Still others asked for criteria in deciding how open to be to fellow priests, parishioners, and the wider community. One gay priest from the Southwest told of his experience with a "homophobic bishop" when fellow priests, his brothers in Christ, outed him to the prelate.

In my mind there is little doubt that more gay priests ought to come out—come out to themselves, to their fellow priests and brothers, to bishops, to their congregations, and to the laity. We need to hear from the celibates and the noncelibate celibates exactly what is going on in their lives. We also ought to hear from the noncelibate celibate straight priests. But in the real world in which we live the net result of honest self-disclosure would be these priests' ouster from ministry. It took a while, but that is exactly what happened to John McNeill.

I understand that some gay priests have decided that they don't want to be thrown out, that they can still do a lot of good as compromised people within a compromised system. Others have chosen to leave altogether. But let me underscore: While rightly angry and frustrated at the hypocrisy—especially as perceived by gay and lesbian people who have to struggle openly in their lives without the cover of clerical status—I do not underestimate, either, the considerable torment and years and years of spiritual, psychological, and even physical anguish that these men suffer. Imagine living in the fear of being discovered in the core and truth of your identity.

These men, too, are victims of the silence of Sodom and the temple of untruth and are entangled within its inner chambers and honeycombs. As one gay priest told me, "The hypocrisy, as I have seen and experienced it, is not simply a matter of a clearly drawn decision to compromise; it is a much more insidious a reality than that." Still, the only strategy, it seems to me, is honesty. Yet, as this gay priest attests, tragically some men are so completely compromised that they are utterly unable to get to that point. Others are bound not only by the pathologies of the church but also by homophobic cultures, for instance, Latino culture, in which self-disclosure of who they are will result in expulsion from family networks.

It is a terrible prison. Yes, there are those who are imprisoned by ambition and dreams of power. Yes, the church is a sinful institution, a prime analogue of structural sin, at least as far as I can see. We must ask—and keep asking—how an institution that claims the gospel as its mission has developed such monstrous conundrums and labyrinths for the servants of the Gospel, and finally denied the truth of the

Gospel itself. Meanwhile, I would rather have the many good gay priests remain in ministry. We members of the laity who are gay can do our part by advocating the need for a safe environment where gay clergy members can be more open and honest, and come out. In a word, we need to show gay priests and religious brothers compassion.

My third reflection concerns the future. We should expect hard-liners in the Vatican and the United States to persist in the blame game, scapegoating gay priests and homosexuality for the scandal of clerical sexual misconduct. While Vatican officials are quick to disconnect celibacy from pedophilia and other pathologies, sins, and crimes, they persist in conflating homosexuality with pedophilia and other forms of sexual misconduct. Sadly, a recent *USA Today* article pointed out that 40 percent of U.S. Catholics see a connection between homosexuality and the current crisis of child abuse by priests. The good news is that 60 percent do not. The scientific evidence, moreover, bears out the majority opinion. No credible scientific evidence suggests a link between homosexuality and pedophilia. Also, a recently released report highlights decades of research demonstrating that homosexual men are no more likely than heterosexual men to force sexual activity with children (Stevenson, 2002).

Even as I write this essay, Catholic News Service reports a Vatican draft-policy proposal that would bar homosexual men from becoming priests. It is hard to imagine how such a policy could ever be administered in a Christian manner. Such an effort will serve only to reinforce the fear of discovery, church repression of honest conversation about gay male sexuality in particular, and human sexuality and gender—gay, straight, bisexual, and transgendered. Do we really want an ecclesiastical version of "don't ask, don't tell"? When and if such a policy comes to light, we are right to ask, just how many of those who draft, review, and approve such an attack on gay seminarians and priests are gay or homosexually inclined themselves?

NOTES

1. Since the publication of *Silence of Sodom,* however, another fine new book, written by James Alison, an English Catholic, has been published. Like Jordan, Alison (2001) is a truth teller and adds considerable insight, honesty, and compassion to the reality of good gay and lesbian life in the church.

2. The estimate of 75 percent seems awfully high. In reality we really do not have accurate figures. Another problem is that these figures presume a model of sexual orientation that is too binary. Also, the figures beg the question of gender identity, not to mention sexual behavior. Finally, the terms *gay* and *homosexual* are far too often conflated.

3. The Vatican Web site has the text of the de facto unions document at <http://www.vatican.va/roman_curia/pontifical_councils/family/documents/rc_pc_family_doc_20001109_de-facto-unions_en.html>.

4. Jordan is now the Asa Griggs Chandler Professor of Religion at Emory University. He wrote *Invention of Sodomy,* his first book on the topic of homosexuality in the church, while a professor in the Medieval Institute at the University of Notre Dame. Jordan earned tenure at the University of Notre Dame. There he witnessed firsthand the effects of clerical closeting on student life, as closeted priests and administrators at the university moved against a gay and lesbian student group, banning it from meeting on campus and refusing to grant recognition as an official student group. During a telephone interview, Jordan spoke of his experience in South Bend with both students and faculty as having a profoundly negative effect on his own academic well-being. It was of primary importance in his decision to leave Notre Dame for Emory.

5. I found it interesting that neither Cozzens nor Wills listed a bibliography at the end of their books. While Wills uses footnotes, Cozzens does not. Jordan went to great lengths to employ both in backing up his thesis. My guess is that Jordan realized, as an out gay Catholic academic, he would face greater, if not more hostile, scrutiny from critics. Yet he writes:

> Lengthy bibliographies serve different purposes. Some are intended to establish the author's credentials. Others testify to an author's bibliomania. This does neither because it is not a systematic bibliography. In it, I mean only to give basic information about the sources cited in the text. . . . There can be no such thing as a complete bibliography for any of those topics [discussed in the book]. These days, in any case, comprehensive bibliographies must be stored electronically. (2000, p. 285)

However, from my professional experience and perspective, Jordan demonstrates both a command and awareness of the vast literature on the topic of homosexuality and the Catholic Church, sources that include social science research on homosexuality in the priesthood, moral theology, historical works, and Vatican documents and the U.S. Catholic bishops' most recent pastoral letter.

REFERENCES

Alison, James (2001). *Faith beyond resentment: Fragments Catholic and gay.* New York: The Crosswords Publishing Company.

Cozzens, Donald (2000). *The changing face of the priesthood.* Collegeville, MN: Liturgical Press.

Eagan, Robert J. (2000). Review: *The changing face of the priesthood. Commonweal,* August 11, p. 21.

Jordan, Mark (1997). *The invention of sodomy in Christian theology.* Chicago: The University of Chicago Press.

Jordan, Mark D. (2000). *The silence of Sodom: Homosexuality in modern Catholicism.* Chicago: The University of Chicago Press.

Kelly, J.N.D. (1989). *The Oxford dictionary of the popes.* New York: Oxford University Press.

Lockwood, Robert P. (2000). Catholicism under attack. *Crisis,* (July/August), pp. 10-15. Available at <http://www.catholicculture.org>.

O'Brien, Dennis (2000). Evidence anyone? *Commonweal,* September 8, pp. 33-34.

Rodriguez, Richard (1992). *Days of obligation: An argument with my Mexican father.* New York: Viking.

Steinberg, Leo (1996). *The sexuality of Christ in Renaissance art and in modern oblivion.* New York: Pantheon Books.

Stevenson, Michael (2002). Understanding child sexual abuse and the Catholic Church: Gay priests are not the problem. *Angles* 6(2). Available at <http://www.iglss.org>.

Wills, Garry (2000). *Papal sin: Structures of deceit.* New York: Random House.

Chapter 5

Anglican Bodies: The Gift of Heretical Liminality and the Risk of Relaxed Vigilance

Jay Emerson Johnson

In the spring of 2003 the Episcopal Diocese of New Hampshire elected V. Gene Robinson as their bishop, an openly gay man in a committed partnership with another man. Several months later, as required by canon law, the General Convention of the Episcopal Church confirmed this election in a contentious vote covered extensively by the news media. As happened with the ordination of women in the 1970s, Robinson's election provoked considerable controversy, including threats of schism. Unlike women's ordination, however, this historic moment has broken a peculiar kind of ecclesial silence among Episcopalians regarding the sexuality of their clergy and has forced Anglican bodies worldwide to confront fundamental questions of church polity, theology, and spirituality.[1]

The "Anglican bodies" I have in mind here admit several interrelated layers of meaning, each of which deserves careful scrutiny. The designation "Anglican," for example, describes a worldwide communion of Christian congregations connected in various ways to the Church of England, scattered over 164 countries and with some 80 million members. Although the vast majority of Anglicans worldwide do not consider English their first language, we still retain the adjective Anglican for our communion and style of theological reflection. Perhaps the moniker "Anglican" helps us to imagine a global network of potentially like-minded Christians whose cultural diversity nevertheless answers to and receives its spiritual identity from the "mother church" in Canterbury. After all, we do have to call ourselves something. Still, this vestige of British imperial influence does seem a bit odd in what we would otherwise describe as a postcolonial era.

The word "bodies" likewise deserves attention. It can refer to the Anglican conglomeration of national provinces loosely aligned with the word "communion." Anglicans enjoy this image, as it summons a sense of ecclesial relation and accountability while maintaining the importance of provincial autonomy; the Anglican Church in Canada, for example, cannot enact canon law for the Anglican Church in Australia. Anglicans thus seem able, often in the same breath, to embrace an episcopal polity, especially when the intervention of a bishop suits our cause, and resort rather stubbornly to congregational sensibilities, especially when diocesan priorities seem at odds with local developments. But I also wish to refer here to *human* and not just *institutional* bodies, the resolutely concrete qualities of which are too often swept away in the machinations of ecclesial politics. On this point, Anglican Christians live with some significant irony. Historically, Anglicans have relied rather heavily on the doctrine of the Incarnation for a host of rhetorical and theological strategies, often reciting this particular doctrinal touchstone like a mantra. Yet Anglican Christians have not necessarily fared better than Christians in any other communion in knowing precisely what to do, theologically and spiritually speaking, with the sexuality of actual human bodies.

As sexuality continues to seize attention and prompt controversy in Christian churches, the peculiarity of Anglican bodies offers a gift to a Western tradition neatly divided between Catholic and Protestant sensibilities. The gift I have in mind is liminality, which lesbian and gay Christians can revitalize in a tradition at risk of squandering the gift's benefits. In this chapter, I wish to give some shape to this queer contribution to Christian traditions by noting first the fragility of this gift in the Anglican Communion and, second, by underscoring the importance of breaking lesbian and gay silence in our institutional church structures.

AN ANGLICAN GIFT TO DIVIDED CHURCHES

Long before postmodern theorists questioned and rejected categorical identities, the sixteenth-century birth of the Church of England paved the way for a malleable religious tradition, rooted in historical sources yet responsive to contemporary developments. Refusing both the Counter-Reformation retrenchment of Tridentine Catholicism and the equally rigid framework of the Puritans, Anglicans staked out a via media, or a "middle way" between extremes. To the casual observer (and even committed members), this middle way can sometimes seem muddleheaded, or as a series of expedient political compromises for the sake of civic harmony. Although this is undoubtedly the case at times, the via media also holds significant promise. By avoiding the excesses and abuses of an ecclesial magisterium on the one hand and the confessional definitions of continental reformers on the other hand, sixteenth-century Anglicans began to craft a broad religious space, unencumbered by any one historical expression of Christian belief and practice. In this sense, Anglican traditions point to the possibility of a liminal Christian identity, always on the threshold of self-definition yet refusing to locate itself in a set of fixed, strictly defined parameters.[2]

To be sure, this gift of liminality emerged as much by historical accident as by design when King Henry VIII sought Rome's permission to divorce his first wife. When such permission clearly was not forthcoming, Henry severed his ties with the Roman pontiff and declared himself and his successors the "supreme head of the church in England." Henry created, in effect, a Roman church without Rome, in which the differences between the two ecclesial bodies seemed rather negligible to the average English parishioner at the time and still do to this day. Only half in jest, Roman converts to Anglicanism will often refer to their new religious home as "Catholicism without the guilt" or "Catholic lite." Not until three centuries after Henry's "heresy" did Rome clarify exactly where the differences lay when Pope Leo XIII declared, in *Apostolicae Curae* (1896), that Anglican ministerial orders are "utterly invalid and altogether void."[3]

Anglicans tend to wince when reminded that our tradition began with a failed marriage. It certainly seems less than laudatory to locate our origins in an act of ecclesial betrayal, a "heresy." Still, given our ongoing controversies with sexuality, we might find some surprising fruitfulness in reconsidering this particular historical moment rather than suppressing or repudiating it. Henry's royal machinations could serve as a historical marker for our continual struggle with what constitutes genuine ecclesial authority and our perpetual search for authentic institutional expressions of Christian faith. Moreover, tracing our origins to a royal divorce could remind us that sexuality and sexual relations remain inextricably bound to the shape and formation of religious traditions. I suspect most Anglicans fail to notice this religious connection with sexuality, or if they do, they quickly change the subject. Indeed, standard historical narratives of Anglican origins tend to disavow any formative role to Henry's sex life, preferring instead to locate the "true" origin of our tradition in the Elizabethan settlement and the creation of the Book of Common Prayer. This shifting of attention from Henry to Elizabeth only underscores our ambivalent posture toward bodies. In a tradition marked by its mantralike invocations of the Incarnation, we eschew Henry, whose first divorce occasioned several others, and instead embrace Elizabeth, the "virgin queen" who never married and whose portraits would seem to inspire an asexual androgyny.

I certainly do not wish to suggest that Henry VIII provides an exemplar of a faithful Christian life. Rather, reminding ourselves of his conflict with ecclesial authority over matters of sexuality and the realignment of ecclesial power it produced could prompt further reflections on the "heretical" gift of Anglican liminality, especially with reference to the unique institutional structure it created for addressing issues such as sex and sexuality. The archbishop of Canterbury, for example, has no direct legislative power over the many national provinces with which he or she is in communion. This relative autonomy among the provinces paved the way for ordaining women in some parts of the Anglican Communion even when the Church of England had not yet approved the practice for itself. It has also enabled the Episcopal Church in the United States to exercise considerable latitude in its treatment of openly gay and lesbian ministers. It even engenders a degree of latitude within the Episcopal Church itself, as some diocesan bishops resolutely refuse to ordain openly gay people, some will ordain them according to a kind of "don't ask, don't tell" policy, and still others embrace explicitly the particular gifts for ministry exhibited by openly lesbian and gay clergy. The controversy over the election of Gene Robinson as the bishop of New Hampshire would now seem to call these liminal practices into question in a new way.

Historically Anglicans have enjoyed the gift of interprovincial latitude without feeling obligated to define it with any precision. In the latter half of the twentieth century, however, we have witnessed a growing sense of anxiety over this ecclesial arrangement. The ordination of women and of openly gay people has sparked considerable consternation in some quarters of our communion concerning what precisely constitutes "being in communion" with the see of Canterbury. This question clearly comes to a head once every ten years, when Anglican bishops from all the national provinces gather in England for the Lambeth Conference, a gathering for conversation, debate, and the drafting of resolutions. Although these resolutions are not canonically binding on the provinces, they serve as a kind of religious weathervane for the communion as a whole, giving us a sense of which way the religious winds are currently blowing. Yet modern and now postmodern forces of globalization have forced us to confront in new ways the mostly unexamined question of our unity and its warrants. As our postcolonial age has thankfully produced African, Asian, and Latin American bishops (rather than English or American expatriates), cultural differences have been playing a much larger role in the debates at the Lambeth Conference. This has been particularly true regarding the role of women in the church and the church's moral teaching regarding same-sex sexual relations. Rather than the more loosely construed image of communion, an increasing number of voices have been advocating *uniformity* in teaching and practice, especially for a return to "traditional values," as the basis for uniting our global network; Gene Robinson has now become the ecclesial equivalent of a lightning rod for this movement.

Given these dynamics, gay Anglicans will surely nod their heads sympathetically while reading *The Silence of Sodom,* Mark Jordan's (2000) reflections on the simultaneously homoerotic and homophobic culture of Roman Catholicism. We know that our own Anglican structures and ecclesial patterns can, have, and still do exhibit many of the same dynamics Jordan identifies. These nods of sympathy will also likely carry some condescension as we secretly harbor the suspicion that queer Roman Catholics have not yet found the courage to flee into the arms of their liminal first cousins across the Thames, where the struggle is surely easier to manage. We might even believe rather smugly that we have, as Anglicans, managed to escape the pitfalls of excessive ecclesial authority while still retaining most of the ambiance and accoutrements of a tradition we deeply love. This applies especially well to the high-church movement of Anglo-Catholics, not necessarily among the more-Trent-than-Trent types, but among the "enlightened" Anglo-Catholics who support women's ordination and accept openly gay clergy. Jordan's eloquent description of the "liturgy queen," for example, finds more than adequate resonance in the flagship bastions of Anglo-Catholicism in the Episcopal Church (most notably in New York City, Chicago, and San Francisco) (Jordan, 2000). Like our Roman counterparts, Anglo-Catholic liturgy queens have created a comfortable home in which to conceal and express our gay sensibilities in an otherwise homophobic tradition. Unlike our analogues in Roman communities, however, we enjoy at least the illusion of having escaped the more overt expressions of homophobic ecclesial rhetoric.

It would seem, in other words, that Anglicans generally, and enlightened Anglo-Catholics in particular, manage to create lively and welcoming corners of Christendom where historical traditions (including their dramatic and theatrical expressions) are honored and preserved in a context where they can undergo appropriate modification through the lens of contemporary experience. Indeed, the liminal quality of our ecclesial formation affords precisely this kind of faithful latitude with its many attendant benefits. Yet it also carries significant risk. While we relish our relative ecclesial freedom compared to our Roman Catholic brothers and sisters, this enjoyment can swiftly breed a dangerous complacency and a relaxed theological vigilance.

For many gay Anglicans, our hard-won, though qualified, acceptance within the life of the institutional church (at least in some quarters of the United States) signals the end of our struggle. We are at last *out,* as gay men, and *in* at the same time, either as clergy or active parishioners. As our vigilance relaxes, however, we feel relatively little compulsion to examine any further the traditions that have shaped our institutional life. As Jordan has described them, these traditions employ various mechanisms to create an "ecclesial field of silence" in the culture of Roman Catholicism. For Anglicans, it means learning an elaborate system of coded language. We have learned what particular dioceses mean when they promote "biblical morality." We recognize what certain congregations really want when they encourage "family ministries." We also know where to find the most amenable locales for gay-friendly, traditional liturgies. Until just recently we have turned almost exclusively to major urban centers to find such places, following the scent of incense or listening for the soft rustle of brocaded vestments where our "family" of liturgy queens go about their ecclesiastical business.

The intimate link between homosexuality and high-church liturgy has weakened considerably over the years, yet it still deserves our attention when considering the sexuality of Anglican bodies. We ought to note, for example, and much like Jordan's description of Roman culture, how Anglo-Catholics created a relatively safe space for gay *men* by nurturing homoerotic fraternity without dismantling the mechanisms of male power. Gay men have not only found (qualified) acceptance in these various outposts of highly stylized sacramental life but also exercised positions of authority in ways historically unavailable to us in other areas of society. This has not, however, been the case for women. The embrace of women's ordination in some, but certainly not all, corners of the Anglican Communion has come as a great relief for many of us and would appear to signal the end of yet another hard-won battle. At the same time, by restricting the parameters of this struggle to the question of access to ordination, we risk missing an opportunity to interrogate those traditions more broadly, with reference to the theology of the ordination rite itself, for example, or to the theology of pastoral ministry, or to the configuration of congregational leadership. Here, too, a relaxed vigilance, though understandable after many years of struggle, carries significant risk as all of us still suffer traditions deeply marked by patriarchal imbalances and as women—especially lesbian women—cope with virtual invisibility in the parish job market.

The cultural and ecclesial debates over same-sex marriage offer another case in point. Considerable legal ramifications (such as shared property) and familial relations (such as adopting children or the right to hospital visitation) clearly make marriage a question of social justice, and it remains on the forefront of lesbian and gay struggles in American society. Yet relaxing our *theological* vigilance on this issue risks truncating our reflection on what we want marriage to mean or signify in religious communities of faith. Our work in this particular arena surely entails more than changing the pronouns in the marriage rite while leaving the rite itself unexamined. At best, this would stand as a missed opportunity to examine the *institution* of marriage and whether, from a theological and spiritual perspective, we actually want to be grafted into that particular historical constellation of meanings.[4]

The issues surrounding ordination and marriage raise additional questions regarding the full range of our sacramental and spiritual life within the institutional church, stretching our imagination and push-ing us to examine that life more closely. Do we hope for nothing more than substituting an openly gay priest for the closeted one? Can we imagine anything beyond the subtle rearrangements of the status quo, adjusting our tailor-made cassocks to fit the shape of women's bod-ies? Does the gift of liminality offer nothing more substantive than the shadows of medieval Catholicism, the experience of "Catholic lite"? When Mark Jordan imagines the Holy Spirit prompting papal conversion on the question of homosexuality, his imagination hits a brick wall. He rightly acknowledges the mind-numbing extent to which our theological traditions and spiritual practices would need to change to allow for an open embrace of same-sex desire in the church (Jordan, 2000). The effects of such an embrace would necessarily rip-ple throughout every aspect of our theological and institutional life. Gay Anglicans understand Jordan's point only obliquely and have be-gun only recently to recognize the mixed blessing of our (qualified) acceptance. By finding ourselves walking more freely within the halls of institutional power, our passion for critiquing the power itself begins to wane.

Groucho Marx once quipped that he would not want to belong to a club that would accept someone like him as a member. Lesbian and gay Christians would do well to ponder Marx's tongue-in-cheek jab at institutional life. As we seek to contribute to the life of the church and to its mission in the world, whether as ordained clergy or active parishioners, the institution itself deserves further scrutiny, especially the traditions that have shaped its hostility toward homoeroticism and same-sex relationships. By working so hard for so many years for in-stitutional acceptance, we may have compromised our ability to cri-tique that institution in which we seek full membership. Women have been pushing gay men on this question for some time. Eager to find our place at the ecclesial table, gay men *as men* have been able to ne-gotiate the politics of male-dominated structures in ways women can-not. This kind of accommodation to power can quickly mask the deeper issues lying at the root of ecclesial homophobia. They run at least as deep as the pervasive suspicion of sex and sexuality and of bodily desire itself, yet extend even further to a thinly veiled misog-yny running throughout our historical traditions. If women and women's bodies have borne the brunt of these fears and suspicions, it certainly helps to explain the barely contained ire the institution bears toward gay men and our bodies. This ire, furthermore, we ourselves can soothe by exercising our ability to act from a position of male privilege. Our understandable eagerness for acceptance and inclusion, in other words, has too often short-circuited our analysis of those ecclesial mechanisms by which misogyny and homophobia are cut from the same cloth.

The sex-abuse crisis in American Roman Catholicism illustrates these mechanisms in a particularly potent way. It is highly unlikely that this scandal will produce significant change in the deeply entrenched mechanisms of the Roman institution that created the conditions for this crisis in the first place. More likely is a further retrenchment of those same mechanisms. Although the institution's hierarchy has begun a long-overdue process of revising its strategic policies of clergy deployment, this hardly addresses the issue at hand. Our efforts over many years to break the assumed link between pederasty and homosexuality would now seem to be unraveling. Each new and sadly predictable call for a more intensive prescreening of Roman seminarians, now explicitly identified as an attempt to "weed out" gay men, suggests that homosexuality itself is at the root of this crisis.[5] Similar to changing the pronouns in the marriage rite, rooting out homosexuality from the institution would simply leave the deeply rooted and problematic aspects of the traditions in place.

The failure of Christian traditions to engage sex and sexuality in any theologically satisfying way—of which the Roman sex-abuse scandal is but one example—ought to strike us as profoundly perplexing. If its consequences were not so tragic, it might even be comical. After all, both Roman Catholics and Anglicans draw on ancient traditions defined by their belief in Jesus of Nazareth as the incarnation of God in human flesh. As Anglicans, we can point to the nineteenth-century figure of F. D. Maurice, whose insistence on the implications of the Incarnation fueled his "Christian socialism" on behalf of the English working class. We can likewise turn to William Temple, archbishop of Canterbury during World War II and champion of applying the incarnational principle to a host of social and economic crises. It was Temple (1934) who insisted that Christianity is the "most materialistic of all religions," by which he meant to stress the radical implications of the Incarnation for every aspect of our personal, social, and institutional lives (p. 478). To claim, in other words, a fundamental union between human and divine, between earth and heaven, and spirit and flesh is to make a rather astonishing claim about the theological importance of material reality itself, including the material reality of human bodies and the human body's desires and relationships.

How then do we account for the embrace of the Incarnation in Christian churches and the simultaneous ambivalence of those churches toward sexuality? Can we make any sense of ecclesial bodies gathered around the Incarnation while virtually eschewing the reality of human bodies and their desires? Perhaps, with Slavoj Žižek, we need to understand this dynamic as a disavowal of the tradition's own inner logic. In Žižek's view, this would help to explain the creation of "heresy" in Christian traditions, which Žižek understands as the refusal to adopt the institution's illogical disavowal:

> In order for an ideological edifice to occupy the hegemonic place and legitimize the existing power relations, it has to compromise its founding radical message—and the ultimate "heretics" are simply those who reject this compromise, sticking to the original message. (Žižek, 2001, p. 8)[6]

Rowan Williams, appointed archbishop of Canterbury in 2002, puts a slightly different spin on Žižek's argument to make a similar point. Theologians, as Williams (2000) notes, seek ways to communicate the faith of their community. Effective theological communication will frequently, though not always, rely on conceptual clarity. The impulse to such clarity will, in turn, increase the possibility of crisis in the community. After all, the attempt to "tidy up an unsystematized speech," as Williams puts it, risks losing a great deal of whatever fails to fit in the proposed conceptual categories. This is precisely the risk Christian traditions have faced from the beginning:

> What the early Church condemned as heresy was commonly a tidy version of its language, in which the losses were adjudged too severe for comfort—or rather (since "comfort" can't be quite the right word here), in which the losses were adjudged to distort or to limit the range of reference of religious speech. (Williams, 2000, p. xiii)

Combining these observations from Žižek and Williams offers a way to think about the precarious status of human sexuality in Chris-

tian traditions. Rather than a logical conclusion of incarnational theology, the homophobic and misogynistic strains of Christian traditions stem from a restriction of the Incarnation's reach (Williams) for
the sake of maintaining institutional power in the complex matrix of
sociopolitical relations (Žižek). As the institution disavows the logic
of its own tradition in the attempt to tidy up its speech, lesbian and
gay Christians must learn to parse the entangled relationships between theological reflection and institutional structures. To do so effectively would mean more than creating access to either ordination
or same-sex marriage. It would constitute a significant gift to an institutional church in need of retrieving the fullness of its tradition.

A QUEER GIFT TO THE INSTITUTIONAL CHURCH

Institutional structures, in and of themselves, are neither good nor
bad, neither beneficial nor deleterious. Yet they are not merely benign, either. Institutions represent more than the practical expression
of an idea in a set of policies or strategies. As Jordan's work reminds
us, institutions create their own culture, their own peculiar ethos,
which no amount of "policy adjustment" will address or touch. An institution, in other words, is more than the sum of its individual members, even more than the sum of its policies and strategic postures.

Walter Wink (1984) offers some helpful insights into these dynamics in his analysis of the language of power in the Christian scriptures.
Wink takes the mythological language of those texts, the language of
"powers and principalities," of angels, demons, and spirits, and applies these concepts to the material manifestations of power, to the inner workings of institutional and ideological structures. As Wink
notes, an institution operates with its own kind of spirituality, regardless of the kind of spirituality its individual members try to adopt.
Wink (1984) illustrates his point by evoking a Marxist analysis of
capitalism:

In Marx's view, the single most important determinant of the
spirit of institutions is the means of production. The spirit of life
or death in a society is not a function, then, of the good will or
bad will of individuals, but the consequence of a determinate
institutionalized spirituality in a determinate material organization of relations between people. The capitalist system, for ex-

ample, is able to produce and reproduce not only surplus value and social classes but also its own symbolic universe, its own spirituality, its own religion. (p. 109)

Engaging the institutional powers of an economic system—a religion—requires more than making better economic policy. Focusing our attention on issues such as welfare reform or the minimum wage, although clearly helpful and needed, is not enough to address the spirituality of a system that molds and shapes its citizens as mere consumers. In Wink's (1984) view, working for social justice will necessarily mean more than rearranging already existing social structures:

> People are not simply determined by the material forces that impinge on them. They are also the victims of the very spirituality that the material means of production and socialization have fostered, even as these material means are themselves the spinoff of a particular spirituality. (pp. 116-117)

As Wink suggests, rather than policy adjustments, the kind of change our economic institutions require is what Christian traditions have called conversion, or the process of radical transformation that liberates a people from the spirituality that binds them to a particular material expression of power. This kind of analysis clearly applies equally well to the institutional manifestations of Christian faith. It is not enough to change or relax canon law to allow for the ordination of women, or to adjust the pronouns in the marriage rite to include same-sex couples, or to enact new policies for reporting child molestations by priests. As important and necessary as each of these "policy adjustments" is, they leave untouched the institution's disavowal of its own tradition, a disavowal that made the policy adjustments so urgently needed in the first place. Failing to take any further steps falls short of the kind of conversion to which God calls each of us individually and to which God calls the institutional church corporately. It falls short, in other words, of transforming an institution that has repressed or rejected the fullness of its own incarnational theology.[7]

In short, relaxing our theological vigilance can blind us to the dangers lurking in any process of global institutionalization, whether in terms of economics or ecclesial communion. As Wink succinctly suggests, any institution becomes demonic insofar as it cares more about its own survival than its mission. Although Rome has lived with this risk of demonization for much longer than Canterbury, the dynamics are the same for both, made worse by the sociopolitical manifestations of globalization.

As the provinces of the Anglican Communion are now realizing with greater clarity, communion-in-difference requires a great deal of hard work and courage. Making uniformity the basis for our ecclesial unity presents a nearly irresistible temptation, as Roman Catholics have realized for some time. This is, of course, not new. Nearly any treatise on church order from roughly the third to the nineteenth century treats this tension between institutional control and local diversity. It describes a struggle that has marked Christian traditions since the first "council of Jerusalem" met to discuss the "problem" of Gentile converts to Christian faith (Acts 15). Yet the modern world has exacerbated this tension by making it more visible, in part through the rapid technological advances in global communication. For global ecclesial bodies—such as Roman Catholicism and Anglicanism—these advances have enabled the church's right hand to know what its left hand is doing. Local diversity can no longer escape the larger institutional spotlight. The blessing of a gay couple's relationship in San Francisco grabs the attention of a bishop in Sydney. A bishop in Singapore takes note of a woman's ordination in Canada. Meanwhile, a traditionalist congregation on the plains of Texas, unhappy with its "liberal" bishop, seeks episcopal oversight from a bishop in Uganda. Try to imagine any of this happening with such alacrity or even accuracy between the tenth-century dioceses in Kiev and Paris. In our supposedly postcolonial era, global ecclesial bodies now exercise far more local influence than our colonial ancestors could have possibly imagined.

Critics of late capitalism are of course quick to question whether the present era qualifies in any way as "postcolonial" and whether colonialism has merely reemerged under a new guise and with added force. Some of the same dynamics have been shaping our global ecclesial bodies for some time, a process that deserves further examination as we seek to articulate the queer gift lesbian and gay Christians can offer to institutional Christianity. We might notice, for example, how the forces of economic globalization fetishize antiquated cultural customs made quaint. To thrive, global capitalism requires the preservation of exotic outposts of local diversity, whether for cheap labor or pristine markets for technological "advancement" or merely the titillations on which a multibillion-dollar travel industry depends. How soon will the "Americanization" of world markets make the system itself implode? How many McDonald's restaurants do we need on the streets of London or Auckland before Americans just decide to stay home? As economists clearly recognize, the threat to globalization comes not so much from pluralism and diversity as it does from universality. The potential disappearance of localized custom and tradition functions as the symptom both of globalization itself *and* the threat to its mechanisms of economic viability and hegemony. In response to this symptomatic threat, the mechanisms of globalization seek ways to preserve these outposts of difference while retaining their accessibility to the contrived "mainstream" of North Atlantic techno-industrialization and for the continued viability of market indices. Cultural difference, in other words, reduces to, or rather emerges more clearly as, *fetish*.[8]

These tensions between local diversity and global conformity now mark institutional church anxieties in new ways. The urge to maintain institutional church power, or merely to preserve the institution itself as an institution, entails the same complexities evident in the process of economic globalization. Consider the image of Australian Aboriginals "performing" at a national gathering of Australian Anglicans, or the image of African Zulu warriors (in full native costume) in consultation with Vatican prelates, or the image of Native American rituals opening the general convention of the Episcopal Church in the United States. These images are, at the very least, deeply ironic as the diversity they purport to embrace is engulfed by the uniformity-based call for universality. The ironic distance of these images only deepens as we view many of these scenes over the Internet, virtualizing even further the reality of cultural and religious differences. These differences have all but disappeared in the fetishistic qualities of postmodern kitsch. In the rush to ease the symptom of globalization, diversity itself becomes a fetish of what has been lost in the institution's universal reach. Or, which is more likely, diversity has become a fetish of what never was but what our institutional imagination conjures about an idealized past. This idealization is precisely what a fetish enables us to accomplish.[9]

A queer contribution to institutionalized Christian faith would employ a similar analysis to the function of gay people in Western society generally and in the church in particular. Gay and lesbian people certainly disturb any preconceived notion of heterosexual universality. As a symptom of disturbing diversity, our lives become a fetish in the very system our lives disturb, whether in television sitcoms, Broadway musicals, or consumerist advertising campaigns. Likewise in our Christian churches, where we frequently find ourselves identified, in iconlike fashion, as the symptom of the human condition in need of redemption, which the church in turn requires to maintain its own sense of mission to "the lost." As still slightly exotic but now "well-behaved" gay men and lesbians, reluctant to cause *too* much trouble for the institution, we risk abandoning our particular gifts in an institution relieved by the success of its mission to save us.

Unmasking these various mechanisms of power, whether of global capitalism or global ecclesialism, treads on some dangerous ground. We risk reinscribing the very power of the institutional dynamics we wish to critique. The risk emerges most clearly in the implication that a religious tradition is defined and measured by the tradition's hierarchy and its institutional structures. The symptomatic and fetishistic qualities of these institutional dynamics remain problematic precisely because, perhaps *only* because, we assume the institution itself determines the conditions under which these phenomena are understood as symptoms and fetishes. The risk of reinscribing institutional power deserves further attention with reference to the tools of globalization, especially as ecclesial "authorities" have greater access to communications media. Who calls the press conferences? To whom do the media turn for "official reaction" from the church? Whose picture appears on the covers of *Time* and *Newsweek*?

Any consideration of an institution's disavowal of its own logic will require not only a consideration of the content of the tradition in question but also an examination of who has defined that content and how. Along that trajectory, the frequent disjunction between official texts and actual practices ought to give us pause. As Rowan Williams (2000) has noted, there is no use in pretending that theology remains distinct from disjunctive practices, "just as it's no use pretending that there is a reading of the Bible that is free of selection and interpretation" (p. xiii). Official Roman Catholic teaching on procreation offers a classic case in point. How will future historians describe twentieth-century Catholicism on this issue? Will they turn to the official teaching of the church, which forbids the use of artificial birth control? Or will they consider the actual practice of countless Catholics happily using the Pill, a diaphragm, or condoms?

Closer to home for Anglicans is the 1979 resolution of the general convention of the Episcopal Church in the United States. Passed by both houses of the convention, the resolution affirmed "the traditional teaching of the Church on marriage, marital fidelity and sexual chastity as the standard of Christian morality" and declared that it is "not appropriate for this church to ordain a practicing homosexual." Similarly, the bishops gathered for the 1998 Lambeth Conference passed resolutions declaring homosexuality incompatible with Scripture and the ordination of noncelibate gay people inappropriate. Although neither of these texts are canonically binding (Anglican canon law is notoriously difficult to enact, let alone enforce), they are meant to serve as an indication of the "mind of the church," and both resolutions stand to this day. Meanwhile, the Episcopal Church enjoys the ministry of hundreds of openly gay and lesbian ministers going about the business of ministry. Where, then, do we locate the task of defining the current state of the tradition? Do we turn to those official pronouncements or to a local congregation where the openly lesbian priest just baptized a child adopted by two gay men? Has the election of Gene Robinson as a bishop violated church teaching or merely broken the silence about the actual practice of the Episcopal Church?

The disjunctions between texts and practices with which we presently live should give us pause when considering historical traditions and the history of their development. On what basis, for example, do we characterize historical Christian traditions as pervasively misogynistic and thoroughly homophobic? Do we turn to the texts or the practices of those traditions? Can we necessarily assume that the daily life of a fourth-century congregation in the suburbs of Rome conformed exactly to the vision of Christian faith enshrined in Augustine's texts? Did thirteenth-century Christians in the south of France model their lives of faith on Aquinas's *Summa*? Surely it is not sufficient, in answer to such questions, to say that we simply don't have much evidence of what those practices really were for average fourth- and thirteenth-century Christians. The historical silence itself ought to give us pause when we read the texts from those periods and shape the questions and the kind of analysis we bring to those texts. In part, this is precisely Mark Jordan's point in drawing our attention to the mechanisms of an ecclesial field of silence, a silence that threatens the revitalization of a tradition defined only by the texts generated by a limited few. The disjunction between texts and practices, in other words, sheds critical light on how the tradition is defined by those who have the power to draft official texts and to determine what constitutes a text as "official."

I am reminded here of Bruce Bawer's book *Stealing Jesus* (1997), in which Bawer seeks to dismantle the move made by fundamentalist Christians to claim the Christian gospel as their own. Reading Bawer's book I experience a nearly irresistible temptation to steal Jesus back, to snatch Jesus away from those theological interlopers. This temptation conjures an image of all of us—Protestants, Catholics, and Anglicans—scrambling around on a religious football field with Jesus as the divine pigskin we keep tossing back and forth. Occasionally we manage to intercept him in our mad dash for the goal line, yet we don't seem to have a clear idea of what it would mean to score.

As a matter of fact, the tradition does not belong to *them*, those fundamentalists. But it does not belong to *us*, either, as "enlightened" Anglicans. It doesn't *belong* to anyone. Indeed, as those of us who insist on practicing our faith and ministering among God's people quickly discover, we actually *belong to it*. Christian tradition marks the ongoing reflection on and expression of the mysterious, inscrutable, delicious, infuriating, sobering, awe-inspiring, ecstatic, and erotic interaction between God and God's own creation. How could such an interaction ever belong to any one group? Indeed, we ought to consider the reduction of this tradition to a handful of official texts as nothing short of obscene and probably blasphemous.

Given these institutional dynamics, gay and lesbian scholarship appears not as a marginal footnote to Christian theology but as essential to the overall health of the tradition. In this sense, gay and lesbian Anglicans cannot afford to relax our theological vigilance as we bask in the (qualified) acceptance our Anglican liminality seems to grant. To be sure, I have nothing but respect for those who feel compelled to abandon institutional forms of Christianity, those who simply cannot bear the hypocrisy any longer. I likewise sympathize deeply with those who, perhaps for reasons of personal safety or ongoing discernment, sit quietly in their pews on Sunday mornings. For the rest of us, perhaps because we are stubborn or we have found a congregation where our incipient courage can thrive, we insist on exploring the full implications of the Incarnation, from which we still derive the hope we need and hear the good news for which we yearn. To recall Žižek, we are the "heretics" who refuse to adopt the institution's disavowal of its own tradition. Or, to recall Williams, we are the ones refusing theology's heretical narrowing and restriction. These refusals prompt an important opportunity for offering a queer gift to a struggling institution.[10]

For Anglican Christians, this queer gift will return to the life-giving possibilities of a liminal Christian identity. By avoiding a nostalgic-like embrace of tradition, which merely fetishizes the past, yet also resisting the impulse to reinvent our traditions, gay and lesbian Christians can draw on our own experiences of sexual embodiment for retrieving, and thereby revitalizing, the practice of Christian faith. As Jordan understands it, this would mean employing our faithful imaginations for creating new kinds of Christian community, reshaping our patterns of ecclesial relation, and forging new pathways for ministry. Gay Anglicans, already well versed in the practice and pitfalls of liminality, can contribute important insights to envisioning this kind of future; indeed, such a future *requires* those insights.

The challenge and the promise of liminality did not, of course, first appear with the birth of the Anglican Communion. It has marked the tumultuous development of Christian traditions from the beginning. Whereas Matthew's Jesus insists that the good householder brings out of the treasure chest that which is both old and new (Matthew 13:52), the same Jesus likewise insists that old wineskins cannot contain new wine without bursting (Matthew 9:17). While the church has taken some comfort in the former image (the old still retains its value), the latter has consistently vexed the denizens of institutional power. Christian history reverberates with many such moments when the Holy Spirit's new wine has ripped the seams of the institution's old wineskin, whether in the obvious example of the sixteenth-century Reformation or in the more subtle shifts rendered by ecstatic mystics. Today, gay and lesbian Christians in the church have been given an opportunity—indeed, a vocation—to call the church to conversion, to reject its long disavowal of its own tradition. No wonder our desires and our faith pose such a threat to institutional power and prompt controversial moments of crisis. The question is not if, but when will this queer wine burst the old wineskins?

Personally, after having left the confines of evangelical Christianity, which by no mere coincidence occurred while coming out as a gay man, I discovered the Episcopal Church and the riches of a tradition, both theological and liturgical, I had not yet begun to imagine. The space for creating and embracing a liminal Christian identity appealed to my own sense of personal liminality as a gay man in a straight world. I still believe this Anglican approach holds rich possibilities for exploring genuine ecclesial authority and authentic institutional forms of Christian faith. At present, I'm relishing these possibilities in a tiny congregation where our sense of shared leadership and baptismal ministry is facilitated by an openly lesbian deacon and her partner. We treasure our diversity as a gift, both young and old, straight and gay, coupled and single. And we do our best to preach the Good News in a liturgy constructed from ancient sources and rhythms yet with a commitment to gender and sexual inclusion.

In at least this one congregation the heretical gift of liminality clearly works and bears much fruit, and I know of other such places where the Holy Spirit seems to be breaking free from her institutional constraints and forging life-giving communities of faith. At the same time we must not relax our theological vigilance. Even in my own congregation, the work of critique and retrieval has only just begun. We have yet to explore fully the treasures of Christian traditions and practices for our own lives as lesbian and gay Christians, the implications of which extend far beyond our inclusion in the institutional church and even beyond the rightly construed urgency for social justice. For at the root of a homophobic ecclesial field of silence we find a truly demonic repression of sexuality, of sexual desire, of the human body itself. The tragic consequences of this repression are only too evident in every suicide of a queer teenager and every betrayal of trust in clergy sexual abuse.

In short, as we explore the gifts an Anglican liminality might afford, the time has not yet come to relax our theological vigilance. For if we can indeed hope for something more than "Catholic lite," what would the Good News sound like? If we can imagine something more than the shadows of medieval Catholicism, what would a queer liturgical practice look like? How would our simultaneously erotic and spiritual sensibilities shape our worship? If we take seriously the implications of the Incarnation and our experiences as sexual bodies, what would happen to the marriage rite? What would happen to

Christological discourse? How would it shape theological reflection on our ecstatic participation in the life of the Trinity? If we learned to care more about Christian mission than the institutional church's survival, could *anything* stop the force of love and social change this might unleash in a world so deeply marked by violence and economic oppression? Can we really imagine sparking this panoply of possibilities and fueling this hope by embracing same-sex desire, theologically and spiritually? If not, more than Sodom will have been silenced; we will have muted the Holy Spirit herself. And this is precisely Mark Jordan's point.

NOTES

1. Although the ordination of women prompted similar concerns about schism, Robinson's election operates from a slightly different dynamic. The Episcopal Church has enjoyed the ministries of many openly gay and lesbian clergy for some time and the Episcopal House of Bishops has included an openly gay member for a number of years—the Rt. Rev. Otis Charles, who came out as gay after retiring as the bishop of Utah. Robinson, on the other hand, was openly gay when elected. The controversy over Robinson would thus seem to have less to do with sexuality per se than with the violation of sexual silence.

2. L. William Countryman (1999) describes well this rather peculiar gift insofar as "Reformation Anglicanism was not so much an idea in search of a community, as a community in search of a revised self-understanding." It is not therefore sufficient, he notes,

> to say that Anglicanism eludes definition. It would be more accurate to say that it positively resists it. And this is more than a convenient metaphor. It seems to have been an animating principle as far back as the Reformation, when it became important for Western Christian communities to distinguish themselves doctrinally from one another. . . . It might be useful to think of Reformation Anglicanism as having defined itself against what it saw as the *over definition* of others. Hence the difficulty ever after in giving it, or discerning in it, sharp outlines. (pp. 32-33)

3. Rather than detailing ecclesiastical machinery at work in these developments, it will suffice to note that while Henry VIII was excommunicated by Pope Clement VII, English priests and bishops were not. This created at least the hope among some Anglican clergy that their ministerial orders had remained "intact" and that an eventual rapprochement with Rome remained viable and even inevitable. *Apostolicae Curae* dashed many of those hopes, as did the emergence in the twentieth century of women's ordination in some provinces of the Anglican Communion.

4. Several years ago the Episcopal Church congregation to which I belong engaged in a yearlong process of communal theological reflection on the *purpose* of blessing relationships liturgically. Our goal, and at the behest of our diocesan bishop

no less, was to draft a liturgical rite for the blessing of same-sex relationships. "Why do we want to bless relationships?" we asked ourselves. "What end does it serve? What does it signify? What, exactly, are we blessing? What kind of gifts do such relationships offer a community of faith and what does the community offer to relationships? What difference does it make to the couple? To the community? What do we learn about God and ourselves by doing so?" And so on. As we began drafting the rite, many of the straight couples wanted to engage a similar process for themselves. Many of the married couples—deeply unsatisfied with the theology expressed in the marriage rite, or at least uncomfortable with its implications—lamented not having the benefit of this kind of sustained reflection for their own relationships, not to mention drafting a more suitable rite for celebrating them.

5. The particular case of Paul Shanley, one of the accused priests to whom the media have given so much attention, has only intensified this problem given Shanley's association with the formation of NAMBLA (the North American Man-Boy Love Association). The Shanley case represents a more general confusion of categories, both in the media and in the church, which lesbian and gay men have been struggling to clarify for decades. Psychosexual dysfunction, pathological repression of sexual desire, pederasty, pedophilia, and homosexuality do *not* work as synonyms. Although we *might* excuse the media for their lack of sophistication on this issue, the fact that the church appears actively to promote this confusion should strike as morally outrageous.

6. Žižek (2001) goes on to suggest that we

> recall the fate of Saint Francis: by insisting on the vow of poverty of the true Christian, by refusing integration into the existing social edifice, he came very close to being excommunicated—he was embraced by the Church only after the necessary "rearrangements" were made, which flattened this edge that posed a threat to the existing feudal relations. (p. 8)

7. Bernard Lonergan's (1994) work on conversion would also be helpful here, especially as it relates to his observations on institutional structures. As Lonergan reminds us, institutions are compatible with both prosperity and misery: "They constitute the commonly understood and already accepted basis and mode of cooperation [among people in groups]. They tend to change only slowly for change, as distinct from breakdown, involves a new common understanding and a new common consent" (p. 48).

8. For this kind of analysis, employing the dual touchstones of symptom and fetish, I am indebted to both Wink and Žižek. The "symptom," according to Žižek (2001), "is the exception which disturbs the surface of the false appearance, the point at which the repressed Other Scene erupts, while fetish is the embodiment of the Lie which enables us to sustain the unbearable truth" (p. 13). Wink (2002) likewise observes how the spirituality of institutions becomes fetishized. This helps to explain, according to Wink, why a society's criminals are frequently punished less severely than a society's political prisoners. The latter actually "question the spirit of the system and so are regarded as the worst criminals of all" (p. 108). Wink's observations apply just as well to the "threat" posed by lesbian and gay lives insofar as we put heterosexual hegemony and dichotomous gender performance at risk.

9. Graham Ward (2002) makes a similar point when he distinguishes between tradition and nostalgia. While tradition enables the working out and forging of

God's realm as we move into the future, nostalgia, by contrast, has no future: "The backward glance is petrifying. It petrifies by fetishizing. The nostalgic gaze sacralizes concepts, objects, forms, and states from the past and reproduces them in a present that simulates and commodifies their pastness" (p. 55).

10. One of the more recent and explicit examples of this kind of work is L. William Countryman and M. R. Ritley's *Gifted by Otherness: Gay and Lesbian Christians in the Church* (2001). Rather than offering any kind of apologia for our existence, Countryman and Ritley understand their task as discerning the peculiar gift we offer to the church, which the church in fact needs in order to thrive:

> The time has come for gay and lesbian people . . . to give up the futile attempt to justify our existence in the church or in the world. . . . It is the church's place to listen now, and ours to speak. And this is not merely about speaking the word of the gay community, it is about speaking the radical word of the gospel, which is about God's outrageous desire to include every variety of person we can think of, and then create yet more. (pp. 24, 29)

REFERENCES

Bawer, Bruce (1997). *Stealing Jesus: How fundamentalism betrays Christianity.* New York: Three Rivers Press.

Countryman, L. William (1999). *The poetic imagination: An Anglican spiritual tradition.* Maryknoll, NY: Orbis Books.

Countryman, L. William and Ritley, M.R. (2001). *Gifted by otherness: Gay and lesbian Christians in the church.* Harrisburg, PA: Morehouse Publishing.

Jordan, Mark (2000). *The silence of Sodom: Homosexuality in modern Catholicism.* Chicago: The University of Chicago Press.

Lonergan, Bernard (1994). *Method in theology.* Toronto: University of Toronto Press.

Temple, William (1934). *Nature, man and God.* London: Macmillan.

Ward, Graham (2002). Between virtue and virtuality. *Theology Today* 59(1): 55.

Williams, Rowan (2000). *On Christian theology.* Oxford, UK: Blackwell Publishers.

Wink, Walter (1984). *Naming the powers: The language of power in the New Testament.* Minneapolis, MN: Fortress Press.

Žižek, Slavoj (2001). *On belief.* London: Routledge.

PART II:
ECCLESIAL MISOGYNY

Chapter 6

Duplicity Writ Large

Mary E. Hunt

Catholic and gay scholarship took giant leaps forward with the publication of Mark D. Jordan's *The Silence of Sodom* (2000). I appreciate the erudition that carries over from his earlier book, *The Invention of Sodomy in Christian Theology* (1997). I commend the graceful, accessible writing style and the aesthetically pleasing format. As he argues in the book, liturgy queens never lose their taste! Nowhere is that more clear than in the beautiful artistic design of his volume. With deep appreciation for his work, I read the story as a catalog of duplicity writ large. I hope this book will help to put an end to it.

The achievement of Jordan's book is its uncompromising exploration of the conundrum that makes perhaps the most homophobic church in the Christian panoply at the same time the most homoerotic. Whether one agrees or not with some of the more speculative arguments—such as the gay hermeneutical approach to the consecration and consumption of the Body of Christ—the research and critical analysis presented prevent Catholics from saying, "Oh, we never noticed." I contend that no adequate analysis of the contemporary Catholic reality is possible without seeing the deeply misogynistic and homosexual overlay that Jordan has exposed so helpfully. This is surely a first step that even some of the most liberal, reform-minded Catholics resist, calling it reductionism and anticlericalism. Now they will need to refute his work in order to persist in their ostrich-like position.

This chapter originally appeared as "Duplicity writ larger: A response to *The Silence of Sodom*," Mary Hunt, *Theology and Sexuality,* volume 9, number 1, September 2002, pp. 9-17. © T & T Clark International, a Continuum imprint. Used by permission of the publisher.

My appreciative response to Jordan's landmark book focuses on three intersecting areas of concern: (1) the Catholic gay structures of duplicity, (2) the economics of ecclesial injustice, and (3) the implications of Jordan's analysis for women. Although I structure my analysis around these general rubrics, there is, of necessity, some analytic overlap.

THE CATHOLIC GAY STRUCTURES OF DUPLICITY

I, like Professor Jordan, am neither ordained nor tenured in a Catholic university. Indeed, I share his opinion of the University of Notre Dame as one of the most hostile environments for same-sex love, consistent with its self-congratulatory misogyny paraded in the name of the Virgin Mary. That other U.S. Catholic universities see it as the flagship is worrisome.

I also concur with Jordan's dim view of Andrew Sullivanesque efforts to excuse and thank church officials for baby steps forward. I refuse to grovel before closeted bishops and ecclesial theologians whose rhetorical sleight of hand in seeming to "improve" church discourse on homosexuality is nothing but a self-hating charade. Rather, I pity them and move on to healthier company.

Like Mark Jordan, I have been "out" and around Catholic institutions long enough to confirm the anecdotal evidence that the "honeycomb Catholic closet" is full of worker bees and queens, virtually none of them women. This is a matter Jordan foreshadowed in *Invention of Sodomy,* which he calls a failure of theologians' imaginations to cope with erotic love outside of its hetero-reproductive expression.

He spells out in vivid detail in *Silence of Sodom* what Robert Goss (2002) shows in his book *Queering Christ,* namely that Catholic seminaries, rectories, and chanceries in the United States, and undoubtedly in other parts of the world in slightly different but parallel ways, are, for all practical purposes, gay clubs. This was driven home to me by a heterosexual Franciscan priest, perhaps one of the few in captivity, who confided how hard it is to function as a heterosexual in the priesthood since favors and promotions seemed related to homosexual bonding. I could only imagine.

Unlike Mark Jordan, I am a woman, whatever that means in this postmodern, transgendered time. But for sake of discussion, I claim that from my feminist perspective his work makes good sense. Indeed, from my starting point the evidence invites even more critique than is offered. I would respectfully suggest a new subtitle: "Catholic Duplicity and the Misuse of Power," since it seems that homosexuality, although an important aspect of the analysis, pales before the lies and abuses that form an integral part of the official Catholic Church.

I attended Marquette, a Jesuit university, as an undergraduate, and the Jesuit School of Theology in Berkeley, California, for the master's in divinity in the late 1970s. I saw up close and personal much of what Jordan reports. I have every reason to believe that twenty years later the same dynamics apply. For instance, I was told that on Jesuit community night in Berkeley it was the custom to begin piously with mass, the liturgy queens' delight, followed by pre-prandials (drinks, to the uninitiated). Then came dinner, post-prans, and for some people, I am told on reliable authority, sex. To put it delicately, most women left after dinner. I concluded, from an admittedly small sample, that most seminarians were gay until proven otherwise. Nothing I read in Jordan's work dissuades me. My Jesuit classmates did not distinguish themselves in their support of the ordination of women, despite our implicit support of them as gay men. Pity.

I would, however, differentiate issues of sexuality from issues of morality and power. I concur with Jordan that homoeroticism plays a key role in keeping the ecclesial erections in place. But what is nowhere explained, nor explainable in my view, is why structured duplicity is tolerated. For example, while the homosexual inclinations of Cardinal Spellman are well documented, what about the ordained seminary professor whose woman companion (read: wife if he had any integrity) is a well-accepted part of the community? Or, what about the priest who may well be heterosexual and oblivious to the sexual dynamics surrounding him because he is drunk most of the time? I pass over the number of times bishops and personnel officers move priests who are accused of pedophilia because they need them to cover a parish in some far-flung corner of the diocese.

None of these real stories take away from Jordan's argument. They simply suggest that deeper even than its homosexual nature is Catholicism's structured duplicity. In each case, and surely with homosexuality, lying is the lynchpin. Perhaps more pointedly, "the silence of Sodom" is but one form of lying. Whether it causes or creates the conditions to tolerate the others is not clear to me. But that "don't ask, don't tell" goes well beyond homosexuality both in the military and the Catholic Church is painfully clear.

Proof that none of this is particularly new comes from the old canonical designation of certain sins "most specially reserved to the Holy See." One of them is "forgiving an accomplice in a sin of impurity," a way out of the Catch-22 created by having sex with clergy. A priest simply cannot forgive his own lover, but must resort to higher authority, in this case the Sacred Rota, where such cases are handled. Of course, most Catholics never hear about such things, but I can attest to the fact that they are taught seriously, if ridiculously, in some seminaries, down to the formula to be used: "Titus, a man, and Bertha, a woman. . . ." This obscures what I would imagine to be the more frequent "Titus and Timothy" cases. So, church gentlemen protest too much when they deny, as Mark Jordan points out, that their priests are sexually active.

Perniciously, churchmen now often have women as spokespersons and let them convey the message while the men cower offstage. Indeed, some of the women may not know what goes on behind closed doors. For example, on a recent television show about priests with AIDS, the U.S. Catholic Bishops' spokeswoman, Mercy Sister Mary Ann Walsh, when asked about priests and sexual activity, resorted to the old Ivory soap commercial that claimed its product was 99.44 percent pure. Such naïveté is incredible, leading to the unhappy conclusion that duplicity, not sex, is rampant. Duplicity, as well as sexuality, seems to keep the hierarchical, clerical power structure erect.

It is the power structure that concerns me most. Corporations with CEOs, boards of directors, regional and middle managers are at least honest about how and why they function as they do. But the Catholic Church, which mirrors their model, cloaks it in the rhetorical resemblance that Jordan discerns so astutely. A bright line is drawn horizontally across the upper part of the pyramid. Above the line are the ordained; below the line are the laypeople. Above the line belong decision-making, jurisdiction, and sacramental authority; below the line are compliance and contribution. Above the line are men in a homosocial pecking order; below the line are women and nonhomoconforming men. Homosexuality exists above and below. But until and unless the fundamental power model is changed to reflect equality and justice, minimal conditions in the Christian Gospels for what Elisabeth Schüssler Fiorenza (1993) has named "a discipleship of equals," I am skeptical that even this necessary exposure of gay clerical privilege will be sufficient to make change. For the ordinary Catholic, the line is simply blinding.

THE ECONOMICS OF ECCLESIAL INJUSTICE

This leads me to a language most Catholics understand, namely, money, or what I euphemistically refer to as the economics of ecclesial injustice. I was struck in Mark Jordan's work by the almost complete absence of economic analysis. One could argue that Jordan makes his case perfectly well without it. I, however, believe that it is a crucial missing piece, not only in his approach but also in a broader one that I assume he would encourage. A personal anecdote will illustrate what I mean.

My father was a cradle Catholic and a self-made businessman. No one ever accused him of being a feminist. Indeed, my decision to study theology was met with some skepticism, as he felt an intelligent woman would be more useful to the family as a lawyer. I learned early in my career to explain theological and theopolitical issues to him in economic terms.

My father was not the first to promote the ordination of women. However, when I explained to him that I was working three part-time jobs, had a fellowship, and was taking out student loans to complete my training, while my Jesuit classmates received room and board, tuition, money for books, and a living stipend, my father quickly changed his tune, questioning the blatant inequality. It was similar to what he saw in his wealthy Florida parish where the needs of immigrants were juxtaposed with the luxury of the rectory.

He watched in disgust as priests he knew were gay carried on campily as if no one noticed, their duplicity more repugnant to him than their sexuality, their collars granting them privileges their secular gay brothers could not assume. Indeed, my father came to tolerate my same-sex love long before he ever countenanced the economic injustice that permeates Catholicism. In his later years he stopped attending mass altogether because the rank hypocrisy of the whole Catholic system galled him. I like to think his view is genetic.

That laypeople have no real say in how their money is spent, that women are kept from decision-making positions, that employees of

Catholic schools are, for the most part, grossly underpaid, that huge sums of diocesan money go into insurance claims for pedophilia cases, that millions are spent on church architects and vestment designers, that Catholic hospitals cost women millions in unprovided reproductive health services are just a few of the real economic consequences of what Mark Jordan calls "the silence of Sodom." It is an expensive form of collusion that I consider immoral.

Perhaps the single most obvious conclusion I draw from Mark Jordan's analysis is that the Catholic priesthood and its theological arm is really a large system of gay male prostitution, perhaps more economic even than sexual. Catholic seminaries and religious orders are tax-exempt institutions that discriminate legally against women and nonhomoconforming men. Such operations are expensive and they provide a remarkably generous ecclesial welfare system for their adherents, which, in turn, makes it much more difficult for those outside the system to gain access. Just the time and money involved in theological studies through the masters in divinity, much less the PhD and postdoctoral time to specialize and write, assures that most Catholic students are either gay men or rich.

THE IMPLICATIONS OF JORDAN'S REMARKS FOR WOMEN

Since I am neither a gay man nor rich, I conclude my reading of the text with some reflections on the implications of Jordan's analysis for women, especially Catholic lesbian women.

First, I concur completely with Jordan that such analyses are gender specific, so he was correct in limiting his gaze to the gay homoerotic culture in which he exhibits a certain expertise. My own grasp on the lesbian equivalent is equally firm. But I would invite both of us, as gender categories shift beneath us, to reevaluate our parameters periodically. It seems we may know more about each other's reality than we assume, and together we can see a bigger picture than either of us can see alone.

Second, I agree that misogyny is a component of homohatred. I would argue that without it there is no Catholicism as we know it. It is not just anyone who is excluded from the gay clerical club; rather, it is women, including lesbian women. The reality of women is denied consistently, beginning with the birth of Jesus that is mythologized to erase agency from his mother. The choice of women's names and the stereotypic drag personae of campy priests cannot be explained, as I see it, apart from an unconscious hatred and/or trivializing of qualities associated with females. I believe we need to probe this more deeply and eradicate it as part of the problem.

Third, I have pondered what a female, i.e., lesbian, equivalent of this gay homoerotic culture would look like in Catholicism. I may be missing something obvious, but in fact I do not believe it exists. Of course there are lesbian nuns, but I suspect many nuns, in the immortal words of Sister Theresa Kane when she courageously addressed the first meeting of the Conference of Catholic Lesbians in 1984, could say that as a woman religious, her sexual preference has been obscured from her. Of course, her sexuality is none of my business, but that it was obscured from her is my concern lest it happen to others as well. This frank admission by a revered woman leader is damning of a church that systematically distances women from their own bodies, from other women, and from the knowledge that celibacy is not a sexual preference but a way of operating regardless of one's sexual self-understanding.

Convents certainly have had their share of romantic intrigue, sexual experimentation, and the like. But the collective lack of power for Catholic women, including religious women who are just as "lay" as the rest of us until the first woman is ordained, cues me to the fact that it is power not sexuality that is at play. Now that Mark Jordan has established the link between homosexuality and power, it remains for Catholic lesbians to explore this further.

My suspicion is that the Vatican's easy if incorrect coupling of lesbian and gay issues, their failure to differentiate between two quite different experiences, not to mention their abysmal ignorance of bisexual and transgender realities, is simply their view that women do not exist apart from men. Likewise, their worry that a female priest would disrupt the nuptial imagery of Jesus the bridegroom and the church as his bride betrays their biologistic thinking rendered absurd with the rapidly growing number of same-sex marriages around the world. One can conclude only that their blinders are self-perpetuating, since in such homosocial environments men need not deal with lesbian women at all. Worries of cosmic lesbianism at the altar that plagued the Episcopal Church when its first women were ordained simply do not occur to the Roman boys who are so busy making it work their way.

In Jordan's analysis, the stereotypic "fag hag" is noticeably absent. I was relieved, because I despise the image. But sadly, women who enable gay men's duplicity abound in church circles, especially among those who seek to "minister to" the gay, lesbian, bisexual, and transgender community, a concept I find loathsome and imprecise. I mention this unfortunate term "fag hag" as another example of misogyny that runs deep in some parts of gay male culture and surely has its ecclesial expression in some well-intentioned women who function as enablers of clerical and liturgical culture. I urge Roman Catholic women to cease and desist from patriarchal arguments about working inside to change the system, to reevaluate whether they are really needed for ministry, and if so, for what kind. I suggest instead that they face the fact that they are perpetuating a sick and dying system, even for laudable motives, and stop doing it.

Many Catholic women have already kicked the dust from their Birkenstocks. The Women-Church movement of which I am a part is one good example of women, including lots of lesbians, moving beyond the style wars and the transubstantiating performances of gay Catholicism. We simply do not take the institutional, what Elisabeth Schüssler Fiorenza (1993) has called the "kyriarchal," church so seriously. It does not have the grip on our souls that it does for men who have more of a stake in it. Rather, we create our own communities and liturgies, our own social change work and interfaith connections. There is a visceral sense in which the Roman Catholic Church is not ours. Now, thanks to Mark Jordan's fine work, we know a little more about why.

Feminist theologians have been asking hard questions about fundamental theological issues for decades. Joanne Carlson Brown and Rebecca Parker (1989) raised the possibly that the Atonement is really divine legitimization for child abuse in work reminiscent of Kierkegaard whom Jordan quotes, opening what is now a healthy and hefty debate by which the Catholic community is seemingly untouched. Oh, I forgot, these are women theologians, and Methodist ministers. Why would the kyriarchal Catholic Church pay attention to them?

Ironically, it is not so much on the level of sexuality but on the level of obedience that we part company with our gay brothers. Although

Catholic women do not have a lot of power, neither do we give it away. More than 80 percent of childbearing-age Catholic women use a form of birth control prohibited by official teaching; Catholic women have abortions at slightly higher rates than non-Catholics. Lesbians from the Catholic tradition are notoriously candid about church matters.

Jordan's description of Catholic churchmen was, sadly, more like reading about little boys who had yet to find their voices than about mature men who ought to be in charge of other peoples' lives. There is a certain perpetual adolescence to it all. Even the most outspoken seem skilled only at being defensive, able to write a letter to a superior or protest to a bishop, but not very loudly. The adolescence is spiritual as well as psychological, resulting in a flaccid church. For example, in light of the war in Afghanistan and Iraq, the hierarchy remains committed to the notion of a "just war" when strong words condemning violence are needed in light of the stakes.

I am used to the company of Catholic women—heterosexual, lesbian, bisexual, celibate and sexually active, mature and fearless— adults in a church that needs to learn to hear and tell the truth. Audre Lorde (1984) taught us, and we have taken her words to heart: "My silences had not protected me. Your silence will not protect you."

To Mark Jordan we owe a debt of gratitude for candor and clarity about that to which we Catholic women do not have, nor do we ever want: access. With Jordan, we are creating something new out loud.

REFERENCES

Brown, Joanne Carlson and Parker, Rebecca (1989). For God so loved the world? In Joanne Carlson Brown and Rebecca Parker (Eds.), *Christianity, patriarchy and abuse* (pp. 1-30). New York: The Pilgrim Press.

Fiorenza, E. Schüssler (1993). *Discipleship of equals: A critical feminist ekklesialogy of liberation.* New York: Crossroad.

Goss, Robert E. (2002). *Queering Christ: Beyond Jesus ACTED UP.* Cleveland, OH: The Pilgrim Press.

Jordan, Mark D. (1997). *The invention of sodomy in Christian theology.* Chicago: The University of Chicago Press.

Jordan, Mark D. (2000). *The silence of Sodom: Homosexuality in modern Catholicism.* Chicago: The University of Chicago Press.

Lorde, Audre (1984). The transformation of silence into language and action. In Audre Lorde, *Sister outsider: Essays and speeches* (pp. 40-44). Trumansburg, NY: The Crossing Press.

Chapter 7

Always a Bride, Never a Groom

Robert E. Goss

The "feminine" excess is forgiven or expected because they [priests] are officially "unsexed." As modern eunuchs, they are permitted to take on the stereotypes of women.

Mark Jordan (2000, p. 199)

Mark Jordan (2000) writes:

In Seville, where sodomy persecutions were left to civil authority, a Jesuit active as a prison chaplain between 1578 and 1616 noted the high incidence of sodomy in the religious orders and the diocesan priesthood. He reports the view that Jesuits rarely sin with women because they can so easily find partners among their students or novices. (p. 126)

Some traditions never die. Shortly after my ordination, I met Frank Ring, another Jesuit, and we fell in love. Our story has remained a part of Jesuit recreational talk and lore for some time. On Valentine's Day 1978, two gay friends, Matthew and Joe, threw a shower-wedding for Frank and myself. We had few belongings—our books and some money for securing an apartment. Matthew and Joe came up with the "queer" albeit camp idea of a shower for the two of us. Ultimately, this was a practical idea, but the unexpected social and personal consequences would be felt for years.

This chapter is a modified version of "Become a priest and find a wife: Catholic anxieties over (fe)male priests," in Goss (2002), *Queering Christ: Beyond Jesus ACTED UP* (pp. 35-54).

Friends attended what promised to be an unusual event—two Jesuits in love and wanting to exchange vows to live together in union. A priest friend celebrated mass, where we formally blessed the rings that we had exchanged months before in a quiet bedroom ritual. At that time we did not call it a holy union, but it was a blessing of the new journey of combining our lives.

There was a wedding cake with two macho construction workers embracing. It became an infamous wedding that was heard around many Jesuit recreation rooms throughout the United States. The Jesuits in attendance of the ritual that night were on phones providing details to other Jesuit friends in many communities. The story came back through numerous trajectories, each carrying more bizarre renditions than the one before. Let me expound Frank's favorite rumor: A Jesuit priest married a young scholastic; the rector of the Jesuit community performed the wedding ritual with numerous Jesuits in attendance, while the Jesuit community threw the wedding reception. At the time Frank and I had not left the Society of Jesus because it took months to complete the necessary paperwork, sending it to Rome for processing and return. I received a stern warning from the Jesuit provincial, who was swamped with calls and protests over the wedding from numerous Jesuit priests. He warned me I had to remain celibate even when I left the Jesuits. I was not celibate while in the Jesuits; I was certainly not intending to start now.

Many Catholic priests in America, Jordan claims, participate in a culture colored by gay tastes, and the camp wedding shower was not lost on gay Jesuit subculture. The elaborations on the story of the wedding provide more insight into Jesuit gay subculture. The story was exaggerated and embellished for a number of sociopolitical reasons, including the turmoil of changes in the post-Vatican II church in the late 1970s. While the story became more blown up in its retelling in Jesuit recreation rooms during cocktail hour, the obsession with the story is revealing about the closeted lives of those Jesuits who rehearsed it with delight and horror. Homosocial organizations—such as the Roman Catholic Church and the U.S. military—use homophobia to police and regulate the sexual lives of their members. We made a public commitment, and this touched a repressed nerve. Some Jesuits covertly engaged in sexual relationships within and outside the order, while others longed for the intimacy of our relationship.

The notion of a priest marrying a young Jesuit scholastic, though Frank and I were only three months apart in age, played on the transgenerational sexual fantasies of priests for younger men. When several months later I attended a heterosexual wedding of a laicized Jesuit priest who was a teacher and mentor, I heard from Jesuit friends that Frank and I had appeared on BBC television. We had become public, fallen Jesuits, stigmatized by our public sexual lives. Other Jesuits, who were covertly sexual, remained honorable within a closeted and punitive system for those who betrayed the secret. Stories were embellished, and the Jesuits attempted damage control by conducting a superficial witch-hunt to remove gay scholastics to prevent such future recurrences. Frank and I were neither the first nor the last wedding of two Jesuits.

A GENDER-BENDING MATRIX

Eve Sedgwick (1990) has observed that male desire is perpetrated by a trinity of conditions: homosocial consent, the regulation of homophobia, and the promotion of misogyny. Homosocial consent is the conscious complicity to participate in homosocial organizations, its brokered rules, and unwritten taboos. This trinity of social conditions provides the circumstances for the creation of culture of clerical camp that supports alternative gender-bending in seminaries, rectories, and male religious communities, yet these social conditions perpetuate patriarchy with homophobia and misogyny. Clerical homosocial consent agrees to the unwritten rules of the Catholic Church: "Don't ask; don't tell. Don't get caught in a public scandal." Homosocial consent, institutional allegiance, the threat of expulsion, closetedness, and silence provide the complex social dynamics of the Catholic priesthood and its hierarchy that prevent public disclosure of the reality of gay priesthood.

Many homosexual Catholic boys intuit naturally in their youth that they are not attracted to the idea of heterosexual marriage. Still other options remain for homosexual Catholic youth, for there is the option of entering religious life or the priesthood. Eve Sedgwick noted:

> Catholicism in particular is famous for giving countless gay and proto-gay children the shock of possibility of adults who don't marry, of men in dresses, of passionate theatre, of introspective

investment of lives filled with what could, ideally without diminution, be called the work of fetish. (1990, p. 140)

When Catholic youth enter religious life or the priesthood, they assume a prestige and status within the Catholic community with the added benefit of an all-male environment where their homosexual desires can covertly be explored and where an alternative masculinity is accepted as normative.

Mark Jordan (2000) aptly places Catholic clergy and seminarians in a transgendered role: "When it comes to clothes, we assign Catholic priests to a mixed or third gender. We have been taught to indulge them as if they were the stereotyped trophy wife of the distant suburbs" (p. 199). It is a culture where men wear dresses, homoerotic rituals are performed, and aesthetic desires are appreciated. In many houses of formation and seminaries, residents are encouraged to develop their aesthetic interests rather than athletic pursuits. Jordan writes accurately about the campiness, homosexual aestheticism, and gender-bending found in rectories and religious houses, for seminaries and clerical culture are breeding grounds for future "ecclesial divas."

In his writings and talks about priesthood, John Paul II encourages candidates for the priesthood and priests to model their lives after Mary, yet in his encyclical Priestly Ordination (Ordinatio Sacredotalis) (1994), he maintains that women cannot be ordained to priests. Because the function of women is ordained as caregivers, Edward Ingebretsen (1999) writes, "Proponents for the ordination of women sometimes forget the fact that putting a Roman collar on a woman only further complicates her performance of social gender by entwining it within the complex weaves of another system of gendered authority" (p. 82). Although priests may not be real men by the narrow cultural norms of masculinity, they cannot be biologically women either. Women are feared not because they provide a sexual distraction to the divine or threat to priestly vocation but because they threaten Catholic priests with revelation of their gender performances of (fe)masculinity.

Women must be kept out of cloisters and rectories to maintain this homosocial bastion because they also present a threat in revealing that the clergy is not a heteromasculine institution. Ingebretsen notes the terrible secret of the church's misogyny: "In the current ecclesiastical lockup women cannot be permitted to become priests because that would make apparent what is in fact the case—that, at least according to public appraisal, there are women priests already" (1999, p. 86). Thus women are excluded from the priesthood not because they pose an erotic distraction but rather that they might expose the Roman Catholic practice of ordaining (fe)males as priests.

Gay men find themselves attracted to the all-male clergy with flowing vestments and baroque chasubles, decorated with lace and crushed velvet. The clerical environment is thoroughly queer, even transgender. Many young seminarians often dress up the Infant of Prague, an image of young Jesus anatomically unsexed, in lacey copes, camp liturgical drag, and a gold crown. It may be the equivalent of gay men playing with Barbie or Ken dolls. Symbolically, it may have deeper psychological self-representations, portraying their vocational desires of being the infant dressed in ornate vestment and reenacted in cassocks and baroque chasubles. At liturgy, they represent Christ *(alter Christus)* to the community. Priests may be culturally failed men, like gay men, but with the one major difference of a sacral status that allows for their deviant performance of masculinity. It allows them to enter the liturgical stage, dressing as Christ and transgressing the cultural roles of masculinity, but Catholic deniability prevents the laity from seeing their true drag performance.

Seminaries and religious orders are filled with aesthetically sensitive and effeminate young men whose tastes in liturgy and theology range from neoconservative to antimodern. Jordan (2000) notes:

> "Effeminacy" is not an attribute of a subset of priests. It characterizes the highly visible actions required of all priests. These queer actions become camp not just through deliberate exaggeration, but because they are punctuated by loud assertions there is absolutely nothing queer about them. (p. 186)

They may not be visible to the Catholic public that has been socialized to think of the queer actions of priests as sacred and normative, but they are readily visible to queer folks, fully accustomed to gender-bender performances.

Yet diva performances are typical of Catholic prelates and their sycophantic circles of closeted clergy. Consider the recent "Spice Girls" controversy in Melbourne, Australia, when the epithet was coined among Catholic priests and made public to describe the inner circle of clergy around then Bishop George Pell, now Archbishop in Sydney.

These closeted priests supported Pell's policy of denying Communion to openly queer Catholics, and Mary Helen Woods, a close friend of Pell, made these remarkable observations about the Spice Girls:

> They love their ceremonies and they love their incense and they love dressing up, and if they want to describe that inner circle as the Spice Girls, I can sort of see where the comment's coming from. . . . People are attracted to a powerful bloke, they tend to be a bit girlie about it . . . (Wilson, 2001, p. 5)

Most dioceses have their own rendition of the Spice Girls, flamboyant, closeted, publicly homophobic, and feminine. While in a protest with Soulforce in November 2000, against the National Conference of Catholic bishops, numerous effeminate seminarians in their cassocks passed through our picket lines but refused to make eye contact with their gay brothers. Their fear around homosexuality was apparent in their failure to acknowledge us.

Diocesan seminaries and religious houses of formation have traditionally been bastions of misogyny. Presuming heterosexual attractions, seminaries and religious houses control female distractions and temptations by creating a segregated male society. Many seminaries and religious houses had set up cloisters, boundaries of living space where women were not allowed. In past times, when women violated male cloister, the space had to be reconsecrated. Cloister spatially defined women as impure and threatening; they were perceived as sources of temptation and sin.

Patterns of heterosexual behavior were tightly regulated to secure celibacy, and the success can be measured by the subversion through the promotion of homosocial patterns of living. Within this homosocial environment, guarding against heterosexual desire, seminarians and clergy create and perform alternative masculinities. It is the homosocial and gender-variant dynamics of all-male prison life. During my theological studies for ordination, I lived with a group of New York Jesuits who were sharp-tongued, misogynistic, gossiped a lot, and often called Jesuit friends "girlfriend" or female names. I have found similar behaviors and patterns among the circle of drag queens that I know in St. Louis.

Traditional Roman Catholic theology supports the concept of priest as the liturgical impersonation of Christ. The priest is a "drag

Christ" in his liturgical role. Though modern Catholic artistic depictions of Jesus may be feminized, fair skinned with rosy cheeks, the Catholic laity is programmed to understand Christ as sexless. Thus the traditional identification of Christ with the clergy becomes a theological block and psychological denial of the possibility of a homosexual, noncelibate clergy. How can "father" be gay? How can so many priests have died of AIDS-related illnesses (Thomas, 2000)? Yet the denial remains a staunch assertion of Catholic faith along with the dogmatic assertion of the sexlessness of Jesus. Church pronouncements condemn homosexuality, and such public theological hatred deflects suspicion from a homosexual, gender-bending clergy and reinforces faithful denial of the Catholic laity. This theological and psychological logic is deeply flawed but effective in keeping the laity in a state of sexual denial about their clergy, though the current sex abuse scandals have deeply eroded that deniability.

Catholic liturgical culture has fostered some extremes among seminarians and priests, competing with fancy frocks, lace, and baroque vestments in the performance and pageantry of homoerotic rituals of celebrating the Lord's Supper. Drag shows take place not in the gay bars but in churches and cathedrals where ritual pageants occur on as grand a scale as the Miss Gay America pageant. These pageants are orchestrated into hierarchies of feminine expression.

Church ritual has remained a suitable stage to perform homoerotic ritual. When a priest lifts up the bread host, he changes the host into the body of Christ with his words and intentions. Intimately touching the body with affective love and sublimated erotic devotion, he distributes the body of Christ to the laity to be ingested, an act of erotic consummation. Jordan (2000, p. 207) notes how the act of consecration of the eucharistic bread elevates the image of the priest who lives as failed cultural males:

> And the priest at the altar possesses no longer just his own dangerous and despised body, but the body of Jesus. He possesses it by making it, and he possesses by impersonating it. The priest holding consecrated wafer has become Jesus holding his own consumable and divine body.[1]

Two not so veiled symbolic configurations are at work in the psyche of the priest. John Paul II uses the theological rhetoric of Mary as the model for ideological virginity to sustain a celibate priesthood;

the priest, like the figure of Mary, through his ritual repetition of liturgical formulae, gives birth to Christ's presence on the altar. Mary, the Mother of Jesus, ironically becomes the model for the priest, and feminist theologian Rosemary Ruether (1983) made the observation decades ago:

> Celibate males are the primary powerholders of the Church. They represent the "male feminine" in the hands of antiprocreative males.
>
> Female virgins are marginalized as humble servants of the male celibate control over the "spiritual feminine." After all, they are still female and potentially sexual. Married couples become a lower case in the Church. Within the "laity" women are at the bottom of the ladder. They are lower than slaves and tend toward the demonic. So it is not contradictory, but understandable, that a male celibate culture that exalted the symbol of the "spiritual feminine" as Mary and Mater Ecclesia. (pp. 144-145)

The priest usurps feminine spiritual power for himself, and he represents Mary in his subaltern identity as a (fe)male. His appropriation of Mary, albeit a queer performance, attempts to appropriate the value of heterosexuality while denigrating sexuality. Simultaneously, he elevates himself as the drag Christ as he dawns his vestments to liturgically represent Christ and inserts the host into the mouths of the faithful. The priest inserts his own body into the mouths of the communicants; the distribution of communion becomes an act of sex as the communicants take Christ into their mouths.

Moreover, there is a real tension within the clergy between those who would like to be more out as gay and those who do everything to keep the issue of clerical sexuality and, in particular, homosexuality out of the public light. These are different and competing styles of homoerotic cultures. Members of both clergy groups, I might add, have suffered heavy casualties from AIDS-related illnesses, and there is no way to measure which group has been more sexually active.

Traditionalist homoerotic clergy are often "rubric queens," who are fascinated with the smells and bells of liturgical worship, its drag, and the orthodox performance of rites—maintaining female exclusion and competition from the altar. In contrast, modern gay clergy have been pastorally sensitive to queer Catholics—very conscious of the queer exodus from an abusive church, trying to quietly change attitudes, celebrating Eucharist for outlawed groups such as Dignity or lawfully sponsored outreach groups, quietly blessing same-sex unions, and fighting the ever-increasing move of the hierarchy toward the right. Those clergy who have become public about their sexuality or opposed the hypocritical theological homohatred have been forced out of the active priesthood. Although the traditionalist clerical group, at least at this time, holds all the power or is in favor with the hierarchy, it is not necessarily celibate, only more circumspect in sexuality and covert in erotic liaisons. Traditionalist priests may not frequent the gay haunts for anonymous sex, but they sleep their way up the corporate ladder of the Catholic hierarchy. How many promotions of priests and bishops have taken place through sleeping with clerics higher in the hierarchy!

FALLEN WOMEN

Along with many others, I was socialized in the marital arts of cruising within Jesuit recreation rooms, an environment of sharp wit and humor, theatrical performances, repartee, and campiness. Combining this environment with alcohol, there is a potential for an erotic linking up between men. Similar patterns of male behavior can be observed in gay bars: drinking excessively, male banter, some discrete cruising, and an occasional offer of a back rub. Offers of back rubs, as I have discovered in conversations with ex-seminarians and former priests, were universally a euphemism for a sexual encounter. In the Jesuits, I was mentored to an erotic love of men through these encounters. Many of these encounters were moments of grace, intimate human encounters of men in love with Christ and with one another. The terrible encounters, however, were with those Jesuits who denied that it ever happened the next day and kept themselves at a distance from their complexes of guilt and shame. I remember having sex with a Jesuit in a swimming pool; it was ecstatic, wonderful sex. We both longed for male intimacy, touch, and love. His homophobic piety would be triggered after such sexual occasions. The next day, I would be a stranger. Such a pattern is often duplicated in anonymous gay sex. But several weeks later, he would creep into my room late at night for another dose of guilt and shame.

Ingebretsen (1999) notes the strong parallels between openly gay priests and fallen women:

> The priest already occupies a socially degraded position by virtue of his social femininity. He is further disembodied, neutered by ecclesiastical fiat and social usage . . . the gay identified priest, not unlike the "fallen woman," becomes caught up in the operation of a socially punitive narrative that presumes a ravenous, all-sexualized life. (p. 85)

Symbolically, misogynistic institutional Catholicism identifies the openly gay priest with the abject, the fallen and sexualized woman. The gay priest's social femininity is extended to some imagined, "ravenously sexualized woman." Frank and I became "fallen women," gaining notoriety and exciting Jesuit erotic imaginations. Some same-sex couples remained quietly under Jesuit administrative radar for years, and others pursued life together outside of the order.

Institutional Catholicism has fine-tuned the rhetorical strategies of compartmentalization and deniability to prevent widespread insight into the homoerotic nature of its clergy and leadership. The real closet of the Catholic Church is not homosexuality but the exclusion of women and the failure to value what is gendered as female. It is the closet of alternative masculinities and fear of female gender-bending. The Catholic male anxieties of the penetrated (fe)male need to be addressed, for if the church is able to uproot its institutional misogyny, then it may live at peace with a queer and noncelibate clergy.

THE BRIDE OF CHRIST

God is so masculine that in Him we are all feminine.

C. S. Lewis

Clergy have often been suspect of their male performances, for they are less than "macho" men because they do not define themselves by heterosexual sexual encounters. Catholic priests are public failures of heteronormative male gender in a culture in which religiousness is equated with the feminine and masculinity is equated with male sexuality and dominance. Catholic religious and priests wear cassocks and vestments; these forms of archaic clothing are perceived as feminine. This deficiency of masculinity is intensified by the patriarchal assertions of the maleness of God. In a binary-gender system of belief, the maleness of God becomes problematic for fundamentalist and conservative Christian males by rendering them subservient and feminine to a male God. In other words, if God is the top, religious men are the bottoms; they are penetrated men and thus like women. They are passive men without full male status.

Jewish scholar Howard Eilberg-Schwartz (1994) has raised questions about how the feminization of religious males by a masculine God has produced male anxieties about the blurring of gender boundaries and underlying fears of homoeroticism. In *God's Phallus*, Eilberg-Schwartz develops a thesis that the father God of Judaism and of later Christianity legitimized male dominance but that it also destabilized notions of masculinity.

> The primary relationships in Israelite imagination were a male God and individual male Israelites, such as Moses, the patriarchs, and the prophets. Men were encouraged to imagine themselves as married to hence in a loving relationship with God. A homoerotic dilemma was thus generated, inadvertently and to some degree unconsciously, by the superimposition of heterosexual images on the relationship between human and divine males. (p. 99)

God's maleness was, thus, problematic for Hebrew men when the scriptural tradition speaks about God's marriage to Israel (Hosea 1-2, Jeremiah 2:2) or God's sexual intercourse with Israel (Ezekiel 16:8), who is imagined as a woman. God's maleness feminized Israel, the collection of Hebrew males. Eilberg-Schwartz uses the story of Noah's nakedness to demonstrate a general Hebrew anxiety of not subjecting a father to a male erotic gaze (Genesis 9:22-25). Ham gazes upon Noah's nakedness just as he would gaze upon a woman's nakedness and experience sexual desire. His male gaze has feminized Noah by making him the object of sexual desire, and this masculine gaze at other men is unacceptable within ancient Hebrew gender codes. Hebrew anxieties over the "womanizing" of males are reflected in the biblical taboo of homoeroticism in the proscriptions against anal intercourse (Leviticus 18:22, 20:13) and in the stories in

Genesis 19 and Judges 19. Penetrated males disrupt cultural codes of masculinity based on cultural codes in which males are penetrators.

Eilberg-Schwartz uses the Noah story as a hermeneutical strategy on why God's body must be veiled, how ancient Israelites did not depict or imagine God's male body, particularly his sexual organs and facial hair. For example, in Exodus 33:21-23, God allows Moses to see only his back, to view neither his face nor his sexual organs. It is similar to Ham's brothers, Shem and Japheth, who walk backward to avoid gazing upon their father's nakedness. The veiling of father God's body is a necessary strategy to preserve the male conceptualization of deity and to preserve Israel from becoming feminized, thus preserving its male identity and status.

Eilberg-Schwartz's notion of collective male anxiety about the paternal images of God may provide us with a key to the Catholic institutionalized terror of modern homosexuality, its misogyny, and even the primal psychological needed to maintain an asexual Christ. Mark Jordan (2000) hints at a similar trajectory of interpretation when he writes, "Male homosexuality must always be particularly threatening to men in a religion of the God who has assumed a male body. It threatens to resexualize our relationship with Christ, hence our life in God" (p. 205). In the fifth century, what disturbed John Chrysostom about males engaging in sex with other males was that it overturned gender hierarchies and norms. He wrote, "I maintain that not only you are made into a woman, but you cease to be a man" (in Boswell, 1980, p. 157). Chrysostom expresses quite a contemporary feeling of misogynistic male Christian anxiety about men who act like women. Such males are colloquially referred to as "bottoms": they are penetrated males, penetrated like women and lacking full male status.

Theological traditions originating in the Deutero-Pauline letter to the Ephesians identify the church as the "Bride of Christ." At a later period, medieval Christian thought identified the church as "Holy Mother." It raises a similar problem articulated earlier by Eilberg-Schwartz about the male collectivity of Israel married to God. The collectivity of Holy Mother the Church is certainly an all-male caste. Until very recently, much of priestly spirituality was monastic, based in a mystical tradition that comprehended the soul as feminine, as the bride, with Christ as the bridegroom. The spiritual lives of male celibate priests have for centuries been derived from, nurtured by, and consummated in terms of an explicitly sexual/erotic ecstatic union of a bride and bridegroom gathered from reflection on the Song of Songs. Many priests are formed in their spiritualities to see themselves as the brides of Christ.

Medieval Christian bridal mysticism, based upon the Song of Songs and prevalent monastic spirituality, was, and still is, used in the formation of Catholic priests and many religious orders. They have been encouraged and formed to seek an erotic consummation as brides of Christ as in the Song of Songs: "Let him kiss me with the kisses of his mouth" (Song of Songs 1:2). Priests in training were formed spiritually and encouraged to see themselves as "brides," to be penetrated and kissed by the bridegroom. Comparative religious historian Jeffrey Kripal (2002) felt estranged as a heterosexual male during his Catholic seminary years from the homoeroticism of Christian medieval bridal mysticism; he notes that within such a mystical tradition, heterosexuality is heretical. The biggest secret for the Catholic laity is that they already have a married clergy, theologically and spiritually; their priests are the "brides of Christ."

The real threat of our shower-wedding to the Jesuits was not only our betrayal but also our revelation as brides of Christ. We became fallen women, divorced and remarried, making public clerical marriage and muddying the metaphor of brides of Christ. These brides were no longer passive, silenced, or secretive, since we revealed our sexual versatility, breaking the ecclesial and cultural gender codes. We broke the code of silence by becoming public in our love. We queered the bride image with two construction workers on the cake. We had become grooms as well as brides of Christ, with a clearer appreciation of our gender transgressions and the appropriation of traditionally feminine roles in a household.

Homosocial institutions organize their identities and energies to limit the performative ranges of feminine masculinity and use homophobia publicly to deflect suspicion, while keeping women subordinate and abject. Because Catholic priestly (fe)masculinity has provided an alternative to the cultural performances of heteronormative masculinity, no bishop or cardinal could ever be accused of making Catholic Christianity more "masculine." The Catholic hierarchy maintains a (fe)male hierarchy among the clergy in what is certainly a top-down or top-bottom hierarchy. The priest can safely occupy a socially degraded position of (fe)masculinity as long as he plays by the unwritten rules: "Don't tell, don't be visible, and don't get caught in a scandal." Priestly compliance echoes the Pauline injunction for women to keep silent and the Deutero-Pauline exhortation that wives be obedient and submissive to their husbands. In this case, priests are mandated to be compliant and submissive to their bishop.

For example, a Jesuit priest at a Jesuit college got drunk with the son of a trustee of the college, and they found themselves in bed together. As recounted by my inside Jesuit sources, the two were so drunk that they were unable to do anything sexual. Though the Jesuit community defended the drunken Jesuit, Rome forced his expulsion from the order. He broke an unwritten rule: "Don't get caught in a public scandal." Catholic hierarchs will look the other way as long as it does not demand their attention or public attention, thus requiring disciplinary action to maintain the "silence of Sodom."

The Vatican is not concerned with theology, only management and control of a clerical crisis that has begun to reach epic proportions in the American Catholic Church, as priests came out in the 1970s and the 1980s. Such priests betrayed the ecclesial culture of duplicity and lying about their sexual lives, and this was intolerable to an institution that prided itself on hiddenness and secrecy. Church leaders became alarmed at the revelations, prompting a modern-day Peter Damien, Cardinal Ratzinger (1986, 1992), to write several letters against homosexuality. The traditional system of pleasures (aestheticism, ritualism, intellectual and artistic pursuits, safe space to express an alternative masculinity, etc.) functioned to solicit voluntary submission. Jordan (2000) correctly writes, "Gay priests and religious are formed in the pleasures of submission to male authority. Who can be astonished, then, that sexually active gay clerics and ex-clerics seem so often to prefer the leather or S&M cultures?" (p. 218). Gay priests and religious submit to their bishops as wives to their husbands. Many priests enjoy the masochism of submission to a Catholic top, while those defiant and out priests have been stigmatized as fallen women, no longer obedient to their hierarchical husbands. Gay priests need to break the codes of silence and submission.

The Catholic bishops and cardinals attempt to keep their priests neutered and passive through a variety of ecclesial fiats, internal rewards for silence, and brutal punishments delivered to those who do not comply. The Catholic hierarchy has formed unholy alliances with the Christian Coalition and the Mormon Church to financially support the Knight Initiative in California (2000), which defines marriage as one woman to one man, fights to repeal civil unions in Vermont, and supports other anti-queer ballot initiatives. Its aggressive theological homophobia and social policy of homohatred are primarily directed to the Catholic priesthood to prevent a competing queer culture that would become more visible. At the same time, the hierarchy is equally invested in keeping women out of power and excluding them from priestly ordination. Open queer folks and women threaten to unravel the misogynistic, homosocial culture of (fe)masculinity.

Eve Sedgwick (1990, p. 3) writes, "Closetedness is a performance initiated as such by the speech act of a silence." American Catholic denial mechanisms are firmly entrenched, with a finely tuned rhetoric of sodomy that sets up a symbiotic top/bottom relationship between Catholic bishops and religious leaders and priests. Fear and complicity have become tools for a deadening silence that kills the spirit by preventing Catholic priests from exploring publicly alternative masculinities and integrating their sexuality with spirituality in healthy practices. Although other minority masculinities, such as dyke masculinity, gay male drag, or female-to-male transsexuals, destabilize the fundamentalist system of binary gender, priestly (fe)masculinity has not threatened the binary gender system because it has made its peace with masculinist culture where men, even (fe)males, are in control. It has sold out to misogynist culture to control and exclude women. The clerical refusal to be a man is wedded with a deeply ingrained misogyny and maintains the oppression of women at is own privilege. It performs an oppositional (fe)masculinity that has not realized its full potential. It signifies that femininity is a lack of masculinity and power but fails to represent a fluid range of being masculine and feminine in the world rich with novel expressiveness and tonalities. The more that Catholic priests distance themselves from their own misogyny, the more their (fe)masculinity may one day become a resistance (to dream even bigger) and a parodic critique of the homosocial structure of the Catholic Church with all its secrecies and exclusions.

It is obvious to queer Catholics that we need a Catholic Stonewall where gay priests and Catholic laity stand up against clerical misogyny and public homohatred. Perhaps they need to burn their dresses in the front of the cathedrals, exchanging their baroque vestments and lace surplices for real gowns, and refuse to participate any longer in institutional exclusion and violence toward women and queer folks.

Misogyny and homohatred go against Jesus' ministry of nonexclusion and his care for the outsider. The Roman Catholic Church has institutionalized a silence of Sodom, and the only way to dismantle it is for priests, women religious, and laity to say, "Enough! We no longer submit!"

NOTE

1. John Paul II (1993) echoes a similar sentiment: "Thus he [the priest] feels led to give himself to the faithful to whom he distributes the Body of Christ."

REFERENCES

Boswell, John (1980). *Christianity, homosexuality, and social tolerance.* Chicago: The University of Chicago Press.

Eilberg-Schwartz, Howard (1994). *God's phallus.* Boston: Beacon Press.

Goss, Robert E. (2002). *Queering Christ: Beyond Jesus ACTED UP.* Cleveland, OH: The Pilgrim Press.

Ingebretsen, Edward J. (1999). "One of the guys" or "one of the gals"?: Gender confusion and the problem of authority in the Roman clergy. *Theology and Sexuality* 10(March): 71-87.

John Paul II (1993). The Eucharist is at the heart of the priest's spirituality (June 9). Available at <http://www.sjbrcc.org/jp2preu.html>.

John Paul II (1994). Apostolic letter on reserving priestly ordination to men alone (Ordinatio Sacredotalis) (May 22). Available at <http://www.catholicculture.org>.

Jordan, Mark D. (2000). *The silence of Sodom: Homosexuality in modern Catholicism.* Chicago: The University of Chicago Press.

Kripal, Jeffrey (2002). *Roads of excess, palaces of wisdom: Eroticism and reflexivity in the modern study of mysticism.* Chicago: The University of Chicago Press.

Muesse, Mark (1996). Religious machismo: Masculinity and fundamentalism. In Stephen Boyd, W. Merle Longwood, and Mark Muesse (Eds.), *Redeeming men: Religion and masculinities* (pp. 89-102). Louisville, KY: Westminster/John Knox.

Ratzinger, Cardinal Joseph (Congregation of Defense of Faith) (1986). Letter to the bishops of the Catholic church on the pastoral care of homosexual persons. In Jeannine Gramick and Pat Furey (Eds.) (1988), *The Vatican and homosexuality: Reactions to the "Letter to the bishops of the Catholic church on the pastoral care of homosexual persons"* (pp. 1-10). New York: Crossroad.

Ratzinger, Cardinal Joseph (Congregation of Defense of Faith) (1992). Some considerations concerning the Catholic response to legislate proposals on the non-discrimination of homosexual persons. *Origins* 22(August 6): 174-177.

Ruether, Rosemary Radford (1983). *Sexism and Godtalk: Toward a feminist theology.* London: SCM Press.

Sedgwick, Eve Kosovsky (1990). *The epistemology of the closet.* Berkeley: University of California Press.

Thomas, Judy (2000). AIDS in the priesthood. *Kansas City Star,* January 29. Accessed at <http://kcstar.com/projects/priest>.

Wilson, Ashleigh (2001). Gay priests cannot stay in office, Pell warns. *The Australian,* May 14, p. 5.

Chapter 8

Pandora's Gauntlet:
Curiosity Enough to Care
and Hope Enough to Question

Marie Cartier

Although I think Mark Jordan's *The Silence of Sodom* (2000) is an amazingly insightful and courageous work in terms of exposing and highlighting the insidious "don't ask, don't tell" policy the Catholic Church holds over gay men, particularly gay ordained men, I also believe that its embedded sexism makes issues around homosexuality in the church very different for women, and therefore lesbians, than for men.[1] For example, I did feel "called" when I was growing up and felt as if I should be a priest. When I talked to a nun about it in my small-town New England second grade Catholic school, I asked her, "If God is in every person, Sistah, then isn't God in me, too? And so, can't I also be a priest, as well as my brother, who already gets to be an altar boy?" She responded by saying, "There are some mysteries, Marie, that we are not meant to understand."

There are *still* some mysteries that I do not understand. Am I still not meant to understand them? In this chapter, I will highlight these mysteries, in service to a deeper understanding and as an offering toward that understanding.

I do not understand how the church rationalizes not allowing women to be ordained by declaring that a priest must reflect the physical image/embodiment of the human face of God, evidenced in his son Jesus, and men therefore are closest to that image. If priests really need to be in the image of God, then as the 1970s feminist ordination movement used to say, the only people who get to be priests are working-class men of color, because that's what Jesus looked like in his human form as far as we know. If I was interested in being a transgendered man, in this time of gender change, would my reconstructed gender allow me access finally to the priesthood?

I do not understand why the Catholic Church "allows" men to have clandestine homosexual liaisons, as is powerfully exposed in Jordan's book. Through different examples, but particularly through his excellent detailing of stories of priests in the upper echelons, Jordan reveals Catholic priests' privilege in being able to cruise with a certain level of impunity in gay bars, etc. I have personally known people who have encountered this—priests openly exposing their Catholic affiliation without fear within the gay bar culture. My first boyfriend, for example, came out with a Catholic priest.

I was away in Provincetown, Massachusetts, a well-known East Coast gay hangout, for the first time with my first girlfriend. Upon returning, I ran into my first boyfriend. It was a weekend of firsts. He had participated in his first sexual experience with a man—a priest, who he would later say was an awful first experience, "very weird," and would not elaborate.

I remember thinking then how strange that we were Catholics having this bizarre weekend of "firsts." My old boyfriend said that the priest was completely open in the bar, completely open about his behavior. In fact, he was much more open than my old boyfriend and many of the people in the bar that night—he was actually bragging about being a priest and bragging about being gay.

The priest felt free to be in drag, to openly approach my friend, and he was securely within the upper echelon of the priesthood. As Catholics we were at the time well aware of his authority and would not have entertained turning him in for many reasons—not the least of which was that we were also gay—but he also still had a strange remnant of authority over us.

When my old boyfriend revealed the details of the "weird night," which included being told "not to tell," etc., a strange silence surrounded the event. We would not talk much of it in the years to come. I think this had to do with the fact that the priest's actions were absolved before they occurred—absolved by his invisibility within the parish. He simply did not exist as gay there and so could not be confronted with his behavior.

I find this very hard to understand, for this is not the case for Catholic women religious. Sexism is evident when women ensconced in the power structure of the Catholic Church as nuns in religious orders are removed from each other and placed in separate convents when they evidence what is called "a particular friendship," the church's euphemism for lesbianism (Curb and Manahan, 1985).

Jordan does elaborate on the difference between seminaries and seminarians, which much more closely resemble convents for nuns in their living arrangements and power structure than, for example, parish priests and those within the hierarchy of the church. For my purposes here, however, the availability of a power structure, similar to nuns in some respects regarding chastisement around particular friendships, is not as important as the *lack* of another living arrangement other than the convent for women. So while Catholic men and women may both choose a more "disciplined" life, the alternative—a less "disciplined" life—is not available to Catholic women. No structure exists for women to move into that resembles the more powerful one for men—a structure which by contrast is more open and less closeted, a structure which therefore allows and excuses the type of behavior encountered by my old boyfriend.

Although this is documented in several books, among them Curb and Manahan's (1985) groundbreaking *Lesbian Nuns,* I also dated a former nun and have been friends with former nuns who have personally told me of the extreme pain and isolation they felt when separated from their "partner," in an exposed "particular friendship." Many of them lost contact with each other forever due to the erasure of a Catholic woman's secular identity upon her entrance into religious life, and her reestablishment in another geographic location due to the accusation of a "particular friendship."

Although some nuns throughout history have enjoyed a kind of masculine freedom to participate in (perhaps) romantic attachments with other nuns, or other women, this is very rare and usually so exceptional that the romantic attachment alone can make Sor Juana de la Cruz a contested figure in history simply because of her supposed attachments; but I would also argue her masculinity in making such a choice within the convent is seen as rare, threatening, and finally, perhaps, heroic.[2]

I do not understand how men and women are both "allowed" to have problems within a church that declares their sexuality a sin, as with lesbians and gay men, but that the sexism inherent in the church can be erased in many discussions with gay rights advocates of Catholic homosexual activism. Since sexism is "allowed" to structure the hierarchy of the church, men, and therefore some gay men, have completely different access to power and therefore some privilege that is not accessible to the Catholic woman.

As a member of an activist group in Southern California working to change the church from the inside of a Catholic parish in terms of increased visibility and acceptance of homosexuals, I have been engaged in many discussions in which bringing up the sexism within the church is seen as clouding the discussion, i.e., sexism is seen as an issue separate from the church's homophobia.

I have been made to feel that dealing with issues of women's ordination is putting too much on the plate of the homosexual rights activist. However, if, as we also said in the 1970s, "women hold up half the sky," then women make up half the homosexuals within the church, whether or not those homosexuals are ordained religious. So, women's ordination should be a front-line agenda item of the work that gay rights activists do in terms of exposing the underbelly of the church's homophobia, sexism, and repression of its homosexual and female parishioners.

I went through a faith crisis in junior high, because of feeling called and wondering where I was called to. I was not called to be a nun; that was not my feeling. So where? I went on a retreat, a common Catholic youth occurrence, where teenagers go away to think, meditate, pray, and—in the 1970s—sing. At this retreat I ended up yelling at a nun over and over, demanding that she "give me Confession!" Why couldn't she give me Confession? She was trembling and upset, called in the priest, and he gave me Confession.

I was furious at her. If she was in fact "God in every person," then why was the priest more of "God" than she was? Why did he have the authority, and not her? I argued with both of them, cried, and left the retreat upset and questioning. I felt I had hurt her feelings and wished I could just accept the sexism in the church—and be a nun—but I could not. I wanted the power of the priesthood, the power that I saw necessary to make social change and that I did not see at the time in the convent.

I do not understand the current trend within gay rights groups of the newly formed "welcome home campaign" the church has instituted in the United States, in terms of their tolerance for the church's "don't ask, don't tell" policy.

When Proposition 22 was on the ballot in California in the late 1990s (a ballot measure which assured that marriage between only a man and woman was legal and therefore once passed negated any homosexual domestic partnership legally recognized and authenticated in another state, such as Vermont) it was well established within California that it was the Catholic Church particularly that allocated funds for a mass-media campaign that was instrumental in swaying the vote toward passage of Proposition 22.

Gay rights activists within the church were split over the church's participation on the measure, not in terms of acceptance or approval of the church's role, but in terms of the level of tolerance for the church's actions. I talked at length to a peer of mine within this moderately activist group I currently belong to who said that the discussions around Proposition 22 deeply divided the gay rights activists within the church and compelled many of them to leave, because of internal pressure resulting in a conscientious objector status.

It is interesting to note an event that happened at a media-covered protest which I attended concerning this issue. I was part of a crowd in front of the Los Angeles Gay and Lesbian Center, standing next to a gay man extremely upset that Proposition 22 passed. Marriage was now officially legal only between a man and a woman in California. I was also upset; in fact, my picture with my head back against my tall butch lover and tears streaming down my face ended up as the cover picture for a *Los Angeles Times* article the next day. The young gay man looked at me and said plaintively, "God made us, too!" in response to this obvious denial of our civil rights. Of course I agreed with him, put my arms around him, and chanted with him. Later I would think of that night as I argued with similar young gay men about the response of the church to women's ordination. I often wanted to just plaintively say to them "but God made us too," meaning of course women, and have them put their arms around me and agree with me, and agree to work with me.

After the Proposition 22 battle, interestingly, the church put into full swing its "welcome home" campaign for gay people; it is in effect a welcome to a home in which one is asked to "don't ask, don't tell," perhaps and unfortunately so replicating many of our real biological homes where we are also asked to acquiesce to a "don't ask, don't tell" mandate. I particularly do not understand this tolerance by gay activists for the church's abuse of power when it is obvious that, at least in this case, the church used its power not only to circumscribe the lives of its homosexual population within the church itself, but in this case of California law, the church used its power and empowered homophobia, as a church to circumscribe the entire unmarried partnership population of California, not just the church's own Catholics.

That some gay Catholics tolerated this abuse and transgression from the realm of the sacred to the secular serves only to highlight what happens when an oppressed population tolerates its own internalized oppression. In order to sit at the feet of the church in acquiescence and acceptance of a proposed "welcome home" campaign, some gay Catholics allowed the church unquestioned authority over not only their lives but also the lives of people outside the church. This serves to show how necessary is a critique such as Jordan's and how necessary it is for us as Catholic homosexuals to look critically at our nostalgia for a church that never was for us the home that it promised to be, and continues to fail in being that home.

I do not understand the power that a baptized homosexual Catholic has, who decides to not wield that power in critical discourse over the church's homophobic positions and actions, especially when the church makes secular campaigns such as Proposition 22 its own agenda. As Catholics, we have a baptized investment, and authentic inroad, into one of the most powerful institutions in the world.

When I am asked how I can be a Catholic, I say simply, "I can be a Catholic in the same way that I can be an American." America also does not allow me as a lesbian woman to marry. The Catholic Church does not allow me to marry. It also does not allow me to head its parishes or be on its governing boards as a bishop, cardinal, or pope. This is not so different from how America treats its women. We so far have never been president and reflect a very small, but growing, constituency in the Senate and House. Women also represent a very small, but growing, activist voice in Catholic activist discussions. I can be Catholic, not recovered Catholic, but live fully and present as a Catholic dissident voice, as I can live and be fully and actively as an American voice, albeit a dissident voice, within American democracy.

I do not understand the erasure of Catholic cultural identity in discourse regarding participation in, and claiming the right to participate in, Catholic world action. As an Irish citizen, I hold dual citizenship in Ireland and the United States and believe I am culturally Catholic. Being Catholic is an integral part of my embodied identity politic.

The impossibility of my claiming this identity for some of my feminist and lesbian activist sisters confuses me. Why does it appear that there is a general acceptance of a Jewish (for example) cultural claiming of identity, but a Catholic cultural claiming is seen as somehow, for lack of a better word, uneducated?

"How can I be a Catholic?" I am repeatedly asked. I am asked this question and then lectured to on the abuses of the church toward women, as if I do not know this, and as if that is all the church is; and I am lectured to with a sort of tired authority, as if only I could understand and comprehend finally what the lecturer is speaking of, then I would finally decide *not to be Catholic*.

Catholicism for me is not as simple as its lists of abuses, especially from someone who is uneducated about Catholicism. This lack of education on their part becomes apparent as soon as I am allowed to speak—strangely in defense of the church that is correctly being chastised but to which I still hold allegiance. I reply that I am Catholic, because I am an Irish citizen. I am also Wiccan, practice Buddhism through my karate practice, and am a deeply spiritual being. But Catholicism is a core part of my identity, and if asked my religion, I often still say simply "Catholic."

I say that I am Catholic the way the performer Madona is Catholic. The church can not get rid of me. It has to accept me, through my baptized entry, as well as my birthright entry. I do not understand the erasure of this political position from people within the United States. The Catholic Church is not only a sacred institution but also holds great secular power, within the United States as well as in countries such as Ireland, where it has become the core struggle for identity for a decidedly working-class, underprivileged population. People have died for my right to be Irish and Catholic. Whatever complexities (and there are many) I feel with Irish national politics, I do not question my identity as both Irish and Catholic.

I do not understand the general ahistorical attitude toward the church's attributes when we discuss its faults. Often we assume that these negative aspects of Catholicism form the entire entity of the church for us as homosexuals. The reality is that the church is a big institution with a long history of commitment to social justice, such as the work of the activist Dorothy Day and her creation of the Catholic Worker Movement.

The church is the largest human rights organization within South America. It is also the catalyst and foundation for many indigenous religions such as voodoo and Santeria that give women much more authority than they have in the traditional Catholic Church. However, it is my belief (developed in a separate paper) that it is in usurping, but changing and still embodying, Catholic discourse that these religions can hold as much power as they do, and give women as much power as they do when women assume leadership in these religions.[3]

The Catholic Church is a large organization—with many faults, and many attributes. There is power in being a dissident Catholic, as Jordan proves with his book, providing critical discourse about the church's problems and highlighting the church's good qualities. I do not understand placing that power aside without a fight.

In summary, in this chapter I have addressed and attempted to illuminate these "mysteries" that I still hold as not understandable within the church. Particularly, I still hold them as problematic for me—as a lesbian, as a feminist, as an activist, and as a dual citizen of the United States and the Republic of Ireland.

Finally, let me address my second grade nun: Sister, although there may be many mysteries we are not meant to understand, there are also many mysteries that are meant to be revealed. The mystery of the church's enduring ensconced and tolerated homophobia has been revealed in large part in Jordan's book *The Silence of Sodom*. The illumination of this mystery offered by his book goes far in terms of its possible eradication. Let us hope, Sister, that the church's sexism and abuse of women is further illuminated in continued work by scholars such as Jordan and others. Because, Sister, I do think that's a mystery we are meant to understand.

NOTES

1. Jordan (2000) is very careful to note that he will not deal with women's issues within the church and places that clearly, and his reasons for doing so, in the introductory chapter. Because Catholicism is preoccupied almost entirely "with male-male desire," Jordan chooses in this volume to concern his analysis precisely with "male-male eroticism in modern Catholicism." I do not mean to suggest that he should have done otherwise. I think his analysis here is brilliant in terms of how the church treats male-male desire, and that is a sufficient topic for his book. Having said that, I believe that much has been left unsaid and needs to be lifted up by another scholar regarding the issues of women, particularly lesbian women, in the Catholic Church. This chapter highlights some of those points.

2. I have done work in this area, particularly historically, and presented a paper, "Unpacking Alicia Gaspar de Alba's Sor Juana's Second Dream: On the Necessity for Fiction in Resurrecting Queer Lineage," to both the Fifth Triennial Conference on the History of Women Religious, 2001, and the 2002 Regional American Academy of Religion Conference, Western Region.

In this paper I argued that Sor Juana de la Cruz, Mexico's patron saint, after the Virgin de Guadalupe, used the nun's habit as a form of masculine dress, was cross-dressing, and was in a relationship with the Viceriene of New Mexico. Although this argument has been made somewhat before, especially in the film *I, the Worst of All,* and in the novel I used as an example, I specifically wanted to argue that we rarely read women's writings as if they meant what they said, but we instead read them through the secondary sources, which in Sor Juana's case are voluminous, clouding her original words to the point of obscurity. I was arguing here for the use of fiction as a methodology in order to "imagine" that the contested figure *really meant what she said.* This argument is particularly poignant for queer female figures, as they are burdened not only by their queerness but also by their femaleness.

Some very wealthy and well-known figures, such as Sor Juana, may have led the privileged life that some of the men we are discussing here enjoy regularly—for example, my old boyfriend's first experience. However, it is important to note that when Sor Juana's masculine life threatened the male authority figures above her in the church, specifically by imagining and publishing a Chistology that was more solvent than that of the reigning male church father, she was severely punished and her masculine authority, in the form of writing, was taken away from her. She also was removed from contact with her, I believe, female lover, the Viceriene. This is the only example I can think of regarding this kind of authority being wielded by a religious nun, and she is from the fifteenth century.

When I presented this paper to the History of Women Religious, there was a long silence after my presentation, and finally, one nun asked tentatively how Mexico treated its lesbians at that time. I answered that Mexico did not know it had lesbians at that time, and that was part of Sor Juana's ability to be one; the habit made her invisible. I would suggest the same is true today, not just in Mexico but everywhere. Part of that is the fact that being lesbian would be a privilege. Nuns are not supposed to exercise that kind of authority in their choices. That level of authority and choice would be as damning as actually being lesbian.

3. In this paper, I compared the power that women are enabled to hold and shape change with using a "revised" pantheon of saints within Santeria and voodoo, as opposed to the way the traditional Catholic Church pantheon of saints circumscribes the movement and power of women.

REFERENCES

Curb, Rosemary and Manahan, Nancy (1985). *Lesbian nuns: Breaking silence.* Tallahassee, FL: The Naiad Press.

Jordan, Mark D. (2000). *The silence of Sodom: Homosexuality in modern Catholicism.* Chicago: University of Chicago Press.

Chapter 9

A Welcome Voice Breaks the Silence in an Exclusively Male Clerical Tradition

Lorine M. Getz

Finally, a critically insightful volume that I have been awaiting for more than thirty years has been authored by Mark Jordan and published by the University of Chicago Press. *The Silence of Sodom* (2000) is a creative, courageous, and useful volume in a nearly half-century-long series of emerging commentaries on and critiques of the contemporary American Catholic Church.[1] Of these, Jordan's work is the first to provide a clearheaded and well-articulated exposé of the secret and, I believe, fundamental homoerotic interrelationship between homosexuality and the sociocultural and religious milieu of the all-male priesthood in the contemporary American Roman Catholic Church.[2] Until now for me, as one trained in and greatly influenced by the church, for many other lay believers, and perhaps even for some heterosexual male clerics, this relationship has been deliberately obfuscated by authorities with insider knowledge who create a visible, self-serving culture of homophobia, heterosexism, sexism, and misogyny in the church. As Jordan's research boldly reveals, that interrelationship between homoeroticisim and homosexuality is based in and maintained by a conspiracy of silence and oppression, with the silencing of gay priests and the complete exclusion of females from the ranks of its ordained clergy.

For historical, social, philosophical, sociological, religious, and other reasons, this important critical volume could have not been so thoroughly researched, clearly argued, and published earlier. For many American lay Catholics and even for some members of American Catholic clergy and hierarchy, as well as for many other religious individuals, institutions, and denominations around the globe, this work may seem to come at a propitious time. This is an era when the media buffets us weekly if not daily with shocking revelations of alleged homosexual abuse of boys and young men over at least the past three decades by members of the ordained Roman Catholic clergy and by members of Catholic religious orders of men, seeming to reveal from different perspectives and for other reasons than Jordan's, the clear presence of homosexuals and homosexual activity among the Catholic "celibate" clergy.[3]

Jordan (2000) mentions the "scandals of pedophilia" (p. 94), carefully distinguishing it from homosexuality and referring correctly to the hysteria that combines the two. However, Jordan's task in *Silence of Sodom* in not to address the individual or widespread and perhaps even patterned sexual abuse of male children and youths at the hands of some members of the all-male Catholic clergy and religious orders. Rather, Jordan sets himself to the careful examination of the inherent homoeroticization of Catholic liturgy and clerical mores. He does not find the presence of the homoerotic or the presence of a growing homosexual subculture in the church in and of themselves troubling. For Jordan what is so troubling, leading to another kind of oppression and abuse, is their silent suppression and vocal denial. The homophobia and related misogyny in the church's official teachings and its public utterance create *dis*ease and *dis*honesty among its most trusted authorities and representatives.

Skirting the issues related to homoeroticism, the stand taken by Roman Catholic Church authorities related to contemporary allegations of sexual abuse in the church has been to highlight the male pedophiles and to blame the homosexuality of some members of the clergy for these immoral and criminal offenses. To obfuscate the facts the Vatican is now calling for the elimination of homosexuals from the priesthood and the seminaries. But attempts to conflate the form of sexual abuse by and of males with issues of homosexuality in the Catholic Church are clearly unfounded. Certainly not all sex abuse by the all-male clergy finds its victims among boys and male youths. Perhaps sexual activity by members of the clergy with children and youths would not be as male focused as it appears to be were the opportunities for such inappropriate sexual interactions more equally available with girls and female youths.

Historically, pedophiles are predominantly heterosexual. Although less current in the media headlines, sexual abuse of girls, female youths, and women by Catholic priests is not unknown. Believed to be largely underreported, the actual numbers are not known. Moreover, current research, particularly that done by religious sociologist Anson Schupe (1998), indicates that sexual abuse of children and youths of both sexes by male and female members of other American religious institutions is every bit as, if not even more, prevalent than what is now being reported by male victims of Catholic clerics. In some of the world's major religions in which the clergy are not all males, sexual abuse is not so categorically restricted to males, nor are their victims so overwhelmingly male children or youths. Within Protestantism, for example, the accused abusers are not limited to or concentrated among the clergy, many of whom are either female themselves or married men, but are rather spread among nonclerical volunteers, youth workers, etc. These individuals are generally less educated, less disciplined, less organized, and less silenced than their counterparts in Catholicism. Certainly regardless of the religion or the gender of the perpetrator, no excuse can be made for the sexual abuse of anyone, much less naive and defenseless children.

However, the records seem to indicate that, though the sexual abuse of children and youths (and women) by "religious" persons, especially by religiously affiliated male persons, is a significant social phenomenon, its specific occurrence among members of the Roman Catholic clergy has a fundamental and unique basis in the construction of the homoerotic notion of maleness, the exclusive maleness of its clergy, and the impenetrable silence surrounding its secret sodomitic milieu. That question, with its specific characteristics in the unique circumstances that form the contemporary American Catholic religious milieu, requires a separate study different from and beyond the focus of this particular work. However, the publication of *Silence of Sodom* provides a hermeneutic tool for such a study that otherwise would have been unavailable.

How could this widespread illegal and immoral phenomenon of clergy sex abuse have been happening for so long without direct corrective intervention by the church's hierarchy and/or public notice and outcry accompanied by the intervention of civil authorities? Is this a heinous anomaly in an otherwise divinely instituted and sacrally governed institute of religion? According to Mark Jordan's thesis, homosexuality coupled with homoeroticism not only comes as no surprise but is part and parcel of the institution itself, embedded in the very heart of the institutional "mystery," method, and membership of the most elevated and exclusive ordained male clergy. That sexual, and particularly homosexual, abuse has been so internally pervasive and tactically accepted, but largely undetected and/or never openly countered externally, has to do specifically with the silence and secrecy of the powerful institution that is the American Catholic Church.

Before examining other aspects of the text, *Silence of Sodom,* I wish to situate the import of this volume for me personally. I grew up in an uneasy religious environment, the first of six children born of a "mixed marriage" in the pre-Vatican II days when ecumenism was not yet in fashion, a daughter when a son was more desired and certainly expected, at least by my male parent. I have done my time in numerous Catholic religion courses, from studying church history to Catholic social living classes in the local parochial school. At the same time, I attended forbidden classes and events at the YWCA (Young Women's Christian Association) and swam regularly at the not-quite-so-forbidden YM&WHA (Young Men's and Women's Hebrew Association). I also participated in CCD (Confraternity or Christian, here read "Catholic," Doctrine) classes and Catholic summer camps, such as Camp Fatima and Camp Rosary, but in attending public school, I found myself considered on the one hand guilty of grave sin for hanging out with pagans (not only my friends at the YWCA and YM&WHA). My dad, a Presbyterian, was troubled by my failure to embrace Protestantism and for going to classes and functions at the Catholic church. I grew up deeply bothered by the clash of opposing "Christian" denominational mores and values throughout my most formative years, yet I kept my religious troubles and questions mostly to myself.

For a brief period, while observing the youthful vitality of a new Presbyterian church on our street in contradiction to the much older Catholic church complex across town to which I journeyed by public bus weekdays for grade school or for CCD classes and where I often met weekday funeral corteges on my way into class, I dreamed of declaring myself wholly Protestant (and therefore "American"). However, when a car killed a Protestant child and his funeral was held at the seemingly young and totally alive neighborhood Presbyterian church, I decided that religion was too complex and frightening for a child to deal with, and I put my religious struggles aside the best I could. I continued to attend Catholic Mass and took the sacraments, lived with and loved Protestants, and kept my questions of divided loyalties and conflicts of values to myself. Finally, at the age of seventeen I decided to join a Catholic convent because the nuns were the only women of any sort that I had come into contact with who studied and knew anything about religion (though some Presbyterian ministers were women, I had never seen or even heard of any at that time). Though I knew privately that I entered the convent to learn why so-called Christians hated one another, my pastor, who wrote my letter of recommendation, admonished me never to let that notion be known, but rather to say if ever questioned by the nuns that I was entering their order because I felt "called."

I was oddly out of place in the convent novitiate, having come not only from the family of a mixed marriage but also from a public high school. I found that my pastor was correct that I could not address my most fundamentally religious question there, but I did have some useful time out of the hubbub of a very busy family to reflect and to study what I could in my private quest for religious truth, by combing the convent library for hints. In the meantime, Vatican II happened and, for a very short time, I felt hope!

Eventually, for many reasons, including my discovery that none of the members of this order of religious women held degrees in Catholic theology or were willing to discuss my larger "Christian" questions, I left the convent to pursue my undergraduate and graduate degrees in religion and theology on my own. I completed my undergraduate degree at a Catholic university, where earlier, as a professor of pharmacy, my dad had been their first Protestant faculty member. I matriculated in education, since at the time their departments of theology and philosophy had both been "closed" by the local bishop for allegedly engaging in the heresy of "modernism."

From there I went on to master's and then doctoral work, both pursued in Catholic theology, but both in ecumenical consortia where I dipped as fully as was permitted first into Protestant theologies and then into world religion courses, contact, and contexts. Curiously, my religious questions were limited to the spiritual and intellectual spheres.

Though I had occasionally dated boys in high school and had crushes on several female teachers along the way, I had little to no interest in sexuality. If there were sexual relationships of any kind in the convent, I never knew about them. Novitiate warnings against "particular friendships" were obscure and irrelevant to my quest. My focus was on sainted women of the church—progressively the Blessed Virgin Mary, Teresa of Avila, the Beguines, Joan of Arc, and later Flannery O'Connor. All of them were, at the least, as they were presented to me, females who were spiritual and sexless.

However, that was not all that was going on in my world. For a brief time between obtaining my MA and my PhD, I had attended classes in a world religion department at a secular university, intending to complete a PhD in literature and religion there. In my first semester of doctoral work I was elected as a student representative to the department's faculty council. At the first council meeting of the year, I learned that the members of this world religion department had a general fund to which they (the all-male faculty) contributed with some regularity in order to send female graduate students whom they got pregnant to England where they could obtain legal abortions. I was shocked and horrified. Before the end of my first semester at this institution, and while I was still mulling over this revelation, my appointed thesis advisor with whom I had taken no classes and whom I had no reason to suspect of untoward behavior, died of a sudden illness. As he would not be replaced and I could not find another advisor in the area of my proposed thesis, I had to leave that institution— and I left it somewhat wiser a female graduate student in the field of religion!

At my new university, I kept quiet about my theoretical insights regarding female student and male faculty sexual interactions in the name of religious inquiry, but prudently chose a closeted, obvious to me and to every other student I knew, gay Catholic clergyman as my new advisor. This was after an initial interview during which a heterosexual professor on the same faculty made unwanted sexual advances during a preliminary discussion on my possible course of study. Though, like nearly every other doctoral student, I ran into snags, confusions, disappointments, and delays during the course of completing the PhD, I had no complications from my advisor relating to my sexuality or his.

During this time, however, I did work as a teaching assistant for several members of the undergraduate faculty. My first spring semester in this capacity, numerous male undergraduates sought me out one at a time to tell me that the professor was "after" them, making sexual demands, requiring that they come to his home after hours, even in some cases insinuating that failure to cooperate would result in a failing grade. Mostly they were shocked and terrified. I mulled over my responsibility as a teaching assistant and decided to take their claims to the most respected elder priest-professor I knew and one whom I thought I could trust. On hearing me out, he merely smiled knowingly and said, "Tell them not to worry. Father is like this every spring. If they just do their work and keep away from him, they will come to no harm. He threatens often, but he never lowers grades for those who choose to ignore him." With undergraduates, there were enough other classes and activities that these students' problems seemed to resolve themselves, or at least I did not hear more about these problems.

However, I came, in this context, to meet a young man who had years ago been the boy-lover of a priest faculty member. That young man, now engaged to be married to a young woman, recounted years of hellish existence, dominated physically, psychologically, socially, economically, and especially spiritually by this priest whom he both held in highest esteem and came to loathe. The young man said that he had been rescued from his terrible fate only by the U.S. government, when it had drafted him into the Army to serve in the Vietnam War. I could only imagine the horror.

While I was completing the work for my PhD, a young male classmate of mine at a previous university enrolled for the PhD in theology at my new school. When he spoke to me of choosing a priest-professor for his thesis advisor whom I knew to be an active homosexual and who was rumored to be secretly seeking "spiritual" relationships with some of the male graduate students, I cautioned my friend against this choice strenuously. He proceeded not only to choose this man as his advisor, but also eventually relayed that he had been chosen by the priest to participate in some sort of "religious" ménage à trois. In this relationship the priest-professor would be God the Father, another male student God the Son, and my friend, God the Holy Spirit. He felt trapped. Ultimately, when he could neither find his way out of the relationship, nor live with it, he killed himself. The priest, I heard, went on to replace him with another young man as his Holy Spirit figure.

Concurrent with all of this, my next younger sibling, the much wished for first male child in the family, was also away at college. He then continued living out of state, busy launching his own professional career. We learned later that during this time he was quietly trying to figure out his sexual identity away from the view of the rest of the family. Finally, at the age of twenty-eight, and while I was still mired in obtaining my PhD, he came to the solitary conclusion that he was gay. As he told me later, at first it scared him. He was, after all, not only a practicing Catholic and a member of a by now totally and staunchly Catholic family (my dad had converted), but also an Eagle Scout and the leader of a Catholic Boy Scout troop in the town where he lived. He withdrew from everything—our family, the Catholic Church, the Boy Scout troop—and sought answers. He did research, checked out the best psychotherapist he could find on the matter, visited other churches, but found no solace or help. Finally he came out to me, then some of our other siblings, then finally our parents. His revelations were met with acknowledgment of what had privately been suspected by a few, with horror and blame for some others, but finally with loving acceptance by the whole immediate family. However, it was tacitly acknowledged that the news should go no further in the family, social, and church circle. He returned permanently to his single professional life in another city. We kept in touch by phone. He went public in his chosen city and became known as an advocate for gay rights. He set up a twenty-four-hour hotline at his home, worked tirelessly to get boys and young men out of male prostitution, sought money for AIDS research, cofounded a lesbian and gay center in his town, started a gay and lesbian newspaper, and ultimately founded more than forty nonprofit organizations to help gays and lesbians find and claim their rightful places in society. When he died tragically of sleep apnea, even his detractors came to his funeral and openly acknowledged his foresight, leadership, and great courage. Today he is recognized as the grandfather of the gay and lesbian movement in his state. His city and its surrounding county have for decades had an exceptionally low rate of AIDS, due in large part to his early efforts to fund research and do outreach through education, newsletters, and the work of the gay and lesbian center. I negotiated for the family, and we held his funeral at a large Catholic church in his city. A gay priest, who had quietly helped my brother with some of his social and educational initiatives, said the mass. I preached the sermon. Several of my brother's dearest friends and business associates who attended the service commented afterward that they never knew he was Catholic. The tragic irony was not lost on me.

It is nearly twenty-five years since my straight male friend committed suicide to end his entrapment in a would-be homoerotic trinity and was grieved silently by his family and friends at a Protestant church service away from the cause of his sudden and tragic demise; twenty years since my gay thesis advisor died alone of medical complications related, among other causes, to cirrhosis of the liver, and was heralded as a brilliant member of the faculty and loyal member of the clergy in a Roman Catholic Mass on the university's campus; and a decade since my brother died of a condition that was medically known but never treated seriously or effectively, perhaps because of his public gay identity, and buried from a Catholic Church he could never find an authentic way to attend. How much more I could have understood during those long decades had I the benefit then of reading and understanding the meanings and implications of Mark Jordan's *Silence of Sodom*!

Jordan's examinations of the secrecy and oppression related to homosexual culture of the clergy, his study of the homophobic rhetoric of the church, and his revelations of the homoerotic elements entailed in the celebration of the liturgy have named for me aspects of these elements within the clerical structure and lived experience of the all-male church authority that I have encountered through others but for which I had no language or system of meaning.

I place *Silence of Sodom,* in terms of its value to me as a scholar of religion as well as a female practitioner, beside the early contribution of Mary Daly's *The Church and the Second Sex* ([1968] 1985). In it Daly, like Jordan, radically critiques a fundamental aspect of the institutional Catholic Church. In her case it is its misogyny. The structures and purposes of the two works are strikingly similar. They both illuminate and articulate aspects of the Roman Catholic Church that I have experienced and/or witnessed firsthand, but about which I had no language, no hermeneutic, no critical frame of reference. To both of these scholars, I owe a debt of gratitude.

More than forty years ago feminist author Mary Daly called first for mutuality and partnership on recognizing the sexism inherent in the institutional church. Later, on realizing the elemental misogyny and related homoeroticism in the patriarchal Catholic Church, not only in its human institutional form but also at the heart of its dogma, liturgy, indeed, at its very core, she left the church and its religious trappings. Now, nearly a half a century later comes writer and researcher Mark Jordan, who, amid the homophobia, the sex scandals, the code of silence, and oppression within the institution, also discovers the fundamental relationships between homosexuality and homoeroticism. However, instead of leaving the Catholic Church, Jordan calls for rebuking the institution's sins, unscrambling homoerotic speaking, developing a new language, and creating a new time for homosexuals in the Catholic Church.

Curiously, Jordan (2000) does not consider Daly's arguments and her final decision. He states, "Feminists and lesbians have led the way in this as in many other aspects of the church life" (p. 238). Here he chooses to see the moderates and reformers who have stayed—the members of Women-Church, etc., not the Dalys and myriads of other more radical members who have followed their wisdom and visions to their ultimate ends outside of the structures of deception and oppression. I will be interested to observe Jordan's own future with the Catholic Church. Will he go back to read more closely the words of the feminists as radical as himself, those who decades ago called for fundamental change in the structure and operations of the institutional church's authorities but found their request rebuffed, ignored, or insufficient? Will his personal inside track on the homoerotic and his own gender identity enable him to accomplish what Daly, as a radical feminist, could not in conscience do? Jordan's male privilege in this patriarchal and misogynist religious institution, coupled with his correct assessment and appropriation of its homoerotic core, will be sufficient for him to gain acceptance, overcome the enforced homophobia, silence, and oppression, engage the new language he seeks, and remain within a changed church, more in conformity with reality as he understands and experiences it, now that he has made the truth he has discovered publicly known.

What I call for here is honest and multifaceted conversation among all those courageous researchers who seek the truth in the face of a complex institution of colossal historical and cultural import, impacting the lives of many Catholics.

NOTES

1. See, for example, James Kavanaugh (1967), *A Modern Priest Looks at His Outdated Church.* Kavanaugh, a Catholic priest, faced ecclesiastical perils such as defrocking and/or excommunication and was called a man of great courage for un-

dertaking his study at the time. His book is an examination of current Catholic Church rules and practices regulating heterosexual issues ranging from birth control to married clergy. In *The Church and the Second Sex* ([1968] 1985), Mary Daly analyzes the role of women in the church, exposing the sexism and misogyny inherent in the institution and calling for reform. In *Beyond God the Father: Toward a Philosophy of Women's Liberation* (1973), Daly focuses on the church's theological center: its belief in a patriarchal God and the accompanying doctrine of an all-male Trinity. By definition as a lay Catholic woman and not a member of a religious order, Daly faced no ecclesial threats; even as a trained theologian and philosopher, because of her sex she had no recognized power or authority in the Catholic Church. A decade later, in *The Desolate City: Revolution in the Catholic Church* (1990), Anne Roche Muggeridge called for revolution to resolve the escalating clergy-laity dissention and the crisis of authority, and to bring about what she sees as necessary changes in the institutional church.

2. This relationship was first articulated by Mary Daly in *Gyn-Ecology: The Metaethics of Radical Feminism* (1980). See especially Chapter 1, pp. 19-20, Chapter 2, p. 74 ff., and Chapter 6, p. 185 ff. Daly did not recognize any possible positive aspects of homoeroticism such as those cited by Jordan, nor did she discuss any of the negative effects of keeping the homosexuality of the clergy silenced and hidden relative to the experiences of gay men in the church. Rather, her emphasis throughout is the distorted effects of the related experiences of patriarchy and misogyny on females in the church. More recently, Randy P. Connor (1992) has examined the relationship between homoeroticism, androgyny, and the sacred in a cross-cultural study that looks at diverse eras and cultures from the Paleolithic era to contemporary Yorba practitioners. His study includes the roles of shamans, priests of a variety of sorts, magicians, and artists. However, he includes Christian practitioners only in a general way, never focusing specifically on members of the Roman Catholic clergy.

3. For an early, but in-depth, consideration of this clergy sex scandal in the Catholic Church, see Berry (1992).

REFERENCES

Berry, Jason (1992). *Lead us not into temptation: Catholic priests and the sexual abuse of children.* New York: Doubleday.

Connor, Randy P. (1992). *Blossom of bone: Reclaiming the connections between homoeroticism and the sacred.* San Francisco: HarperCollins.

Daly, Mary (1973). *Beyond God the Father: Toward a philosophy of women's liberation.* Boston: Beacon Press.

Daly, Mary (1980). *Gyn-Ecology: The metaethics of radical feminism.* Boston: Beacon Press.

Daly, Mary ([1968] 1985). *The church and the second sex,* Revised edition. Boston: Beacon Press.

Jordan, Mark D. (2000). *The silence of Sodom: Homosexuality in modern Catholicism.* Chicago: University of Chicago Press.

Kavanaugh, James (1967). *A modern priest looks at his outdated church.* New York: Pocket Books.

Muggeridge, Anne Roche (1990). *The desolate city: Revolution in the Catholic Church,* Revised edition. New York: HarperCollins.

Schupe, Anson (1998). *Wolves within the fold.* New York: Rutgers University Press.

Chapter 10

Where Have All the Young Girls Gone?

Mary Ann Tolbert

Attention to the sexual abuse of girls and young women has been largely absent from the ongoing debate in the media over clergy sexual abuse in the Roman Catholic Church. This absence begs for explanation, especially since across U.S. society in general "current studies indicate that girls are three times more likely to be sexually abused than boys" (SIECUS, 2002). Although reliable statistics about clergy sexual abuse within the Catholic Church—or any church—are hard to come by, A. W. Sipe, a former Catholic priest and current psychologist who has been studying sexuality in the Catholic priesthood for twenty-five years, reported to the *Boston Globe* that from his work he would estimate that more than twice as many priests are sexually involved with females as with males (Paulson, 2002). If Sipe's estimate is true or even close to true, the absence of public attention to the situation of clergy sexual abuse of girls and young women becomes even more remarkable.

A clue to why the plight of female victims continues to be largely invisible in the current crisis might be found in the striking comments of Cardinal Francis George of Chicago during the meeting of U.S. Cardinals with Pope John Paul II in April 2002. Cardinal George said:

> There is a difference between a moral monster like [the Rev. John] Geoghan [who engaged in sex with boys] . . . and someone who perhaps under the influence of alcohol engages with a 16- or 17-year-old young woman who returns his affection. That is still a crime . . . so the civil law does not distinguish. But in terms of the possibility of reform of one's life, there are two very different sets of circumstances. (Sennott, 2002)

As George notes, civil law does not distinguish between these acts, since both are understood as sexual abuse of minors, but for George their moral weight is quite different. My guess is that many Americans would agree with him. By considering the different moral weight many people, both within and outside of the Catholic Church, seem to give to sexual relations with boys versus those with girls, I think we can begin to see some of the reasons why the victimization of girls and young women has been largely absent from the coverage of the current clergy sex abuse scandal.

I would like to suggest that underlying and supporting the moral difference George sees between the sexual abuse of boys and that of girls are the assumptions of a pervasive heterosexism. Heterosexism can be defined as the belief that *only* sexual desire between men and women (i.e., a heterosexual orientation) is normal, healthy, truly intimate, mutual, rewarding, and to be publicly acknowledged (Sears, 1997). Under this cultural ideology, sexual relations between people of the same sex are viewed as inherently abnormal and unhealthy. Even at their very best, same-sex relations can be only a debased imitation of the true intimacy and mutuality available to opposite-sex relationships. Alternatively, those who reject such heterosexist ideology recognize same-sex desire simply as a normal, persistent sexual variation with the same potential for intimacy, mutuality, and healthy living available to any sexual relationship. It is important to note that being heterosexual does not inevitably lead to an acceptance of heterosex*ism*; only people—be they heterosexual, homosexual, or bisexual—who accept the exclusive claims to normality and morality of heterosexual desire and relationships are informed by a belief in heterosexism. However, heterosexism has been conventionally and pervasively adopted by much of U.S. culture and is certainly the major public self-articulation of U.S. "sexual morality." Consequently and not surprisingly, the current debate over clergy sexual misconduct has been largely framed by the media and by church leaders within that convention.

The assumptions of heterosexism have had at least two powerful effects on the present debate: First, they have tended to dismiss or trivialize the victimization of females by male clergy while dramatizing the plight of males, and second, ironically, they have disallowed any suggestion of mutual affection between priests and the sixteen- or seventeen-year-old *males* they may have become sexually involved with. In the first place, because heterosexual relations are in the majority, as the statistics show, more females are abused than males, making their abuse less newsworthy because it is more pervasive.[1] Moreover, since heterosexuality is assumed to be the "normal" orientation of everyone, female victims of sexual abuse, especially teenage victims, are often portrayed as complicit in their own abuse by their "seduction" of older males. Indeed, sexual abuse can be presented as simply a mutual return of affection, as Cardinal George's quotation indicates. It is the normality of heterosexual relations that also encourages George to suggest that the use of alcohol might be sufficient to permit a priest to slip over the edge of his vows with a young woman. Because heterosexual desire is so natural and pervasive, very little enticement is needed to bring it into play. All of these assumptions about the normality, naturalness, and mutual affection of sexual relations between men and women serve to blur the lines between morally and psychologically appropriate sexual relations and relations of sexual abuse in the case of young women and older men.

The same cannot be said of male-male sexual relations. Under heterosexism, male-male sexual relations are always unhealthy and abnormal, whether the object of desire is a boy, a young man, or an adult male. Here the claim for abuse seems clear and persuasive. Because in the heterosexist view that no young man could actually be naturally attracted to another man, sexual relations between priests and young men must always be marked by abuse of power, never mutual affection. Moreover, the abnormality of homosexual desire means that no morality-loosening substances, such as alcohol, would ever lead to this kind of act; only a depraved personality would participate in such sexual abuse. The naughty but understandable scenario of the tipsy priest and the seductive teenager works only as long as the teenager is clearly identified as female. If the teenager is male, the priest must be a monster and the teenager an outraged victim. Heterosexism makes the case of the male victims much stronger, more dramatic, and thus much more "newsworthy" than that of their female peers.

However, Cardinal George's scenario of returned affection between priest and female teenager, seen in its most positive light, might sometimes describe the beginning of a lasting and mutually rewarding relationship—provided, of course, that the priest is willing to renounce his vows and vocation, as many have indeed done, and marry the woman he loves. Under the assumptions of heterosexism, the same positive light could never shine on the relationship between a priest and male teenager. Even the possibility of real affection, much less the view of lasting future commitment, is ruled out completely. Nevertheless, many priests have indeed left the priesthood, not to marry women but to live in faithful, long-term relationships with other men. This far from unknown scenario of same-sex mutual affection and fidelity is completely absent from the current debate because heterosexism makes it positively unthinkable.

Sexual abuse of children is intolerable, whether those children are boys or girls. As contemporary psychology has insisted and many documented cases have shown, actual pedophilia is defined by the sexual desire for children, often of either gender. Most child molesters are not sexually attracted to adults at all. Their sexual "orientation," such as it is, is not "hetero," "homo," or "bi"; it is instead a desire for children. Such child molesters must be removed from the clergy or any other professions where they seek and gain contact with children. However, if the assumptions of heterosexism are removed from the present debate, the type of situation Cardinal George suggests for the sixteen- or seventeen-year-old and the male priest becomes much more complex; gender can no longer be the deciding factor in judging the morality of the situation. Teenage girls, just like boys, can be and have been sexually abused by priests, and that abuse must not be trivialized. At the same time, teenage boys, just like girls, have sometimes experienced and returned real affection in those sexual relationships. Moral judgment about the presence of abuse in either case must rest on other factors besides gender—factors that include consent, maturity, commitment, mutuality, trust, and the lasting beneficial effects of the relationship for both participants.

NOTE

1. The bizarre studies by Paul Cameron in the mid-1980s that are used by some conservative Christian groups to prove homosexuals commit the greatest number of acts of sexual abuse and that boys are abused more than girls have been thoroughly discredited by other studies and are generally ignored by most researchers. For a thorough critique of Cameron and his group, see, for example, Gonsiorek and Weinrich (1991) and Herek (1991). Much of this critique is helpfully summarized in Gregory Herek's Web site, available at <http://psychology.ucdavis.edu/rainbow/html/facts_cameron.html>.

REFERENCES

Gonsiorek, J.C. and Weinrich, J.D. (1991). The definition and scope of sexual orientation. In J.C. Gonsiorek and J.D. Weinrich (Eds.), *Homosexuality: Research implications for public policy* (pp. 1-12). Thousand Oaks, CA: Sage.

Herek, Gregory M. (1991). Myths about sexual orientation: A lawyer's guide to social science research. *Law and Sexuality* 1: 133-172.

Paulson, Michael (2002). Vatican stance on gay clergy criticized. *Boston Globe,* March 4.

Sears, James T. (1997). Thinking critically/intervening effectively about heterosexism and homophobia: A twenty-five-year research retrospective. In J.T. Sears and W. Williams (Eds.), *Overcoming heterosexism and homophobia: Strategies that work* (pp. 13-48). New York: Columbia University Press.

Sennott, Charles M. (2002). Pope calls sex abuse crime. *Boston Globe,* April 24.

Sexuality Information and Education Council of the United States (SIECUS) (2002). Misconceptions surrounding child sexual abuse need clarification to protect our children. Press release, June 11. Available at <http://www.siecus.org/media/press/press0020.html>.

PART III:
POWER GAMES
AND CALLING NAMES

Chapter 11

Breaking the Silence in Public: A Case Study

Michael Kelly

One of the problems faced by those who would "break the silence of Sodom" is finding a platform from which to speak. Many openly queer people have lost their careers, their platforms, and their audience precisely because they would not remain silent. When justice and integrity demand they continue to speak up, these queer Catholics often find they have no context, no status, and no authority to support their speaking. Church leaders, by contrast, have media advisors, clerical spokespersons, diocesan newspapers, journalistic supporters, and, in a few cases, professional public relations firms to help them make their voices heard both within the church community and in the public arena.[1] Coming out and speaking up can seem, paradoxically, like being forced into irrelevance and ceding ground to the bishops and the bureaucrats.

On the other hand, the princes of the church today have to cope with modern realities that bring them deep discomfort: an educated laity and a free press. The mass media, for all their tendencies to be in thrall to those with power and influence, are ultimately interested in stories that will sell papers, and they are, at the end of the day, beyond the control of the church. Furthermore, a new generation of journalists is demonstrating that it is not overawed by ecclesiastical display and that it sees the church as an appropriate subject of investigation, analysis, and, at times, exposé. Such journalists are increasingly discovering what Catholic insiders have always known—that the church is not some monolithic structure ruled by godlike autocrats who are slavishly obeyed by the simple faithful—but rather that it is a diverse, argumentative, creative, vibrant community where many voices and perspectives vie for influence. They are also discovering that highly educated, articulate, and media-savvy Catholic laypeople can offer them good copy by openly challenging the church. For disenfranchised, marginalized, queer Catholics, this opens up radical new possibilities.

A CASE IN POINT

Over the past five years I have discovered that the skills I once used to correct senior high school essays, teach creative writing, speak to faculty, parish, and parent groups, and educate teachers in basic theology have prepared me extraordinarily well for engaging the mainstream media. One aspect of this development has led to me writing occasional freelance opinion pieces for the editorial pages of several of Australia's major newspapers. I discovered that no magic was involved—just relevant issues, good, focused writing, and a helpful editor or two.

Early in 2001, I began to e-mail and phone my journalist friends concerning the developing international discussions about gay clergy. This is a very simple and useful way of alerting members of the media to contemporary church issues; sometimes the issues are too arcane, but occasionally one hits the spot. For example, I was instrumental in prompting a widespread media discussion of the Vatican's suppression of the Third Rite of Reconciliation throughout Australia through several carefully placed phone calls. In a similar way, I prompted a tough exposé of the right-wing Catholic group Courage, with its endorsements of "reparative therapy" for homosexuals.

At the time the BBC had just screened the documentary "Queer and Catholic,"[2] which uses Donald Cozzens's book *The Changing Face of the Priesthood* (2000) as a starting point for a serious study of homosexuality among Catholic clergy. I was concerned that this issue, which was emerging as a major controversy in Europe and the Unites States, was not being adequately covered in Australia—a situation our right-wing church leaders, such as Cardinal Archbishop George Pell, would have found rather congenial.

After many discussions, numerous faxed articles, and some uncertainty on all sides, an associate editor of one of Australia's major newspapers tentatively commissioned a substantial article—with no guarantees, since I was not an established feature writer. It was time for me to bite the bullet and break the silence of Sodom.

Over the next two months I wrote a 3,000-word article about gay priests. I made a point of discussing it with several gay priests I knew well—two in Australia, two in the United States, and two in England—so that I had grass-roots criticism and support along the way. Shaping this essay required some difficult and sensitive choices. What one might say in a scholarly article or a church publication looks very different in the stark black and white of Saturday morning newsprint. The advice of these gay priests was invaluable in discerning the tone and emphasis of my writing, as I will discuss later. After some minor editing by journalist friends, I submitted the article.

The first response of two senior editors at the newspaper was excitement: "Extraordinarily powerful and deeply moving." "The best thing you have written for us." "Impressive journalism, an important study." Immediately discussions began about running the full article as a major weekend feature. All that was needed was confirmation by the boss, the editor in chief, and that, they believed, was a foregone conclusion.

Over the next two months, however, it became clear that even for a mainstream newspaper in a country as secular as Australia, the issue of gay priests was almost too hot to handle. Without detailing all the discussions that took place, suffice it to say that some senior editors, who never questioned the quality of the writing and the importance of the issue, were extremely wary of provoking the right-wing rump of the Catholic Church. Questions of defamation and libel, for example, worried them, as did the possible reaction of readers. For some weeks it looked as if the article would never be published.

For me, this part of the whole experience was deeply disempowering. It felt as if my voice was being silenced a second time by the church and its closeted clerical power brokers, this time through their hidden, subtle influence in the public arena. Breaking a silence as deep, as defended, and as sanctified as the "silence of Sodom," however, was never going to be a simple or a safe project, and what awareness I, in my naïveté, lacked, these editors offered in their caution.

At the same time, a good story just will not lie down, as any seasoned journalist knows. Finally, after personal discussions between the editors and some of my priest consultants, who must be congratulated for their honesty and integrity in standing by what I had written, the letter was published on August 18, 2001, as a major feature in the Saturday edition of the *Sydney Morning Herald,* Australia's leading broadsheet, under the title "Father I Am Troubled: The Secret Life of Gay Priests." It is reprinted here as I submitted it, with only minor adaptations to the format to improve clarity.

MY LETTER

"Father I Am Troubled: The Secret Life of Gay Priests"
by Michael B. Kelly

One cold Thursday in May I had a surprising conversation on the Internet. I had clicked into a local gay chatroom and was soon swapping messages with "Bill." He was keen to meet. I declined and was just about to sign off when "Bill" told me he had an unusual job.

Bill: Look, I'm a priest.
Me: [I took a breath. How do I handle this?] Catholic?
Bill: Yep
Me: Resigned or still in ministry?
Bill: Still in
Me: [I need to go gently here—this man could be making himself very vulnerable.] Must be tough at times......so, how do you handle all the teachings and rules?
Bill: I knew you'd ask that !!! Actually, I'm a traditional Catholic. I believe and teach what the Church believes and teaches
Me: So, how come you're in this chatroom?
Bill: Well, I've been celibate for 17 years—I'm starting to explore a bit
Me: Fair enough. [Now I find myself caught between irritation and compassion—but I have counselled gay priests and I know what they can go through. Maybe I can help this guy a bit.] So, how do you cope with your desires? 17 years is a long time
Bill: Don't know.....go to Confession??? Still working it out.
Me: Fair enough...I understand
Bill: But I don't try to rationalise what I may do
Me: You just do it and then condemn yourself for it? [Damn. Too strong. Lost him.]
*** "Bill" has left private chat ***

This story is true, and "Bill" is far from unique.
Gay priests exist. They minister in every country and at every level in the church. Some of them live in total celibacy. Some have occasional affairs.

Some have a committed lover. Some frequent sex clubs and beats and hope they won't get caught.[3] Some of them, like "Bill," reach out for sexual intimacy through Internet chatrooms. Some of them love solemn ceremonies in cathedrals, and some work in rough parishes, helping homeless kids and getting up in the middle of the night to calm family rows and patch up shaky marriages. All of them have traditionally been united by one thing—silence. That silence is finally being broken.

In *The Age*[4] last year Paul Rogers, a former Melbourne priest who is now married, spoke openly of gay priests, many from conservative circles, who regularly "get their rocks off" at a certain sex club, then support the refusal of Communion to gay Catholics who openly affirm their sexuality.[5] In a recent ABC "Compass" television program a former Sydney seminarian spoke about having his first sexual experience with a fellow seminarian—a story common amongst gay priests. The recent "Spice Girls" controversy made public a situation long discussed amongst Melbourne clergy, who coined the term to describe priests in the "inner circle" around George Pell, who are perceived by their colleagues as being closeted homosexuals and who, in the words of one of Pell's friends, Mary Helen Woods, "love their incense and their dressing up" and are rather "girlie." Some of the priests most critical of such clerical camp are themselves gay, but live it out very differently, committing themselves to grass-roots pastoral work.

Some of that takes place in gay bars. I personally know priests who have heard confessions and counselled young gay men in smoke-filled venues in inner-city areas. I know priests who have a committed lover, others who live celibately, others who use their day off to visit a certain sex club where, as one prominent priest told me recently, "You could practically have a senate of priests meeting some Monday nights."

Stories like these are simply the local version of a worldwide and age-old phenomenon that is finally being discussed.

In 1999 a book called *The Changing Face of the Priesthood* rocked the Catholic Church in the United States. Written by Father Donald Cozzens [2000], a highly respected seminary rector and professor of pastoral theology, it was an incisive study of the crises facing the Catholic priesthood today, from paedophilia to aging to resentment at the Vatican's abuse of power. It was Cozzens's chapter on sexual orientation, however, that fanned into flame a long smouldering controversy.

For more than 10 years researchers had been reporting that a substantial number of priests were homosexual. However, Cozzens's experience and status as the "ultimate Catholic insider," as one Catholic journal put it, gave his statements a power that could not be ignored by the church establishment.

Cozzens quotes studies that found from 23 percent to 58 percent of priests, and 48.5 percent of priests and 55.1 percent of seminarians are gay. These figures are similar to estimates made by Richard Sipe, the most respected researcher in this field, who was a monk for 20 years then became a psychiatric specialist in the field of clerical sexual habits [Marr, 1999]. In 1990, after counselling priests for twenty years, Sipe estimated that 30 percent of priests were gay and said that without these men "the church as we know it would cease to exist." He went on to predict that by 2010 more than half of America's priests would be gay. Many researchers say that figure has already been reached, and most of them agree the percentage of gay seminarians is higher still.

On the basis of several decades of working closely with priests and bishops, Cozzens says that in addition to figures like 50 percent, it must be recognised that the percentages are even higher in religious orders, and that there are also "priests who remain confused about their sexual orientation and men who have so successfully denied their orientation that in spite of predominantly same-sex fantasies, they insist they are heterosexual."

With admirable frankness he moves the discussion forward: "At issue at the beginning of the twenty-first century is the growing perception—one seldom contested by those who know the priesthood well—that the priesthood is or is becoming a gay profession."

Not surprisingly, Cozzens has his critics, yet even they concede that a "significant percentage" or a "substantial minority" or a "disproportionate number" of priests and seminarians are indeed gay.

Many of them are also sexually active. Over the past three decades, as tens of thousands of priests have left to marry, the percentage of gay priests has risen and the observance of total celibacy, amongst both straight and gay clergy, has dropped [Marr, 1999]. These were the years of Vatican II, the sixties, the Pill, feminism, gay liberation, and the collapse of many of the certainties of the past. Only those caught in a vision of the Catholic priest formed by Bing Crosby and "The Bells of St Mary's" could be surprised that the priesthood, too, has changed. Men who joined "minor seminaries" in their late teens and made vows of permanent celibacy in their early twenties have found that, in a more liberal era, their repressed sexual urges, chronic loneliness, and the mixed wisdom and cynicism of middle-age have combined to force them to confront human intimacy in ways they thought they had escaped.

Many priests have left, often to marry, and among those who remain there are many who live double lives. Richard Sipe reports that "roughly 50 percent of homosexually oriented priests are celibate just as are the heterosexually oriented."

Here in Australia there have been no statistical studies of gay priests or of sexually active priests, though in 1999 Janiene Wilson, a psychotherapist working in a Sydney seminary, told journalist David Marr that Sipe's U.S. findings are relevant to the Australian context. Extensive anecdotes and "guesstimates" from Australian priests tend to confirm this observation. This is not surprising, given the similar cultural and ethnic composition of these two Catholic communities.

Information concerning both homosexuality and sexual activity amongst the clergy are extremely difficult for researchers to gather. However, in January 2000, a newspaper called the *Kansas City Star* published a series of articles that showed that in the United States there are at least 400 known deaths of priests from AIDS, and that probably twice that number have occurred—ranging from four to eight times the rate in the general population. In a confidential poll of 800 priests, two-thirds said they knew of at least one priest who had died from AIDS, and one-third said they knew at least one priest who was living with HIV [Wills, 2000].

When one considers that many priests with HIV keep their status secret, and that men with HIV are just one segment of a much larger population of sexually active men, it becomes clear that many priests are having sex.

How do such priests reconcile their sex lives with their vow of celibacy? Some think the vow is just a formal requirement that will inevitably change. Some reinterpret it as an inner commitment to the gospel. Others see it as simply a promise to remain unmarried. Many of them believe that facing their desires has made them more integrated men and better priests. As a gay priest wrote to me recently, "Some of these men pour upon their communities a warmth and compassion they have learnt in occasional life-giving encounters or in the arms of their committed lover."

Inevitably, some people will be shocked by such comments. Right-wing Catholic groups are already starting to claim that "sodomites" have perverted the City of God and they should be shunted out of the priesthood and holy order restored. Even some more responsible commentators talk as if gay priests present an obvious and grave problem for the church—simply because they are gay.

Fr. Donald Cozzens, honest, heterosexual celibate that he is, says calmly, "Throughout the Church's history many priests, popes, and saints were homosexual in orientation . . . without question, gay priests minister creatively and effectively at every level of pastoral leadership." He says that gay priests tend to be "nurturing, intelligent, talented and sensitive"—echoing psychologists and anthropologists who suggest gay men have always offered their communities particular gifts of spiritual leadership. Cozzens adds dryly that those who complain there are too many gay priests never seem bothered that they are criticising God, who is the source of their vocations.

Homosexuality itself is not the problem. Nor, I would suggest, is sexual activity. The real problem is secrecy. Historians like Mark Jordan [2000] of Emory University and the late John Boswell of Yale have established that "men who love men" have always been attracted to priesthood and religious life. Such men have traditionally accepted the imposition of silence and secrecy as the price of maintaining a congenial haven during hostile times. We should remember that for many centuries both church and state punished "sodomites" with exile, torture and death by fire. Even in Australia in the late 1970s men caught having sex with men were still being dragged before the courts and having their reputations, careers and lives destroyed.

In such climates, sensitive, spiritual young men who felt no particular desire to marry readily saw priesthood as a natural and holy option. Having been one such young man myself, I know that most candidates for priesthood sincerely seek to devote their lives to prayer and service. Most accept the church's teaching that homosexuality is "unnatural" and that sex must be restricted to marriage, and most believe the love of God will be enough to sustain a lifetime of celibacy. Some of these men are very young. I was 17.

In time one discovers how urgent sexual desire can be, how persistent the longing for intimacy, how subtle the love of God. One either leaves or begins to look around for strategies of survival.

One soon discovers that individual priests live with a "zone of privacy" around them. Everyone gets along by never becoming too close or knowing too much. As long as sacred protocols are observed and certain beliefs officially promoted, what one thinks or does privately is politely, deliberately ignored.

When one lives for years in a rigid but very rewarding system, as priests do, this arrangement can come to seem sensible. However, over the centuries this wedding of institutional inflexibility with private license has created an entire culture of secrecy, duplicity and fear that has ended up punishing those who tell the truth and rewarding those who defend the teachings, structures and deceits that keep the system together.

This is the world of the clerical closet, where the left hand refuses to know what the right hand is doing, where bishops who vigorously condemn homosexuality are privately known to be gay themselves, where no one is really surprised when a conservative parish priest dies of a heart attack in a gay sex club—as happened in Melbourne a few years ago. In this world many clerics play covert and complicated games for "the good of the Church," often doing emotional violence to themselves and to others as they publicly condemn what they cannot integrate in their own hearts.

Mark Jordan [2000, p. 91] warns against imagining the clerical closet as "a suite of inner rooms sheltering all the gay clergy. There are no well-established rituals or sweeping histories or even enduring networks of support. There is no inside. The varieties of sexual lives in the clergy are too complicated and too compartmentalised." For every high camp "lavender rectory" (a term coined by priest-sociologist Andrew Greeley) there is an isolated priest looking for occasional sex at a beat, and another conscientiously striving to sublimate his desires through prayer and service.

The pervasive power of secrecy ensures that homosexuality amongst the clergy is almost impossible to discuss openly and calmly. Those who try are usually accused of sensationalism. Official silence, public denials and repeated condemnations of homosexuality are the standard strategies used by the hierarchy to stop the discussion in its tracks.

In 1995 a dozen American bishops jointly complained that their own National Bishops' Conference was refusing to discuss "rumours of a higher percentage of homosexual men in seminaries and the priesthood." Jordan comments that here we have "bishops complaining to bishops that it is impossible to talk openly even about 'rumours' of homosexuality" [2000, p. 93].

So what has been the hierarchy's response to the work of Fr. Donald Cozzens?

After much initial outrage, many bishops are grudgingly admitting that there is an issue worth discussing here. The Vatican is said to be looking at policies to remove homosexual candidates from seminaries—though this could mean the end of the priesthood. By contrast, some church leaders are claiming that the only issue is sexual activity, since "celibacy makes equals of us all" and sexual orientation in itself is "totally irrelevant."

This has been the approach taken by seminary officials in London after a recent Channel 4 documentary "Queer and Catholic" interviewed Donald Cozzens, along with seminary officials in Rome and England and former seminarians. Faced with an issue that can no longer be denied, the Church claims it doesn't really matter anyway.

Even Archbishop George Pell has taken to claiming that sexual orientation in itself is "morally indifferent." This will come as news to former seminarians like my friend Laurie who was told to leave the Jesuit Novitiate simply because he was gay. It will be news to former priests like Julian Ahern, who was refused Communion then marginalised by Melbourne's hierarchy because he "came out" as gay.

Most of all this would be news to Cardinal Ratzinger, who polices Catholic doctrine on behalf of the pope. In 1986 he wrote an official letter, authorised by the pope, explicitly designed to refute those who claim that the homosexual orientation in itself is "neutral or even good." It is, he stated, an "objective disorder" because it consists of a "tendency to intrinsic moral evil." On this basis the church has sacked gay teachers who come out, kept gay priests firmly in the closet, demanded exemptions from anti-discrimination laws, and opposed extending civil rights for gay people.

The "celibacy makes equals of us all" approach also avoids the fact that many priests, both straight and gay, are sexually active. Indeed, throughout church history celibacy has been largely "honoured in the breach." When the respected Cardinal Seper told the 1971 synod of bishops in Rome, "I am not at all optimistic that celibacy is being observed," he was stating what bishops from Africa, Europe, Asia, the Americas and Oceania—and certainly Church historians—already knew [Wills, 2000, p. 186]. It is time this was talked about openly.

The church is clearly entering an era of confusion and public contradiction in its approach to homosexuality. The hierarchy can see discussions about gay priests as a public relations nightmare, or they can see this as an opportunity to invite the entire Catholic community to reexamine the church's whole approach to sexuality, chastity, pleasure and power. Whatever they do, the issues won't go away. Modern phenomena such as a free press and an educated laity will see to that.

And here we touch on the fear that underlies much of the hierarchy's handling of sexual issues. The whole structure of doctrines and rules is like a house of cards. The more shaky it starts to look the more fiercely the place of each card must be defended. Permit married couples to use contraception, or allow lesbian teachers in schools, or admit there are sexually active gay priests who are good pastors, and the whole edifice of sexual teaching— which many theologians say has no sound basis anyway, could collapse. The Vatican and its most loyal bishops fear that with it could go claims of sacred authority, infallibility and "Absolute Truth."

The Catholic Church is the last great institution in the West that still campaigns against homosexuality. The discussion about homosexuality amongst its own clergy is just beginning. Things could get heated and messy as the sacred closet becomes unstable, and as ordinary Catholics start to feel they have been deceived. There may be accusations and condemnations from within and without the church.

In the midst of it, I will remember my Internet chat partner, "Bill."

I will think of this man who has ministered for years in an average suburb, working long hours with little support and poor pay, keeping his vows despite his loneliness and his horniness—and all because he believes "what the Church believes and teaches." I will think of his 17-year struggle with ordinary human desires which have been branded disordered and evil. I will think of his tentative search for intimacy. Most of all, I will think of the power of grace, which no ecclesiastical pronouncement, however hallowed, can limit or stop. I will pray for Bill, and I will pray also for myself, that I will see in "Bill" not an opponent or a sinner, but a trapped brother.

THE ARCHBISHOP RESPONDS

On Sunday, August 19, the day after my letter was published, Archbishop (now Cardinal) George Pell of Sydney issued a statement: "On the slanders and exaggerations of Mr. Michael Kelly regarding 'gay' priests." The cardinal ordered that it be distributed to every parishioner in every Sydney parish after Sunday mass. Pell claimed that I slandered and exaggerated the case of gay priests. He wrote:

> The piece . . . smugly claims that 48.5 percent . . . of priests are gay and that half of them are sexually active. . . .
>
> The crux of Kelly's unctuous vilification is that "the Catholic Church is the last great institution . . . that still campaigns against homosexuality." The Catholic Church believes and teaches that sexual activity should be confined to married couples . . . (Pell, 2001)

Archbishop George Pell's response to my letter is a classic example of what Mark Jordan calls "hysterical" speech. As he said of another archbishop's dismissal of claims that there are many gay priests: "The Archbishop's response is an irrational denial. It is hysterical."[6]

Pell's statement, written in heat and haste on the afternoon the letter was published, then rushed throughout the parishes of Sydney for mandatory distribution to every mass-going parishioner, clearly pushes the argument that my essay is deeply shocking and utterly scandalous. Nothing of what I wrote is worthy of serious consideration, and I have smeared the good name of the priesthood. Pell seems to think, or at least he wants his readers to think, that there can be no place for open or public discussion of certain issues that any objective observer can plainly see are valid and important within contemporary Catholicism. Obviously, the editors of the *Sydney Morning Herald* saw them as such. But no, this is all just muckraking, and any decent person will be outraged and treat this article—and apparently its author—with contempt.

Pell's response is astoundingly ad hominem. Where he might have archly criticized the newspaper and its editorial policies, he goes for a raw and blunt attack on a named freelance author—and shows far less caution in "naming names" than I exercised in my own writing. Rather than genuinely engaging with issues, this statement is intended to totally discredit me as a writer and commentator. It is angry, even vituperative ("Kelly's unctuous vilification"), and uses a kind of public language we tend not to expect from church leaders today. It is an intimidating attack—and I suggest it was intended to intimidate. Had its target been a person less seasoned in church politics, it would have been profoundly hurtful and offensive. It is not every day one is attacked like this, in public and in print, by the Catholic primate of one's country.

More important, and here I concur totally with Mark Jordan's comments about the purpose of such "hysterical speech," Pell's statement is intended to stop any discussion in its tracks. The high moral tone that Pell assumes in his last few paragraphs cannot disguise the fighting language with which he began. Any journalist or commentator is given notice that the archbishop of Sydney will not hesitate to defend his version of "the moral integrity of the overwhelming majority of Sydney clergy" (as if that is what is being impugned), and that defense will include public attack.

Significantly, Pell's statement had something of the desired effect. This newspaper has a public relations and marketing wing that promotes its major stories each week. Everyone expected this particular letter to generate enormous controversy in print and on radio and television, and I was advised to hold myself ready for a very busy, high-profile week. Even my priest-advisors were readying me for a big week of "breaking the silence of Sodom."

However, nothing happened. The marketing people told me on the Monday following publication that they could not find any media people who would even touch the story. Sydney has a lively, rough, boisterous radio chat-show culture, governed by several "shock jocks" who jump on any new issue, but they, too, were refusing to tackle it. The PR people were bewildered. So was I.

Over the past five years I have done countless media interviews in which I have critiqued and challenged the church's treatment of queer people, and I know how to deal with a media frenzy, but this time I had not one phone call. Some gay friends suggested the story was actually not as controversial as some of us thought, but Pell's aggressive response and the absence of even one expression of media interest tell a different story. After reading Pell's statement, distributed in tens of thousands of copies, and, perhaps, after a few well-placed phone calls, it would have been a brave shock jock who took on the new archbishop of Sydney.

For all that, I, at least, had the consolation of some very supportive letters from several Catholic pastoral workers and a few priests, and the certainty that George Pell's "hysterical" response would have ensured that thousands of Catholics dashed out of mass that Sunday to make sure they read the weekend paper.

Perhaps despite himself, Pell assisted in breaking the silence of Sodom. More than one person said to me, after reading his response, "Perhaps he doth protest too much"—or more bluntly, "What's his problem?" I am told this was a common reaction among priests, religious, and church workers. One senior journalist and author told me he thought the story itself did not shock the public as the newspaper's editors imagined it would; it merely confirmed what everyone already thought. It was Pell, he suggested, who really did his own damage. Similar to many prelates before him, he may have misjudged an educated laity and a streetwise secular public who are not scandalized by the idea of gay priests but who find bully-boy tactics, ecclesiastical bluster, and sanctified duplicity increasingly offensive and increasingly obvious. Pell may have temporarily intimidated the media, but I doubt that he fooled the people.

REFLECTIONS ON SPEAKING OUT

Breaking the silence of Sodom is a continuing challenge. No one book, article, exposé, or even scandal will adequately bring to light what has long been locked in darkness; no speaking out will adequately find language for what has never been expressed in free speech. Those of us who do seek to speak out find, as Mark Jordan has so tellingly expressed it, a "honeycomb of closets" within the clerical system, layer upon layer of duplicity down through history, and victims, heroes, perpetrators, and plain men hopelessly entangled in a culture that is almost impenetrable even to those who have lived it—and perhaps especially to those who have been formed in it. Analyzing the labyrinth of secrets, fear, and power that is clerical culture is important, but it can also absorb energy and insight that could be better spent elsewhere.

As I have reflected on my experience of speaking out in public, I have become convinced that what we are about in breaking this silence is, even more deeply than analysis or exposé, the changing of perceptions, of assumptions, of "hunches," the creation of a new "flavor" in lay and public imagination concerning the priesthood. Perhaps after reading my article some ordinary Catholics wondered if "Father" might be gay—and did so without hysteria. Perhaps some pastoral workers were able to accurately name the "friendship" they had noticed between a couple of young priests they knew. Perhaps a politician was encouraged to support gay rights despite the Catholic hierarchy's opposition because he felt confirmed in his suspicion that hypocrisy and grandstanding were involved. Perhaps a seminarian felt a little relieved that the truth about the culture he was entering had been spoken out loud. Perhaps some parents decided not to encourage any of their sons to think about the priesthood because it is so clearly dysfunctional. Perhaps a bishop realized that he could not control the free press and felt a tinge of fear that the game might be up, even as he reached for the cardinal's hat.

One thing I do know for sure is that listeners to a popular chat show on Sydney radio 2SM, on the morning before my article was published, heard their host chatting with me about these issues and concluding not only that it didn't matter if "Father" was gay, but that he should be encouraged to live his life openly, form healthy sexual relationships, and so become a better, more honest priest. Radio 2SM was originally a Catholic station ("SM" stood for "St. Mary's," the name of the local cathedral). The irony of this was not lost on me.

In using the media to change public perceptions and hunches about gay priests, we need to be very conscious and careful. The media is, they say, a tiger, and even if you know how to ride it, you are still in for a wild ride. As I shaped my letter, I was very concerned with issues of sensationalism and scandal. On the one hand, I wanted to tell the truth—about episcopal hypocrisy and priests in sex clubs—and on the other hand I did not want to feed anti-Catholic bigotry or demonize many good, pastoral, committed gay priests. Even though I may not endorse the hidden accommodations some priests make concerning sexual activity, I understand how these men came to find themselves in such situations, and I respect, immensely, the struggle for integrity, humanity, and openness of heart that many gay priests live out every day of their lives. As I said earlier, the clerical closet is a complex place and many complex men are caught in it.

In the end, with the encouragement of several sexually active, semi-closeted gay priests, all of whom are deeply committed to grass-roots justice making and to the renewal of the church, I opted to push the point that plenty of gay priests are fine pastors but are caught in a system of duplicity mandated by a conservative, self-serving hierarchical structure. As I put it, "The problem is not homosexuality or even sexual activity. The problem is secrecy." Of course, the problem is more complicated than that, but enforced secrecy endured by good men who just want to have some degree of love and intimacy in their lives is a key part of it, and it is something that the public can readily understand and feel sympathy for. This is not a matter of doctoring the truth, but when one's words may be read by several million people (as is the case with many major newspapers), one has a responsibility to be careful in which direction one chooses to point one's readers.

This need for conscious and careful public speaking has been thrown into harsh focus by the current "sex-abuse crisis" within the Catholic Church. Bishops who once strenuously denied the presence of large numbers of gay priests have rushed with hysterical speed to pin the blame for the abuse on homosexuals who they claim are close to "dominating" the priesthood. Scapegoating and witch-hunts are suddenly in the air, not for the first time in church history. If we, as queer Catholics, are not to add fuel to this unholy fire when we speak publicly about gay priests, we will need to choose our words very carefully indeed.

I have no ready system or solution at hand. However, if I were writing my letter today, I would focus more directly on the duplicity of the hierarchical system, its obsession with secrecy, its misuse of power to protect and enhance its image, and its techniques of control and intimidation. The average gay priest who ministers in a parish and goes off to the sauna once a week is himself a serf within this huge system, and we are now discovering just how vulnerable and expendable a serf he is. As Mark Jordan commented recently, hypocrisy is too weak a word for what the hierarchical system is now doing.

Gay priests can now have no illusions that the clerical system is inherently benevolent or indulgent toward "discreet" queers, or that it will change and reform itself through some sort of evolutionary magic. In the climate of confusion, anger, and fear now pervading clerical culture, gay priests need to feel support from their queer sisters and brothers in Christ. Sometimes we may need to speak up strongly in their defense and against any looming purge, however it may be disguised. At the same time, however, we queer Catholics need to be blunt and honest in requiring that these priests join us in working for structural change within the church, that they behave as brothers and not as indulged children or petty autocrats, that they use the resources and access their silence affords them to support those of us who pay the price for speaking out, and that they work ceaselessly and courageously for change from within.

CONCLUSION

Contemporary culture offers queer Catholics tools and forums unknown to our ancestors. The mass media above all provides us with means to call the hierarchy to account and to critique the church in contexts that, at their best, treat both prince and pauper equally. Archbishops, with all their grand display, their wealth, and their PR companies, can be publicly challenged by a queer, marginal Catholic with a laptop computer and some skill in journalism. Furthermore, in the wake of the current sex-abuse controversy, most of the vestiges of deference and indulgence once enjoyed by the Catholic hierarchy have been blown apart, and the media, the public, and the Catholic laity are ready to listen to critical voices as never before.

Queer Catholics need to rise to the challenge of the age. If ever there was a time when we needed to speak out with courage and prophetic insight, this is it. We must not be afraid to speak in the light what we have heard in the dark. The pious "discretion" and the "family loyalty" that many of us imbibed with our first Communion will not serve us well now; indeed, they were always intended to serve the system and not our deep selves, and they have exacted too many sacrifices. In speaking out without fear, but with dignity, clarity, and integrity, we will not only expose and critique the clerical system but also give living witness that the holy lies and the sacred stereotypes imposed on us are not true.

At the same time, media exposure is a double-edged sword. It will not only expose the duplicity and oppression we wish to critique, but its harsh light will also fall on our own flaws and weaknesses. The more we speak out, the more we will need to search our own hearts, work through our anger and bitterness, surrender our self-righteousness, and let go of our desire to judge and condemn. Again and again we will need to ask for the grace of seeking the reign of God, of facing our own complicity with evil, of removing the plank in our own eyes before targeting the splinter in our brothers' eyes.

The first time I publicly challenged Cardinal Archbishop George Pell over the church's treatment of queer people, I went for a long walk on the beach near my home. I was bothered by my anger, by my sense of righteousness, by the depth of my pain. It was only when I came to see that my confrontation of this bishop could be a kind of dancing with my own shadow that I felt I could go forward with some purity of heart. I knew only too well how Pell came to be who he is as a conservative prelate; I knew it was a path I could have taken—indeed a path that still held a kind of sad fascination. When I felt I could face up to him as my "trapped brother," I felt ready to go forward.[7]

In this going forward, and in speaking out, there is not only confrontation and critique but also invitation and gift. We raise our voices to proclaim the reign of God, the truth that sets us free, the life that is given in all its fullness. However deep our frustration and anger, we need to speak out of our own freedom, hoping above all to do our part in breaking chains, opening eyes, and calling all into the dance. The silence of Sodom must give way, in every age and in every heart, to the glorious song of freedom sung by the children of God.

NOTES

1. The Archbishop of Sydney, George Pell, for example, retained the professional services of one of Australia's major public relations firms, Royce Communications.

2. The Channel 4, BBC documentary "Queer and Catholic" was produced by Mark Dowd, a former Dominican. It screened in the United Kingdom in May 2001.

3. The term *beat* refers to cruising areas—such as parks or toilet blocks—used by some gay men to meet others for recreational sex.

4. *The Age* is Melbourne's major daily newspaper.

5. This refers to the experience of the Rainbow Sash Movement. See <http://www.rainbowsash.com>.

6. Jordan (2000) refers to Cardinal Roger Mahoney's claim that "neither our seminaries nor our presbyterate is filled with homosexuals" (p. 106).

7. I am indebted to James Alison for the term "trapped brother" and for his reflections on moving beyond resentment. His recent book, *Faith Beyond Resentment: Fragments Catholic and Gay* (2001), is highly recommended.

REFERENCES

Alison, James (2001). *Faith beyond resentment: Fragments Catholic and gay.* London: Darton, Longman, and Todd.

Cozzens, Donald B. (2000). *The changing face of the priesthood.* Collegeville, MN: Liturgical Press.

Jordan, Mark D. (2000). *The silence of Sodom: Homosexuality in modern Catholicism.* Chicago: University of Chicago Press.

Marr, David (1999). *The high price of heaven.* Sydney: Allen and Unwin.

Pell, Cardinal George (2001). On the slanders and exaggerations of Mr. Michael Kelly regarding 'gay' priets. Available at <www.sydney.catholic.org.au/Archbishop/Addresses.shtml>.

Wills, Garry (2000). *Papal sin: Structures of deceit.* New York: Doubleday.

Chapter 12

Those Troubling Gay Priests

Bernard Schlager

From the mid- to late-1970s I was enrolled at a Roman Catholic seminary high school in the Midwest. Already a dying institution at that time, the American high school seminary was the first stage in a twelve-year training program for young men considering the priesthood. Many American dioceses and religious orders had sponsored high school seminaries in the latter half of the twentieth century, but soon after the Second Vatican Council in the mid-1960s, with its call for reform in all areas of church life, many Catholic leaders began to seriously question the rationale for and relevance of seminaries for teenage boys. One important factor in the reassessment of the viability of high school and even college seminaries, of course, was the precipitous decline in enrollments at nearly all such institutions during the tumultuous 1960s. At my high school seminary, for instance, an average of 125 students were housed on a large and well-appointed campus designed for well over 1,000 students. In many ways, the demographic collapse of these schools for aspiring priests foreshadowed the severe priest shortage that would afflict every diocese and religious order in the United States by the late-1970s.

Although mine was an unusual choice for a Catholic boy in the mid-1970s, the decision to enter the high school seminary was one that I made both eagerly and without regret. The life of a priest was something that appealed to me for many reasons including, in hindsight, my sense that the homosocial world of both seminary and priestly life would offer what I hoped would be a comfortable retreat from societal pressures to date girls and eventually to marry. In addition, for a teenager with an incipient awareness of his homosexual orientation and terrified that such an orientation might mean that I was destined to lead a life of despair, I, like many others before me, envisioned a priest's life as one filled with social and religious purpose. In other words, I could live as a highly respected member of society without having to deal with or reveal my queer sexual identity which, already at the age of thirteen, I well knew was not only unacceptable in church and society but also considered by many to be deviant and an indication of mental illness.

With the recent pedophilia crisis in the American Catholic Church, the seemingly endless cases of bishops moving pedophiles from parish to parish, and the profoundly disturbing attacks on gay priests and seminarians by Vatican officials and U.S. bishops alike, many colleagues and friends have asked me recently about my own experiences in seminary and religious life (I was also a member of the Dominican order for a few years after I graduated from college). People are particularly curious to know if I experienced sexual abuse at the hands of a priest or if I knew of abusive situations in the seminary. Luckily, I did not, although I must admit that I was aware of one priest at my high school seminary who had a reputation among students for making unwanted sexual advances. Whether the rumors were true I don't know, but it is interesting for me to reflect today on the fact that many of my fellow students did not doubt such rumors. More significantly, in light of recent events, I also have realized that none of us would have seriously considered reporting such rumors to anyone in a position of authority in the seminary. Perhaps, it was simply because we assumed that Father X was gay (and, in addition, attracted to teenagers) and/or because we felt that it was too risky to charge a teacher and priest with such infractions. Whatever the reasons, we, as young teenagers, already understood and observed the Catholic silence surrounding queer sexuality and gay sexual behavior.

I did not come out of the closet as a gay man until I entered the Order of Preachers (the Dominicans) at the age of twenty-two. Although I had entered the order in the closet, I soon discovered that religious life was, for many reasons, the perfect place for me to embrace my identity as a gay man. As Mark Jordan (2000) notes so aptly, "Catholic seminaries have long done what the World War II draft is credited with doing for American gays generally: seminaries teach young gay men that there are other young gay men" (p. 170). Without a doubt, that is the greatest gift that high school seminary, college seminary, and the Dominican order gave me: the comforting knowledge that I was not alone as a gay man and that, should I choose the life of a priest, I could expect to enjoy the support and companionship of other gay men who had been drawn to a vocation of service and brotherly fellowship.

Three of my seven classmates in the novitiate had entered the order as out gay men and, during the nearly three years that I lived with the Dominicans, I found the vital support that I needed to realize the implications of being at once gay and Catholic. In the end, however, I could not stay in an institution that was (and certainly remains to this day) not only homophobic but also responsible for so much of the "homo-hatred" present within the Catholic Church and in many Western and Western-influenced societies around the world. What caused me to leave religious life (and I did so happily) was the seemingly sudden and profoundly painful awareness that the group of men among whom I had discovered and celebrated my gayness were silent supporters of the larger institution that was, in its official teachings and practices, rabidly anti-gay. As soon as I realized this, of course, I had to acknowledge that I, too, had for too long unthinkingly accepted the required silences surrounding sodomy within the church in general and within the clerical subculture in particular.

To be gay in religious life was no sin among the men with whom I lived; to fall in love with other men and embrace physical and sexual affections was also deemed acceptable by many of my religious confreres *so long as* one observed the demands never to talk publicly about one's affectional preferences. In other words, to survive as a gay religious man meant that one should never contradict in any public forum the silent and yet powerful rhetoric of the official Catholic position which condemned all homosexual activity as sinful. Now most, if not all, of the gay men with whom I lived as a young religious thought that church teachings on homosexuality (as with much of church teaching on human sexuality in general) were not only theologically unsound but also destructive of the mental and spiritual health of many gay and lesbian Catholics. However, it was not permitted that we, as representatives of the institutional church, voice aloud our opinions about queer identities and queer loves because the penalties were all too apparent: severe reprimand from leaders within the hierarchy of the order and the church at large and eventual, but certain, expulsion from the order. This is how I first experienced the very real and very effective "silence of Sodom" of which Jordan writes.

As an "out" cleric preparing for the priesthood I realized that I, too, felt shame about my queer identity and, at times, experienced genuine abhorrence regarding my own same-sex desires. These feelings were the result of many years of Catholic education and were well in place long before I entered the seminary as a teenager. Once I entered seminary and then religious life I was expert in parroting back the anti-queer rhetoric that theologians and church bureaucrats have for centuries worked to inculcate among believers. Only when I embraced my own identity as a gay man, however, did the remarkably seductive power of the silence of Sodom become real and relevant for me: yes, I could embrace my queer identity and struggle to integrate my gayness with my vocation to the priesthood, but I could live as gay within the clerical worlds of seminary and religious life only if I agreed to enforce the codes of silence (and shame) surrounding queer identity within the clerical caste.

Currently I work for the Center for Lesbian and Gay Studies in Religion and Ministry at Pacific School of Religion (a member institution of the Graduate Theological Union) in Berkeley, California, and, in this line of work, I have come to know many queer people of faith in training to serve as ministers or who already work as effective ministers in various denominations. All of these people, whether out or not, consider their sexual orientations to be vital aspects of who they are and what they bring to their pastoral ministry. These women and men serve as ministers in such denominations as the Metropolitan Community Church, the Episcopal Church, and the Unitarian Universalist Association; ministers in United Church of Christ, Methodist, Baptist, and Disciples of Christ churches. Even Roman Catholic Church seminarians and priests speak openly, albeit carefully, about their queerness and their struggles and joys as gay religious leaders within a homophobic church. Of course, significant (and sometimes even overwhelming) discrimination against queer people exists in many non-Catholic denominations, but the reality is that a generation of out GLBT people have served successfully as ordained ministers in a variety of denominations to fellow believers of all orientations. Just as women have moved into ordained positions in several church denominations over the past few decades, so too are queer people being ordained by church groups open to (and sometimes downright eager to) affirm the call of queer people to ordained religious leadership.

As is well-known, religious leadership in many societies, cultures, and eras has been an especially attractive vocation for queer people; articulating the spiritual yearnings of humanity and leading others through times of loss and pain are gifts that a significant percentage of us queer people possess in abundance. Whether as spiritual leaders, artists, prophets, or gadflies, LGBT people have often drawn upon their personal experiences of alienation and coupled this with a sense of divine presence in the world to fashion understandings of the human experience that resonate with people regardless of affectional preference or sexual identity.

Although Roman Catholic leaders have long maintained an effective silence on the issue of gay priests, the American public is just beginning to realize that the Roman Catholic Church in the United States has a large percentage of gay priests (perhaps anywhere from 30 percent to 60 percent of all priests in this country are gay). Why such a significant percentage? Clearly it is because the priesthood offers a life of religious dedication and useful social service within a fraternity of like-minded men; moreover, within a church that preaches lifelong celibacy as the only valid option for homosexuals, the life of a priest still makes sense for some men who want to live a life of holiness as defined by their church. It is no longer a secret that many American bishops have sanctioned for years the admission of gay men into seminaries and the priesthood; what is only recently being addressed in public, however, are the implications (or "dangers" as many church leaders prefer to frame the issue) of a predominantly gay priesthood for straight seminarians and priests and for the church as a whole. Having long accepted gay men into its clerical ranks, the church hierarchy is finally being forced to discuss the ramifications of a predominantly queer priesthood.

It is, of course, the current pedophilia crisis in the church that has provided the opportunity for influential members of the Catholic hierarchy to discuss publicly the issue of gay priests and to lay blame for clerical sexual abuse on gay priests. The simplistic argument runs like this: because some gay priests have engaged in criminal sexual activity with boys, all gay seminarians and priests are potential pedophiles who must be drummed out of seminaries and the priesthood. Rather than acknowledge the debt of gratitude that American Catholics owe their many gay priests, the vast majority of whom are good pastors, homophobic church leaders are desperately trying to pin responsibility for the current pedophilia crisis on priests who are gay and thereby minimize their own responsibility for supporting long-known pederastic priests in ministerial posts.

President of the U.S. Conference of Catholic Bishops, Wilton D. Gregory, for instance, has implied that gay priests are simply unhealthy individuals. According to Gregory:

> It is an on-going struggle to be sure that the Catholic priesthood is not dominated by homosexual men, that the candidates we receive are healthy in every possible way, psychologically, emotionally, spiritually, intellectually. Most seminaries are working vigorously to provide such an environment. (Allen, 2002)

Or consider a homily in which Monsignor Eugene Clark, rector of St. Patrick's Cathedral in New York City, not only emphasized the Vatican's position that homosexuality is "a disorder" but also offered his own views that the admission of gay men to seminaries was a grave mistake; these comments were made in a homily whose larger theme was American society as "probably the most immoral country in the Western hemisphere" (Price, 2002).

Another profoundly anti-gay comment was uttered by one high-ranking Vatican official who called into question the very validity of the ordinations of homosexuals. "People with these [homosexual] inclinations just cannot be ordained," he stated in an interview about priests involved in sexual abuse. This psychiatrist went on to equate the situation of homosexual priests with closeted gay men who are married to women; just as these marriages might well be ruled invalid, so too should ordinations of gay men be considered invalid (Henneberger, 2002). Obviously, some Roman Catholic authorities at various levels of the church hierarchy are desperately trying not only to blame homosexual priests for crimes of pedophilia within the church but also to turn attention away from the criminal ways in which many bishops over many decades have transferred accused sexual abusers from parish to parish. But where are discussions or even admissions of sexual abuse perpetrated by priests against girls and women? Why is there no wholesale attack on heterosexual priests for those cases which, although they are not currently being discussed in any significant way by the media or church leaders, are surely significant in number?

Many commentators in the religious and secular media have emphasized recently that nearly all of the sexual abuse cases involving priests and boys in the United States are, in fact, not instances of pedophilia but rather cases of "ephebophilia," that is, the sexual abuse of teenagers. This is a potent argument and one that the likes of Jerry Falwell, who attempted to blame the events of September 11, 2001, on gay people as well as feminists and others, has eagerly seized upon in his crusade to blame gay people for all that is wrong in the world. Whatever the accuracy of these charges, it remains the case that few people are including in their discussions of Roman Catholic clergy sexual abuse those teenage girls who have suffered abuse at the hands of priests. Ephebophilia may well be a crime that some Catholic clergymen have engaged in but, once again, the abuse of teenage girls by heterosexual priests must be included in discussions of the current crisis lest those who would demonize gay priests succeed in turning the discussion of sexual abuse into a blatant attack on gay priests.

Evidence of the double standard operating among some American bishops can be found in comments by Cardinal Francis George of Chicago who drew a distinction between a serial abuser of young children (such as Father John Geoghan, whom George labeled "a monster") and a priest "who perhaps under the influence of alcohol engages with a 16- or 17-year-old young woman who returns his affection" (Sennott, 2002). Is a priest who sexually exploits an underage girl because he abuses alcohol and seduces a supposedly "complicit" teenager less monstrous? Such attitudes not only surely contribute to the continued hiding of crimes against girls by priests but also imply that sex between an apparently straight man and a girl is somehow less serious than other sex crimes perpetrated by adults against other children (read: boys?). Although George is drawing a distinction between serial abusers and seemingly one-time or infrequent abusers, it is no surprise that he would point to a man-girl sexual liaison and imply that mitigating factors might explain such behaviors on the part of a straight priest. Of course, no such mitigating factors would be offered for equally criminal sexual behavior between a gay priest and a teenage boy.

How can GLBT Catholics and their allies respond to such blatantly homophobic and desperate tactics undertaken by some of their most influential leaders? An especially powerful sign of resistance would be the coming out of even a small percentage of the many gay bishops and priests in this country. These individuals could offer themselves as examples of sexually healthy clergymen who are committed to lives of selfless service; lay Catholics can continue to make vociferous and public demands on their bishops to address issues of hierarchical corruption instead of scapegoating their gay clergy. Progressive Catholic theologians, such as Mark Jordan, have a particularly important role to play in continuing to offer theologies that contradict and undermine the homophobic theologies that inform so much of official Catholic teaching and praxis. Or, as Jordan himself frames it, theologians must now speak publicly about the "silence of Sodom" which informs so thoroughly official Catholic theologies of homosexuality. With such voices raised in persistent protest, change *can* happen; Catholics *can* lay the groundwork for a day when their hierarchy at long last abandons its anti-sex theology (which oppresses both Catholics and many non-Catholics alike) and embrace queer people as objectively well-ordered, healthy, and holy people.

Although some in the Roman Catholic Church may boast of a history of timeless and unchanging moral doctrines, the opposite, of course, is true. In the past its leaders have sanctioned slavery while many of its theologians in the Middle Ages vehemently opposed lending money at interest; anti-Jewish tracts have been written by some of the church's greatest theologians and used by church leaders for centuries to demonize Jewish people and their faith; and women, of course, have long been depicted by church leaders as lesser human beings.

It is not unrealistic to believe that Catholics, working with believers in other religious communities, will dismantle homophobic theologies of oppression (which have been crafted over the course of centuries by leaders of all religious traditions) and expose these theologies for what they are: demeaning, violent, and inherently un-Christian. Perhaps the issue of gay priests, so troubling for many current Roman Catholic Church leaders because the existence of such priests exposes a long-standing practice of quietly accepting gay men into the ordained ministry while simultaneously denigrating their sexual identity, will become the catalyst for Roman Catholic leaders to repent of their sinful ways and begin to ask forgiveness for maintaining those oppressive silences that have led to the hateful treatment of their queer sisters and brothers. Only then will the silence of Sodom give way to those new modes of speech that Jordan describes; only then will the Roman Catholic Church be ready to embrace without reserve her queer members, priests and laity alike, who have for so long been denied the recognition and dignity they rightfully deserve.

REFERENCES

Allen, John L., Jr. (2002). The word from Rome. *National Catholic Reporter* 1(35)(April 26). Available at <www.nationalcatholicreporter.org/word/pfw0426.htm>.

Henneberger, Melinda (2002). Vatican weighs reaction to accusations of molesting by clergy. *The New York Times,* March 3.

Jordan, Mark D. (2000). *The silence of Sodom: Homosexuality in modern Catholicism.* Chicago: University of Chicago Press.

Price, Joyce Howard (2002). Church seeking scapegoat, gays say. *The Washington Times,* May 25.

Sennott, Charles (2002). Pope calls sex abuse crime. *Boston Globe,* April 24.

Chapter 13

Lessons from Our Neighbors: An Appreciation and a Query to Mark Jordan

Karen Lebacqz

"Church's sex-abuse case-load booms." "Priest's confession taped by alleged abuse victim." "L.A. cardinal admits erring in abuse case." "Cleric held in rapes." "San Francisco archdiocese discloses 40 accused of abuse." "Pope says sex abuse not just sin, but crime."[1] In Spring 2002, the newspapers in the United States were replete with such headlines of stories about sexual abuse in the Roman Catholic Church. Every day there were revelations of problems at the personal and institutional level. Although recent revelations focus on the Catholic Church, the 1990s were full of revelations and cases in Protestant denominations. What are the factors in individual psychology, in institutional structures, and in the larger social ethos that contribute to sexual abuse of children and adults by members of the clergy?

Sex in the Parish (Lebacqz and Barton, 1990) was an initial foray into causes and contributing factors of abuse in Protestant denominations. Jordan extends our understanding with some superb reflections on institutional structures, particularly on the role of rhetoric in the Roman Catholic Church. However, Jordan's primary purpose was neither to expose nor to discuss clergy sexual misconduct; hence, his work must be supplemented for a fuller understanding. A little-known text issued in Canada more than ten years ago contributes greatly to an understanding of the structural and institutional factors that generate sexual misconduct and permit it to go unchallenged and undetected. William May's (1991) study of child sexual abuse is also helpful. Using these texts helps to outline some structural issues that are of importance for all churches and for other institutions as well.

Jordan's primary purpose in *The Silence of Sodom* (2000) is not to expose sexual misconduct by clergy. His purpose is to examine the rhetoric of the Roman Catholic Church and to demonstrate how this rhetoric silences true gay lives in the church. Therefore, and possibly ironically, *Silence of Sodom* is less an exploration of clergy sexuality than an exploration of factors in modern Roman Catholicism that stifle clergy sexuality. Jordan would say that any clergy sexual conduct in the modern Roman Catholic Church is not true sexual conduct, because of the oppression clergy experience in a homophobic church. Nonetheless, Jordan's insights about church homophobia are useful for those interested in sexual misconduct. "If the church could be so violently wrong about [homosexuality] for so many centuries," declares Jordan, "there must be some deep deformity in church governance" (2000, p. 2). It is the question of "governance" that interests me. What is it in church structures, policies, and practices that permits, even encourages, sexual abuse by clergy and makes it so difficult to prevent and punish? Where Jordan's focus is primarily on rhetoric and its role in stifling sexuality, my own interest lies less in what is said or how it is said than in what is practiced and how.

For that very reason, however, I find Jordan's focus on rhetoric to be salutary. How does our very conversation within churches mask problems, create tensions, violate lives, and prevent truth from being spoken or heard? Why do we view and respond the way we do to revelations of abuse in the churches? In particular, why did events in the Roman Catholic Church hit the national news media the way they did? The many revelations of clergy sexual misconduct in Protestant churches in the 1990s did not make front pages as national news in the same way that current events have. Is the current outrage because most of the victims were *children?* Is it because they were *male* children, whereas many of the victims of Protestant clergy were female? Is it because the perpetrators were *priests* rather than ministers of Protestant churches? Are expectations higher for priests than for Protestant clergy? Is it because our nation is at war and we are afraid of war and feel more comfortable retreating to the arena of sex? Is it simple escapism? Is it yet another instance in which our fundamental heterosexism and homophobia rise to the fore and trump all other legitimate social concerns? Is it because baseball and basketball and hockey and World Cup soccer all happened at once and it became too confusing to keep up with our usual national pastimes?

Whatever the complicated set of reasons for the prominence of current events, the underlying issue for me is what happens institutionally that permits these events to occur. I was fascinated by Jordan's discussion of the ways in which the training of Roman Catholic priests may contribute to sexual misconduct. Young clergy in training are pushed into enclaves of men-only companions, as they are supposed to be celibate and avoid contact with women. Such isolation from the world creates an atmosphere in which abuse can thrive. For those who are gay, these enclaves do not provide models of gay celibacy, nor do gay enclaves outside the church provide such models. How is one to be gay and celibate at the same time? Many gay Roman Catholics may indeed be attracted to the priesthood precisely because an active gay identity "outside" is not respected but as a priest, the young man is offered a model of "redemptive suffering" and avoidance of a disgraceful sexual identity. Further, priesthood brings power in the Roman Catholic Church, so it is one of the few avenues where gay Catholics can find a position that is both acceptable and powerful. Although I have condensed and oversimplified Jordan's insightful discussion of training of clergy, the important point is that same-sex desires may be officially condemned by the rhetoric of the church while at the same time conditions are created under which same-sex desires flourish.

Jordan's focus is primarily on the specific training of Catholic clergy. I therefore find it helpful to supplement Jordan's analysis with the excellent discussion of the Canadian Report of the Archdiocesan Commission of Enquiry into the Sexual Abuse of Children by Members of the Clergy (1990). This commission was established because of allegations of sexual misconduct and abuse brought in the 1980s but extending to clergy behavior over a twenty-year period; it submitted its formal report to the Archdiocese of St. John's in Newfoundland in 1990. The commission understood its mandate broadly: it was to investigate the factors that may have contributed to sexual abuse of children and the factors that may have contributed to the wrongful behavior going undetected or unreported, and it was to make recommendations regarding the selection and training of clergy and the structure and functioning of the archdiocese. Accordingly, in its report, the commission included attention to such diverse issues as sexual stereotyping in schools, portraits of men in the media, views of children widely prevalent in church and society, traditional masculine socialization, and questions of theology, administration, and ethos in the Roman Catholic Church. While evidencing some sensitivity to priests who had engaged in abusive sexual behavior (for example, the commission took note of the loneliness and isolation of priests, their lack of instruction on sexuality, and the stress that many clergy experienced after Vatican II mandated significant changes in church function and structure), the commission nonetheless came down strongly on the failures of church administrators and structures. It argued that "radical change" was needed in the way this particular archdiocese was governed; it also noted that the "authoritarian and patriarchal structures which lie at the very core of Roman Catholic discipline" made such radical change difficult.

Of particular concern to the commission was the fact that allegations of sexual misconduct had been brought to the attention of denominational officials as early as the 1970s. Yet the two archbishops who had served during and since that time had not taken those allegations sufficiently seriously. Some clergy were sent for "treatment" and then returned to parishes. Others were never even reprimanded. Even when several were tried in criminal court and convicted of offenses such as rape, the diocese did not take steps that would indicate the possibility of a serious and widespread problem. "The situation was not properly managed," the commission declared bluntly (1990, p. 113).

What happened in Canada foreshadows current revelations in the United States. Our neighbors to the north dealt with this issue a dozen years ago. Had we taken their experience seriously and learned from it, events might have transpired differently here. Officials in the Roman Catholic Church might have acted sooner, acknowledging and investigating allegations of misconduct and abuse and exposing more quickly their own complicity in the cover-up.

Further, our news reporting on this issue might have been more clear about several aspects of sexual misconduct. One of Jordan's concerns is that public scandals about child sexual abuse are taken to be evidence of clerical homosexuality and of the way clerical homosexuality will be expressed. When male children are sexually abused, we *assume* that the abusers must be gay and that gay men left alone with male children will abuse them. Jordan argues that gay priests do not generally practice nor do they approve of child sexual abuse: "Priests I know who identify themselves as gay tend to condemn pederasts harshly and to urge prompt disciplinary action against them" (Jordan, 2000, p. 97). Thus, public scandals such as those that hit the news media in Spring 2002 should not be taken as evidence of "true" gay identity within the church.

I concur. Ironically, however, Jordan's own focus on gay identity among clerics may only reinforce the notion that sexual abuse and homosexuality are linked. Here is another place where we might have learned from the Canadian study. The Canadian commission found that of men who molest boys, only one-third can be classified as homosexual. Pedophilia and homosexuality are different, and most pedophiles are not homosexual; they are heterosexual. Jordan is correct to suggest that looking at the "scandals" of pedophilia will not tell us much about ordinary homoeroticism in the church, but one can go further than Jordan does at this point. The distinction between pedophilia and adult homoeroticism was investigated with some care by the Canadian commission. They concluded that most of the priests who molested young boys were not homosexual. Moreover, few of those priests were technically pedophiles. Pedophilia in the technical sense is erotic attraction to children. Many of the molesting priests were not primarily erotically attracted to children, but simply were in positions where children were the most readily available for sexual acting out and where the children were too vulnerable to mount effective protest. Hence, the commission pointed to situational factors that contributed to the abuse.[2]

In short, our current predicament in the United States was prefigured in Canada. Attention to the experience of our neighbors might have led to better handling of the issue here on several levels. Particularly important is an understanding of the situational nature of much clergy sexual misconduct and the need, therefore, to address institutional factors that contribute to an abuse-ripe situation. Jordan's study adds some specificity regarding the training of clergy, and to this extent contributes to an understanding of those institutional factors, yet I would also urge attention to the larger arena addressed in the Canadian study.

For example, the Canadian study, although it did not focus specifically on rhetoric in the way that Jordan does, did raise issues such as sexual stereotyping in the schools. Views of children, the organization of sexual relationships in which adult men look for smaller and "weaker" partners, the pervasive influence of hedonistic individualism, the portrayal of males in dominant roles in the media, and traditional masculine socialization with its tendency to emphasize sexual acts rather than relationships; all of these factors and many more were explored as possible contributors to the phenomenon of clergy sexual misconduct and child abuse. The Canadian study makes clear that one cannot look only to the church and its structures, but must also look to societal attitudes, values, and modes of socialization in order to see what causes clergy misconduct. This broader arena adds dimensions to Jordan's focus on in-church rhetoric.

At the same time, writing some ten years later, Jordan is able to go beyond the Canadian study in some important ways. One of these is asking how gay liberation affects clergy conduct. Will the increasing acceptance of positive gay identity in society provide healthy models for gay Catholic clergy, and will this tend to decrease the need for sexual acting-out? Although I affirm the importance of healthy models of sexual identity, I believe that Jordan himself sits on the horns of a dilemma at this point. It is a dilemma that touches the heart of ethical inquiry.

On the one hand, I believe that Mark Jordan is absolutely correct to suggest that we need "new speech" in order to know anything about clerical homoeroticism. He is certainly correct to suggest that the scandals of pedophilia, which currently rock the Roman Catholic Church, will not be the place to learn about the real lives of gay and lesbian Catholics, in and out of the priesthood. But how, then, do we get to know about gay and lesbian lives? It is tempting to say that we need simply to step back and *dis*cover them, but this is not satisfactory, as Jordan acknowledges. Much like contemporary "queer theory," Jordan appears at times to suggest that sexual identity is not simply something to *dis*cover but something that must be created or invented. The problem with "gay liberation" approaches, for example, is that they assume that one can simply liberate what is already there. But if structures have been oppressive, then it is possible that true gay lives and true gay identity is not waiting to be liberated but remains yet to be invented.

If this is so, then there is a fluidity around sexuality: one is not simply "gay" or "straight," but is a sexual being under construction at all times. The dilemma is how, then, would we ever know what is "true" gay or lesbian identity? How would we set any limits to acceptable sexual behavior? Must people be free to try anything and everything in order to "invent" themselves? Although Jordan gives voice to a condemnation of pederasts from a gay perspective, this condemnation stands on shaky ground. The dilemma is how to be totally open about the meaning and expression of gay sexuality while at the same time finding grounds on which one can condemn behaviors by either straight or gay priests. If sexuality is fluid and there are no models to adopt, can one with consistency claim that *any* behaviors are ultimately wrong? If we really know nothing about clerical homoeroticism, and if we must create new communities and institutions in order to permit new speech, then on what grounds do we condemn any expression of sexual interest, whether homoerotic, heteroerotic, or pedophilic? What are the grounds for prompt disciplinary action against priests who molest children? In short, by recognizing that all expression of sexuality has been distorted, and that we must not simply liberate but construct sexual identity, does Jordan open the door to a kind of ethical relativism that fails to set any limits?

I find helpful William F. May's (1991) discussion of "the molested." May takes as his subject for discussion a child who was molested and was eroticized by the experience. Far from shutting down her ability to relate to her own body, she became sexualized and loved the physical experience of the sexual encounter. I confess that when I first read this chapter, it made me angry. It made me angry because such experiences of being sexualized by abuse are very rare. It is far more common for children to dissociate from their bodies and to have great difficulty henceforth in establishing relationships. I have personally known women who repressed the experience for more than fifty years and for whom the revelation late in life of what happened to them as children was unbelievably painful. Why, then, does May take this atypical example? Why does he choose the child who *likes* the encounter, is *eroticized* by it, becomes early on aware of her sexuality and heightened in her sense of bodily pleasure?

I have come to understand that May chose this child precisely because her case was the "hard" case. When a child is abused and henceforth dissociates from his or her own body, the damage done is clear and evident. But when a child is abused and is "turned on" by the experience, the damage is not clear. Is there any harm? Can we still call it abuse?

This question is crucial, because it goes to the heart of understanding whether people are simply fluid and "under construction" at all times, or whether there is a core that can be damaged even when there is no displeasure. May takes the view that a core is damaged even when the child appears to like the experience. He writes, "The eroticized child may consent, cooperate, and seek pleasure, rather than merely submit." But it is precisely because the child may become a compliant, even eager, participant, that May takes her to be still a victim: "Her cooperation shows how thoroughly the predator has victimized her." Drawing an analogy with slavery, he suggests that those who convince a slave to believe that she enjoys slavery "have taken her completely, body and soul" (May, 1991, p. 103).

In an effort to allow open room for exploration of sexual identity, we must nonetheless find a way to say that some sexual activities are wrong. Here, the Canadian commission is also instructive, for they are clear from the outset about two matters: (1) sexual *use* of children is wrong, whether by true pedophiles or by heterosexual or homosexual adults; (2) *many* structures in society, both within and outside the church, have contributed to this wrongful expression and all of those factors need to be examined. Mark Jordan does us a great service in lifting up the restricted roles and "tropes" that have been the framing of our understanding of gay Catholicism in the modern period. There is work to be done in coming to terms with healthy sexual expression for *all* Christians, gay and straight and bisexual and transgendered, Catholic and Protestant and Episcopal and other. At the same time, a sharp line must be drawn against the abuse to which so many of our children are routinely subjected. Girls are regularly sexually harassed in our schools and homes and on our streets. Such harassment is wrong and must be condemned. The sexual abuse of boys is also wrong and must be condemned. Grounds for such a clear condemnation will be found, however, only if we can give up the postmodern tendency to think that all values are fluid and determined only by power arrangements. Jordan's condemnation of the rhetoric of the Catholic church is a step in the right direction. The Canadian commission's attention to a broad spectrum of social constructs and structures is another. May's insistence that human beings possess a soul that can be violated is yet another. All three help to create a structure that permits us to analyze the wrongness of clergy sexual abuse.

NOTES

1. These headlines appeared in the *San Francisco Chronicle* during Spring 2002.
2. The commission utilized Groth's (1978) distinction between *regressed* and *fixated* offenders. Regressed offenders prefer adult partners but because of precipitating stress will turn to children. They also utilized Goldstein's (1987) distinction between *situational* and *preferential* child molesters. They found that the offenders in their study were largely regressed and situational.

REFERENCES

Archdiocese of St. John's (1990). *Report of the archdiocesan commission of enquiry into the sexual abuse of children by members of the clergy,* Volume 1, *Report,* and Volume 2, *Background studies and briefs.* St. John's, Newfoundland: Archdiocese of St. John's.

Goldstein, Seth (1987). *The sexual exploitation of children: A practical guide to assessment, investigation, and intervention.* New York: Elsevier Science.

Groth, A. Nicholas (1978). Patterns of sexual assault against children and adolescents. In Ann Wolbert Burgess, A. Nicholas Groth, Lynda Lytle Holmstrom, and Suzanne M. Sgroi (Eds.), *Sexual assault of children and adolescents.* Toronto: Lexington Books.

Jordan, Mark D. (2000). *The silence of Sodom: Homosexuality in modern Catholicism.* Chicago: University of Chicago Press.

Lebacqz, Karen and Barton, Ronald G. (1990). *Sex in the parish.* Louisville, KY: Westminster Press.

May, William F. (1991). *The patient's ordeal.* Bloomington: Indiana University Press.

Chapter 14

Neither Do I:
A Meditation on Scapegoating

William Glenn

Many years ago, I remember in response to a question of what should one pray for, Daniel Berrigan, the prophetic Jesuit known for taking the gospels as a personal mandate, said: "Take the daily newspaper in one hand, and the Scriptures in the other, and you will know what to pray for." Berrigan probably wasn't the first to suggest such a path, but he seemed, to me, to be living it out every day. Beginning in the autumn of 2001, and moving through the new year, the newspaper and the Gospels both became essential, for their intersection has become the arena where the lifting of the veil on the Roman Catholic Church's many-layered sexual shadow has occurred, to what appears to be the deep chagrin of the hierarchy and the relief of almost everyone else.

It is quite evident that the hierarchy has not employed a public relations consultant, because their response has been so tone-deaf. I have read, almost daily, of the increasingly evident strategy, interwoven into the various remarks and responses of bishops and cardinals to the currently exposed sexual underbelly of the clerical caste. The strategy has become a massive list of public denials:

> *Not* that a multitude of children were violated sexually, emotionally, and spiritually and need and deserve significant care and official and personal contrition.
> *Not* that a significant number of priests found themselves choosing behaviors that one suspects were psychologically and morally and spiritually repugnant to them, but choices nonetheless, in engaging in sex with some of those who placed in

them near absolute trust, and that the behaviors, when disclosed, were denied and subsequently treated as simply sinful, freed of the nuance needed to understand and hopefully
prevent their repetition and delineate their habituation and
nascence.

Not that when boys and their families came forward, in bravery
and in trust, they were counseled to silence and secrecy,
counseled primarily about scandal, about not going public
lest shame and approbation accrue to the institution itself.

Not that something was egregiously wrong with this system in
its refusal to come to terms with the systemic and systematic
causes of this widespread horror.

Not that there is a connection between clergy sexual abuse and a
dualistic regard for the human body that degrades it as the locus of sin while anointing the nonmaterial spirit as the locus
of sanctity.

Not that the total exclusion of women from priestly service, and
hence deep authority within the institution, might be a significant cofactor in the perpetuation of a system unable to recognize its own unbridled decay from within, particularly in its
obsession with all things sexual, and its dogmatic and canonical control over the sexual lives of its adherents, particularly
its female members, and their anima-identified brothers.

Not that it is remarkable that boys are the current focus of the
abuse and subsequent charges, but that the status of girls and
young women, who historically have been the most objec-
tified of persons for others' sexual pleasure, is hardly being
engaged; this focus confirms what women have said emphatically over the past thirty years. Of course, when boys are violated, it is news; the subjugation of women sexually is no
story at all.

Not that requiring lives of sexual abstinence from all who would
serve its sacramental ministry and all who are elevated as
models of holiness might repress in those many individuals
their authentic and holy sexual selves and lead to the damaging consequences unconscious repression produces.

Not that the personal and institutional rejection of one's internal
life and sexual knowing and orientation leads to denial, pro-

jection, and reaction formation, those psychological defenses that characterize one's deepest impulses as evil and, hence, identifies them, if at all, in others who consequently become the marginalized whose task it is to bear that onus, even unto death.

Not that the almost thirty-five-year-old ban on having a real conversation within the church regarding all manner of things sexual (from contraception to abortion to divorce to the politics of annulment to remarriage to sexual relations outside of marriage to homosexuality and to the ordination of women), including all issues in which the fundamental cofactor is the control of the sexual lives of the members, particularly and most evidently the female members, has contributed explicitly to the eruption of these charges at this particular time in the larger culture's overt conversation about human sexuality and has erupted, like mushrooms after the rain, all over the planet.

Not that the placement of church law on par with and equal to Gospel values might produce an imbalanced understanding of the relative importance of ecclesial law over the simpler and perhaps more compelling mandates of the gospel as having their origin in the words and the person of Jesus.

Not that the dogmatic heritage of the institution, going back to its first great conciliar debates, and the equation of politically adduced intellectual understandings with the mind of the Absolute, and the impulse to absolute assurity that such an equation provides, leads to an utterly false sense of having the deified response to all human questions, discounting the subsequent advances of all forms of knowledge (the sciences, anthropology, psychology, sociology, criticism, ad nauseum), and inflates the institution's sense that is has the answer to every human question at all times.

Not that the silencing of theological conversations and a host of theologians in Europe, North America, South America, South Asia, Australia, and elsewhere, when engaged in conversations thought to deviate from the narrowly understood, but tenaciously held positions of the current magisterium, might be having a deleterious effect on all dialogue in the church, and thus prevent the church from receiving the aggregate wisdom of its immense membership in all manner of things, including human sexuality.

Not that the concentration of power in the hands of a very few career-oriented men in the Vatican and in the national churches has led to a profound myopia regarding the lived experience of the faithful compounded by a remarkable refusal to glean wisdom from all other sectors of society to best learn how organizations that thrive work in order to serve their constituents.

Not that the kind of absolute secrecy that the institution has employed in this sexual imbroglio and throughout its affairs has a regular and efficient tendency to return and haunt those who would use it as a cover for an authentic and open process that one might expect a spiritually based organization to exhibit.

No. The strategy chosen and defended by the bulk of the cardinalate in the United States speaks to none of these plausible approaches to the horrific problem. We need a reformation of Catholic sexual theology. We need another Luther to nail ninety-five theses of gender and sexual justice on the doors of all the cathedrals.

Rather, the strategy adopted covertly is to suggest that the presence of homosexuals in the clergy is, in fact, the root cause of this problem and, as it, or rather, they, are rooted out, in whatever way the leadership devises, the body of the institution will once again, as if it ever was, be made pure. It is these stealth homosexuals, not unlike stealth terrorists, who have secretly manipulated the institution to enter and to do their dirty deeds and covertly undermine the otherwise perfect order. They are named the evildoers, over against those within, who by implication are the innocent, the good. The cardinal archbishop in Boston has described the explosion of charges against priests as his own personal September 11. The Catholic hierarchy laid the blame squarely on the unacceptable presence of homosexuals within the priesthood, claiming that gay priests are unfit for priestly service. That places them, actually, in good company with all of womankind.

Homosexuals, homosexuality, or, as the cardinal archbishop in New York put it, "the word they use . . . gay and so forth," these are to be regarded as the heart of the problem; this is the moral rot on the otherwise holy barque; these are the "moral monsters," in the words of the cardinal archbishop in Boston in describing one broken priest; these are the sole cause of this "scandal," as it is presently being called. The cardinal archbishop of Chicago, when pressed on a television news program to offer a defense of the church's post-Vatican meeting position, when pressed about *gay* men as priests, reprimanded the journalist regarding the distinction between *gay* and the clinical and desultory *homosexual,* and reminded him that gay was an appellation to be applied to those, to use the church's definitions, "intrinsically disordered persons" who had multiplied their sinfulness by acting out their sexual desires. *Homosexuals,* as a clinically defined group, are what I'm dealing with here.

I am, to use this clinical term often cited as a pejorative descriptor, a homosexual. But more accurately, and to the counter-point, I am a gay man, whose primary emotional and affiliative attraction is to other men. Gay people are everywhere: in the world and in the churches. They are not yet an occasion of joy but are, I believe, an occasion of grace, for those who dwell within either and both. Homophobia, the fear, and more, the visceral hatred of homosexuality, is, I have thought for years, but a poor stepchild of the fear, and visceral hatred of the feminine, of women, which results in the misogyny that permeates the church and the world.

Several years ago, I was asked to a come to a meeting of community leaders at the White House, and I found myself to be the only man in the group of perhaps two-dozen women invited to share our concerns for our communities with First Lady Hillary Clinton. I was a bit nervous when invited to introduce myself to the assembled and to share the concerns I brought (at the time I was the executive of a central-city AIDS agency in San Francisco). I mentioned in my remarks that I was a gay man. To illustrate the meaningfulness of that qualifier, I told the group that I had come to understand that homophobia, which I battled in my work and in my life, was in fact acutely related to the oppression of women, and that when misogyny was finally overcome, so, too, would be homophobia.

What happened next startled me. Every woman in the group started to nod her head, mostly vigorously, lips murmuring understanding. These women, leaders in a variety of fields, had vital experience with misogyny and knew the fear of the feminine was at its heart, and they intuitively knew that fear of the feminine, the anima, was at the heart of homophobia, as well.

The church's homophobia, once subtle, emerged in the 1980s as strategic and directed. Inherent in homosexuals, according to the church, is the "moral evil" that resulted in Cardinal Ratzinger's 1986 Letter characterizing homosexuals as intrinsically morally disordered. Of course, I have eliminated the Vatican double-talk which distinguishes person from act, a non sequitur that is consistently used to further said control.

At the time of the pronouncement, what struck me as most significant was not the rendering of this condemnation onto gay persons, scapegoating them for the institution's sexual shadow, but rather, the absolute quiescence of the faithful to the scapegoating of their sisters and brothers within, with this unjust and inhuman charge. I was a parishioner at that time in a liberal church community, staffed by several closeted gay priests, and no one in that congregation, neither priest nor lay minister nor leftist agitator-cum-communicant, spoke at Sunday mass, wrote a word in the bulletin, or partook of the gossip to which I was privy, in the corridors, or in the plaza, against that horrible judgment, that indicting projection, that shame-filled marking of innocent human beings.

I, perhaps, need not remind the reader that homosexuals are marked psychologically, emotionally, spiritually, and often physically as having to bear the shame constitutive in the act of being the scapegoat, growing up, emerging, claiming oneself, and, even today, believing the almost imperceptible but enormously damaging effects that scapegoating intends and always produces. Scapegoating creates fear, doubt, cultural and familial isolation, and self-denigration, and scapegoating works. It deflects attention off the scapegoaters and creates havoc not only in the lives of those so marked, but of everyone else, as well. It is really a cultural no-brainer, and its throbbing vitality has been abundantly evident in the pages of *The New York Times,* or whatever paper one reads, in the pronouncements of the cardinal archbishops. But its throbbing vitality has been most evident though mainly imperceptible in the lives of all persons it tags: those *homosexuals.*

We are all coconspirators. We are all deniers, projectors, minimizers, adept at holding the cultural bias against homosexuals in our unconscious shadow, rendering it ready whenever summoned to assist in the cultural task of purifying humanity of its sexual self. Even if that is us. You may be feeling the effects of it as you sit reading these words; its tentacles may be affecting you as they are designed to do. It may be inducing in you fear or revulsion or sorrow or confusion or rage—if not here and now, no doubt elsewhere, perhaps at home, at work, even walking down the streets of the city or town or village in which you live. If you are gay, it demands that you not live at peace, demands that you not live free, and demands that above all else, you, in this lifetime, not be yourself. Of course, it is the antithesis of Christian teaching that one would not be oneself and would deny his or her core erotic attractions. Who else might one take to the Creator in prayer, in life, but one's very own self as one has come to know whom one is? And who would ever deny this to anyone else, especially in the name of that very Divine?

You may feel angry or nauseous or numbed or oblivious or enraged or confused. Or you may believe this has nothing to do with you. But, as with our heightened awareness of the suffering throughout the world, an unexpected grace these past few years, from the waste in Iraq and Afghanistan, to the ongoing chaos of Palestine and Israel, and to the barely on the screen famine in Southern Africa, this is affecting us all, both straight and gay alike, and it is affecting us most intimately.

To grapple with this ongoing storm, I stumbled my way to John 8. In this text's deep-in-our-memory story of Jesus' encounter with the woman caught in the act, as the scripture says, *the very act,* of adultery, that is, of having sex with a person to whom she was not wed (i.e., given in marriage like chattel, part of a dowry, part of a transaction with commercial and cultural and religious significance), Jesus provided an example of wisdom, paradox, nuance, and contemporaneity.

As it is my spiritual practice, I took this passage to prayer, seeking its wisdom, if that is something I would be given the grace to ascertain, and to do so in the midst of cultural and political wars that impinge powerfully on my own sense of self, my own sense of autonomy and security, my own sense of the vulnerability and fragility of the world, of her broken inhabitants, of the very planet itself. And, if the truth be told, my spiritual practice places me in touch with presence and absence, the Divine and how the Divine desires to be known in the very midst of human life.

This poignant and well-known passage seems especially appropriate, on its surface, and in its heart, to what we all deal with each day. It is about sex (well, maybe it is), and the law (well, again, maybe), and about gender (absolutely), and about power and authority (as is so much) then, and now. It is also about shaming and scapegoating and entrapping and encircling and stoning. It is about the shadow, projection, righteousness, and judgment, and about letting go in the most elemental and profound of ways of all that keeps us from being those human beings we were created to be. Women and men. All of us, gay and otherwise.

It is about this law-breaking woman and her all-male and all-powerful, or so it seems, accusers, and it is about this odd rabbi, Jesus. It is about his simple refusal to join in judgment, his curious placing himself *within* the body of the judgers, within the community, and his simultaneous invitation to let go of the need to judge at all. I am with him in most of this. I do not want the woman shamed, encircled, accused, scapegoated, or, most of all, stoned. The very idea is abhorrent, of course, so, so far, I'm siding with Jesus. And I do not want Jesus entrapped, played for the fool, put on the spot, or placed in the juxtaposition of choosing Moses or a slattern. (God forbid!) I am siding with Jesus all the more.

I do not want to pretend that no critical analysis is going on here, that oppressive power relationships do not exist, nor that Jesus is naive as to what in the world he is up against, and what is required to establish the reign of God, that reign of justice and mercy, and maybe, finally, love about which he is continually preaching to the exclusion of about everything else. I believe Jesus could only have been conscious of all of this, too, so I am siding with Jesus it seems quite a bit now. And then he scrawls in the sand, and no matter what he is scrawling, this haunts. He lays an imperative at the feet of the assembled: "You who are without sin cast the first stone" (John 8:7).

As one intrigued by the internal dialogue, I suspect in this instance it must have been something like this: "I'm not saying you can't stone her. I'm not arguing with Moses. I'm not saying she's not guilty as charged. I'm not saying you are not about the very business of enforcing the law. I'm not even saying you shouldn't be trying to trap me, even though we both know what this is really about. I'm not saying I don't have a very clear read on this imbalanced situation, and I'm not saying it is not very evident who in fact here is being served. No, I'm not saying any of these things at all. This is all I'm saying: *You who are without sin, cast the first stone.* You who can afford to judge, be my guest. You who are pure, grab a stone now."

The author notes that they began to drift away, not surprisingly, the oldest drifting first. I believe that part about the oldest leaving first, feeling a little older now, for the old know way too much of what haunts the human heart, and how one's unforgivings bind human lives. The old have had to experience the circular path judgment always takes. The old have had practice understanding the wisdom behind the childhood axiom that as one points one's index finger at another, three fingers are always pointing back. Or at least the old ought to know.

In sitting with this passage over many days, over days of the daily wanderings of cardinals and of their vilification of homosexuals, I become what feels like too aware of the radical demands of this reign of God, the God of Moses and Isaiah and Job, and the God of Jesus, the God whose reign Jesus preaches, which at its heart is about absolute mercy, at its heart is about a God of absolute mercy, at its heart is about a call, particularly to the oppressed, to be persons of absolute mercy. And that absolute mercy requires a conscious, deliberate withdrawal of judgment, of impugning motive, of hardening one's heart, of prematurely placing oneself in an equation with the heart of an absolutely merciful God, and then presuming to reserve judgment, as we might for God, for oneself.

In the passage, the enforcing circle of power, those mandated to keep the community pure and in compliance with what it was presumed the Almighty himself wanted, moved away one by one and slowly withdrew. What a relief! What a denouement! What a catharsis! And what a pleasure that would be if in the current order of things that proved to be the case. But that is not the end of the story. Jesus remains, and he is left alone with the nameless woman. He asks "Has no one judged you?"and she replies, "No." Including himself squarely and humbly in the community of persons called to no judgment, he declares, "Then, neither do I." Jesus adds, "Go now. Sin no more" (John 8:10-11).

The heart of the story is not about whatever transgressions of the law the woman might be guilty of, to which Jesus does not even aver. The heart, I believe, is in these words: "Neither do I." Jesus has not suspended his critical faculties, nor denied his vital feelings, nor ignored oppression as he encountered it in the world in which he lived, nor has he done so in this instance. And so how am I, or you, to echo these words, no, to inculcate them and to live out of them, with all the evidence of crushing sin in the world, social and personal, and oppression of every stripe, including the viscous homophobia that cripples so many of God's children, the scapegoated and the scapegoaters alike. What are we to do?

How, as a homosexual, rather, a gay person, am I to confront the scapegoating I see and experience and yet be one with this odd rabbi who says simply, regarding judgment, "Neither do I." I do not believe we are called to suspend our critical faculties or our vital feelings or ignore the oppression that we see and experience ourselves, or that experienced by any of the least of our brethren. I believe the reign of God, in fact, depends on those very faculties and feelings and willingnesses to encounter oppression head-on. To not do so would retard the reign of justice upon which the reign of mercy depends. But, if like the encircled men, sitting in judgment of a defenseless woman, we think we have the right to judge the hearts of church leaders or cast more shadow on their souls, we are really just like the encircled mob of men. We become queer hypocrites, righteous, chest-beaters, Bible-thumpers, and the finger-pointers ourselves.

The truth of this passage, the invitation at its heart, is to give up all moral judgment, every last ounce. Jesus proposes, instead, might we be filled with the knowledge of God's intimate, eros-charged, encompassing love for our very particular selves, like the ones we sometimes are pretty sure they, whomever they be, are not.

We are called, as always, to see things clearly. Paradoxically, that is the vocation of the oppressed, in particular, who in the crucible of suffering, akin to the cross Jesus would come to know, learn the deeper reaches of the path all humans are called to walk. We are still called to understand the hearts and motives and potent defenses human beings regularly employ. We are called to be, as Jesus elsewhere says, as cunning as serpents and as innocent as doves (Matthew 10:16). We are not called, however, even when scapegoated, vilified, lied about, or abused, to judge our enemies. Nor do we pretend that we do not have enemies, which Jesus never assumed. His commandment was to love them; he did not question whether we had them. His entreaty to the nameless woman was not about her sexual behavior but about what he may have suspected was her temptation to judge those who had just done such a masterful job of judging her. This is the sin, Jesus knew, neither she nor we could afford.

We are called to love our enemies, not to be blind to or ignore the degrading effect of their deeds and public statements, but to find in them that which is to be loved. We try to love them as God loves them, and I and the other authors in this volume are writing messages in the sand, inviting Catholic bishops and cardinals to examine their own failing and take the higher road of love. So harsh is this rabbi in his demands. Yet so compelling and life-giving and all things yet possible and new-making are the rewards his demands provide.

Chapter 15

Scandal Work: Catholicism and a Crisis of Intimate Relations

Edward J. Ingebretsen

The real power . . . is power . . . over men. How does one man assert his power over another, Winston? . . . By making him suffer. Obedience is not enough. Unless he is suffering, how can you be sure that he is obeying your will and not his own?

Felicity de Zulueta (1996, p. 95)

This chapter has two main points. First, I wish to explore how scandal functions as a mode of public discipline, providing a civic rubric, as it were, designed to manage consensus around some point of trauma. I will take, as an example, recent media coverage in the United States where a complicated "scene" of public shaming and misplaced guilt was staged upon the sexed bodies of priests and children. The presentation of the scandal involved ecclesiastical misdeeds as well as narrative misdirection, but each element needs to be considered independently of the other. Following a discussion of the dynamics of scandal, I want to examine the ecclesiastical misdeeds—specifically related to Catholic authority structures—wherein power relations, under cover of a rhetoric of care, exploit priests (pastoral agents) as well as those who seek their "ministry."

THE FURY OF SCANDAL

Nothing is so convincing as facts we already know. The rubric of public scandal operates according to this dictum. The news alert pasted across the bottom of the TV screen is, as a consequence, at pains to announce something that is in fact not the case and to keep from view any evidence to the contrary. That is, what is breathlessly telegraphed as late breaking and shocking is, more often, banal and old. Readers and editors have heard this material (or something like it) in some form or other before. Like an urban legend, news circulated in this fashion banks upon anticipatory assent. Although journalism is a recent genre, it includes elements of oral traditions and social purposes that are centuries old. The exchange of information between individuals and among groups was less about "news" than about other factors: group identity and cohesion, narrative pleasure, emotional titillation. Many of these features still anchor even the most buttoned-up, contemporary news broadcast (Spacks, 1985).

Thus, the "facts" of any scandal recede behind the furious melodrama installed around them. More accurately, consumer interest in these facts is produced within and through the dynamics of that public presentation, particularly by means of the codes or markers by which viewers and readers understand "shocking" or "interesting." Such techniques include interruption of normal sequencing, grim announcers, large-type fonts, and other markers of surprise, shock, haste—all of which solicit, exploit, and direct viewer interpretation, but which do so unacknowledged for the pressure they apply. In other words, narrative frame, rather than content, interests viewers or readers because that is the ideological burden of the genre. Stephen Neale (1989) argues that the teleological sweep of narrative piques curiosity and interest, solicits consensus, and works to "produce coherence in the subject" (p. 110). Part of that coherence is the illusion of reader mastery. As Neale remarks, "In life meaning is problematic, in narrative it is not" (p. 107).

In other words, scandals are rarely about individual and private misdeeds, although these may seem to be the center of attention. Scandal is less a private, documentary mode than a public, disciplinary one, and what often is being disciplined are the social "hot topics" of sex or money. The energy around these is understandable; both are held in high esteem as the chief desired goods of American culture. Despite this fact (or because of it) few people have easy access to either. Scandal narrative works by attaching desires for these "products" to the strongest set of public emotions available—usually, fear and anxiety, sometimes envy. In combination with sex or money, emotional anchors such as these have an almost irresistible lure. Further, the "coherence" produced in the reader/viewer is a function of a narrative whose general plot is already known in advance and whose outcome the media consumer can therefore anticipate. This interaction "between media messages and what the individual already knows and believes about the world" (Neuman, Just, and Crigler, 1992, p. 1) can be called *formula.* Daily "news"—with its historical connections to the penny press, the broadside, and other vernacular media—depends upon such bite-sized, chewable bits of genre. Such boilerplate narrative, with its "already-heard" status, lends a comforting sense of confirmation to the facts. In this respect, then, news is a public example of the less-formal processes of gossip (Neuman, Just, and Crigler, 1992; Lule, 2001; Manoff and Schudson, 1986; Fishman, 1980).

The confirmation is, however, spurious. The rubric of scandal resembles preaching more than documentary, although the credibility of the form rests upon the pretense of documentation that sustains it. Two points, in particular, deserve note. Scandal—like the more traditionally churched rites from which it derives—demands repetition to achieve its pedagogical aim; as preachers know, something heard again and again acquires a status of conviction in which "truth" is really not the issue. In formalist terms, the "coherence" of the genre is produced in the reader-subject, not one necessarily contained by the narrative subject. Finally, like any effective preachment, the rubric of scandal demands a body—symbolic or actual—whose exposition to scrutiny functions as a cautionary tale. Transgression, displayed in public, will be used as an exemplum, an example, demonstration, or warning. But the moral gaze that licenses the display of "public sin" also enables other looks altogether. For example, the cagey preacher can exploit diverse private and commercial interests in sex, fantasy, and horror, all the while remaining (at least in pretense) ignorant of the way these conventional narrative elements are designed to keep an audience's attention.[1]

These two factors—a habit of ritual, dimly remembered, and pragmatic commodity marketing—must be considered as part of the formal properties of scandalous narrative, whether such narrative is found on CNN or in supermarket tabloids. Stories of sex, transgression, murder, and mayhem have existed for as long as there has been mechanical means, oral or written, for plotting, sharing, and selling them (Halttunen, 1998; Cohen, 1993). Pop cult economies have, if anything, only developed new modes of dispensing (and profiting from) such narrative cycles. In the rhythms of commodity culture, the sexed body is everywhere, crosshatched by a mix of desire and taboo. Sexy bodies sell products while eroticized stories anchor "news." Nonetheless, despite its obvious retail possibilities, sex is still largely taboo as a subject per se; as a consequence, its presence in public will always be accompanied by some explicit justification, usually couched as "in the public interest" or as a "need to know." Both markers repeatedly punctuated the Clinton saga, the problematic content of which needed repeated moral management. Scandal is, in sum, a form of marketing that condenses a variety of commercial stratagems; as such it exploits taboo by bending it to other purposes, establishing a moral gaze that subsumes less moral motives into its purview. Like gossip, scandal need not actually be true; however, also like gossip, for scandal to do the social work required of it, to form social opinion and craft consensus, it must be interesting (Lull and Hinerman, 1997).

In other words, it takes two to scandalize. ABC, CNN, or CBS media cameras might lock in one direction, locating monsters in the civic terrain for the sake of staking and eliminating them. Nonetheless, who controls the camera and who profits from its focus also need analysis. In other words, a discussion of the scandalizing body needs to account for the demands made upon that body, often inchoately, by a viewer who may have reason to deny, repress, or not acknowledge his or her interest. Where, and how, does the moralized gaze of the reader/viewer disguise other "looks" (excitement, drama, prurience) that might not be so morally justified? The "outbreak" of pedophilia and the media attention to this "crisis" is a place to explore some of these points.

To begin with a general comment: sex passes without notice as a "base narrative" of many forms of popular media. This fact alone makes any narrative featuring sex suspect in the first place, since what seems centrally important is, essentially, a "vehicle" or "frame." Indeed, one type of sexual tale, that of the sexually predatory priest, is neither new nor late breaking. In its broadest form, a well-furnished genre of priestly sex has existed since the twelfth century—in other words, since the church formally mandated celibacy for its priests. Stories about priests having sex made for satire, fiction, and poetry, and similar plots could be found in theological text, preachment, social polemic, and political exposé. In recent years, documentary and sociological studies have been added to the mix. Narrowing the focus even further, accounts of priests having inappropriate sexual contact with children are not new, either, although this narrative twist borrows much of its energy from the more general category of children and sexual threat. Philip Jenkins (1996) and David Sonenschein (1998a,b) explore in some detail the histories upon which the "contemporary" crisis depends.

In *Pedophiles and Priests: Anatomy of a Contemporary Crisis,* for example, Jenkins (1996) names a section of his introduction "The Discovery of Clerical Sexual Abuse." Jenkins is ironic here. As he explains, what seemed to be a discovery of clergy sex in the 1980s and beyond was no discovery at all; elements of the plot device have existed in narrative form, and served narrative purposes, long before the nineteenth or twentieth centuries (Burkett and Bruni, 1993; Sipe, 1995). Indeed, miscreant priests are regular fare in a number of genres. The Gothic novel (and Harlequin Romance, its modern incarnation) are replete with ambitious, tyrannical, and sexually predatory priests. In the Gothic such ne'er-do-wells embody the Gothic's attack, from the margins, of mainstream class and power politics (Sage, 1988). One of the earliest self-described examples of English literature, Chaucer's *Canterbury Tales,* makes effective satire of lustful and greedy priests. Sonenschein's two volumes of *Pedophiles on Parade* (1998a,b) extensively and exhaustively chronicle Western energy around children and sex. It is also significant, as Jenkins and Sonenschein show, that the use of these narratives shifted dramatically within the political milieu of the emerging United States. Ministers and their sexual misdeeds constituted "Puritan Pornography" (Jenkins, 1996, pp. 25-29). Sexual narrative, given moral cover, made for interesting reading while shaping the contested debates over the exercise of civil authority in colonial America. In *The Invention of Sodomy,* Mark D. Jordan (1997) shows how the narrative of the sexed priest even makes its way into medieval confessional manuals, where, already, its covert titillation was justified by the ostensibly moral focus claimed by the text.[2] Contemporary pop genres indefatigably market the sexual priest in romances, detective thrillers, gothic horror, TV, soap operas, sitcoms, and cinema. An author-sociologist of some repute (a cleric himself) repeatedly focuses upon priestly transgression (notably, *The Cardinal Sins* [Greeley, 1981]; *Fall from Grace*

[Greeley, 1993]). The extensive use of this material in so many diverse media, however, reflects changing attitudes toward the church rather than a necessary increase in priestly sex. Indeed, sex functions in these narratives as it does in other texts more generally, as a metaphor implicating other meanings, intentions, and ploys. In fictional texts such as *The Thorn Birds* (McCullough, 1977), the priest's illicit sexuality dramatizes social, religious, or sexual boundaries that are deemed either too constrictive or too weak. Thus, although sex might seem to be the issue, the priest's sexual activity often intends an examination of something else (e.g., liberality, freedom, humanity, church intransigence). The current interest in priests and the children whom they abuse is a similar case in point, since a clear, double vision is at work. That is, report after report will note, almost by way of apology, that the offending priest's actions are years, perhaps decades old. In one of the more incendiary cases—indeed, the case that began the recent investigation in Boston—the court ruled that the two most grievous charges against the priest could not be brought because the statute of limitations had expired ("Time limit concern," 2002).

So, then, how are viewers/readers to understand these typically lurid tales of sexual despoilation? If they are not meant to be legally adjudicated, what are we to make of them? Perhaps a better question is to ask, How do their public presentations make meaning? In *The Origins of Pornography*, Lynn Avery Hunt (1993) argues that at the heart of the obscenity charge lay a cluster of tensions, mostly political in nature, concerned with protecting the king's symbolic body from attack. That is, although the king's *physical* body could be protected from violence, his *symbolic* body was vulnerable to sexual lampoon and politically sensitive gossip. Obscenity laws became weapons in the king's arsenal. The genre from which "pornography" is derived uses sex narrative politically, rather than erotically, although emotional arousal certainly helps the political. Sex functioned as a kind of sideways glance; the display of intimate relations (usually of a perverse or inappropriate kind) announced the related misuse of social privilege and hierarchic power. Not much has changed since. In this respect, then, the media coverage of the "pedophile-priest," with its insistent although offstage ideological energy, remains truer to the intention of the pornographic genre than does the genitally obsessed text or film now associated with it.

Contemporary scandal industries manipulate sex-narrative—coded as shocking, appalling, or socially distressing—to address other topics sometimes far distant from sex. This is not to deny that sex is an issue. The *Washington Post* reports that since the early 1960s 850 Catholic priests have been accused of sexual contact with minors, while more than 350 were removed from ministry before this year. As many as 218 were removed in 2002 alone on these charges (Cooperman and Sun, 2002). Probably many, even most, of these removals are with cause. Nonetheless, the crisis staged around priests and children extends beyond them, as indicated by how similar this crisis is, in form and content, to others that have preceded it. For example, the furious public response to clergy sexual offenses recalls similar public dramas through the 1970s and 1980s in the United States. Beginning with the Child Abuse Act in 1974, the symbolic body of the child was used to anchor a variety of moral panics, including, notoriously, the pro-life political movement as well as many anti-gay movements (Weeks, 1985). The contest over the child—definitions, rights, responsibilities—became an occasion by which to test, and if need be, to strengthen, social boundaries of adult sex and gender that were then under siege. In the 1980s workplace sex continued the discussion.

One reason for the gripping nature of the current case is the way it distills sex-boundary anxiety with eloquent narrative economy. The priest is forbidden sex while children are ideologically, and sentimentally, presumed to be nonsexual, even beyond sex. In addition to narrative pleasure, however, it is also probable that the furor around sexual priests has psychological benefits for an amnesiac culture. That is, like parallel scenes centered upon incest, child abuse, or other unlawful intimacy with children, excoriating the priest deflects attention from the ephebophilia that is a pervasive feature of commodity culture. Sonenschein (1998b) matter-of-factly labels American pop culture pedophilic.[3] It is a sobering thought that, as statistics indicate, one of four female children in the United States and one of six male children face some kind of unwanted sexual encounter during their early youth.[4] Priests who take sexual advantage of children or young persons are indeed reprehensible; they are, however, not alone in their desires or, apparently, in their actions. Because of the social vulnerabilities surrounding them, however, priests and ministers are powerless and easy targets for misdirection and scapegoating.

The priest's role as the perceived "agent" of intractable Catholic authority ratchets up the energy around charges of child sex, of course, and this returns us to Hunt's observation about the resilience and capaciousness of sexual narrative. Its uses are many. Again, without question many of the published reports of priest behavior are true. I argue, however, that the scandal format is *already* a genre whose designs upon viewers and readers anticipate whatever "meanings" are to be derived by the inflamed recitation of particular cases.[5] Genre criticism shows that while cultures change over time, narrative elements remain constant, perhaps even predictable. Such predictability or repetition, however, is not simple duplication. Chaucer's lusty friars differ from the clerical philanderers of Rush's *The Best-Kept Secret* ([1957] 1980), while Chaucer's and Rush's explicitly heterosexual transgressors are not the homosexual (and child-abusing) clerics of Jason Berry's *Lead Us Not into Temptation* (1992). How formulas stay the same, even as they serve different narrative purposes, demands our attention.

BODIES UNDER SCANDAL, BODIES UNDER LAW

Jason Berry (1992) argues very explicitly that the crisis of child molestation is a result of the "infestation" of the clergy by homosexual priests. At one point he asks if Jesus would "approve" of "ecclesiastical culture [that] harbors child molesters [and] tolerates homosexual activity" (p. 367). Berry is not alone in his thinking, even though statistics and sex research do not bear out the conclusion. Research suggests that clerical sexual misbehavior with children and homosexuality are not related issues, even though there are vociferous attempts (from both within and outside the church) to collapse the two. Indeed, the casualness with which homosexuality displaces the actual energy of the current scandal underscores my point about the sinuousness of scandal as a narrative form. It arrives on the consumer's screen preloaded, as it were, with designs upon its viewers or readers. Since Chaucer, the sexual priest has been useful in many different narrative contexts. Only very recently, however, has that libidinous priest been directly pinioned as "homosexual." This point needs to be considered. For example, Florence Rush's exposé, *The Best-Kept Secret* ([1957] 1980), excoriated priests and the church for a history of abusing women and children. Rush was writing in the height of Cold

War paranoia where homosexuals were, like communists, the cultural "bogeyman." Given the culture of the time, that Rush criticizes Catholic clergy for their philandering, while giving scant attention to the possibility of "homosexual" priests, seems to be a remarkable omission. Could it be that, in Foucauldian language, the "homosexual priest" had yet to be invented? Or better, could it be that the homosexual priest had not yet been found to be socially useful? Berry's similar exposé, a half-century later, decries a priest who is no longer a philanderer but a pedophile. The shift is significant, although it goes generally unremarked either in church or secular media (Ingebretsen, 1999; Meachem, 2002).[6]

When charges were first made in January 2002 about clerical misconduct in Boston, media outrage was directed less at offenses by priests than at the Catholic authorities who seemed either to dismiss sexual misconduct or to treat it cavalierly (Ferdinand, 2002). One ranking cleric turned the argument back upon the victim, suggesting that parents should have been more careful. Since then, the media debate has settled upon the plotline that it is gay clergy who are "responsible" for the church's moral crisis. Father John Geoghan had a three-decade history of being relocated from parish to parish, and even from diocese to diocese, following multiple convictions for child abuse.[7] When the story broke, it was not long before the pope's own press agent predictably condemned homosexuals for the church's woes—this despite the fact that Cardinal Law's disregard of existing civil, as well as church law, was the issue that caused outrage. Dr. Joaguin Navarro-Valls remarked in an interview that "people with these inclinations [homosexuals] just cannot be ordained" (in Henneberger, 2002).[8] This comment, with Vatican authority behind it, was quickly seconded by ranking clergy, bishops, and cardinals (some of whom are themselves most certainly homosexual in orientation). Absent from the debate was any protest from the rank and file of priests, with the exception of the occasional heterosexual panic outburst. One priest declared to a classroom of startled children, "I'm not gay . . . I'm normal, just in case you were wondering" (Rosin, 2002, p. A14). Straight or gay, the silence of rank-and-file priests reflects the likelihood that any speech they make upon the matter in this climate can, and probably will, be used against them.

Addressing the congregation during mass at St. Patrick's Cathedral, the chief pulpit in Catholic Manhattan, Monsignor Eugene

Clark blamed the scandal on "disordered" homosexuals; likewise Cardinal Anthony J. Bevilacqua's remarks concerning homosexual pathology, stress, and alcoholism were as follows:

> We have found that, when you have someone—even using the example of an alcoholic, oriented toward alcoholism—they may be wonderful in the seminary but when they get into the tension of the priesthood there is a tendency at times to seek some kind of outlet, and that's why some priests who have never touched a drink as candidates, when they become priests, they have fallen into alcoholism. (Cassels, 2002)

Bishop John M. D'Arcy, Diocese of Fort Wayne-South Bend, Indiana took a wider swipe, aiming at homosexuals and "especially effeminate" men (Smith, 2002). Here, very evidently, is the specter of gender failure that has driven the anti-gay cleric church discussion since Vatican II. Bishop Wilton Gregory, president of the U.S. Conference of Catholic Bishops, cast the issue apocalyptically: "This is an ongoing struggle. . . . It is most importantly a struggle to make sure that the Catholic priesthood is not dominated by homosexual men" (in Meacham, 2002, p. 23). Cardinal Adam Maida of Detroit suggested that the "problem" is "not truly a pedophilia-type . . . but a homosexual-type problem." Maida said his conclusions derived from "social scientists" (in Whittington, 2002). Despite the occasional note of apology and distance from such language, one concludes that these well-placed Catholic officials speak with the explicit approval of their betters; the noisy gong sounds off with at least a nod from the keeper of the church, who, in fact, owns the bell as well as pays the ringer. Catholic clergy, and especially bishops, are not in the habit of making public statements that disagree with the Magisterium. Indeed, although "liberal" Catholics and prelates might shy away from the remarks of their leaders, these comments have direct correspondence in church doctrine—notoriously typified in the "Letter to the Bishops of the Catholic Church on the Pastoral Care of Homosexual Persons" (Ratzinger, 1986).

Going unmentioned, and certainly undiscussed, of course, are these various officials' willingness to ordain homosexual men in the first place. There are pragmatic reasons for doing so: (1) to fill a declining cadre of priests, and (2) to capitalize upon the homosexual's fabled sensitivity, compassion, and (need I say it) compliance. Taken as a whole, pronouncements about gay priests made by bishops and cardinals of rank demonstrate that homosexuals serve in church ideology very much as they do in civil society, as scapegoats. Scapegoats are rarely the source of the melodramas in which they star. Indeed, long-standing willingness to ordain gay men (Bishop Gregory, cited previously, has ordained them himself; some now sit beside him as his brother bishops) suggests that the church welcomes these men and the work they do. (This, however, raises another issue; if the number of homosexual clergy is rising, one wonders why fewer and fewer straight men want the job.) Accepting the homosexual's ministerial labor, while distancing church administration from him in public, are not irreconcilable positions. To the contrary, they are mutually supportive. One can materially profit from servants in one's home and still keep them out of the living room, fretting about the "problems" associated with these kinds of people. Profiting from homosexual labor does not contradict public denunciation—even in the most "liberal" of terms—of "the homosexual problem." In fact, recent strategies announced to remove gay clerics means, of course, exactly the opposite. The church can ill afford to lose any more priests, and so it wants to keep them—homosexuals, too—on the condition that they remain silent. There is nothing new here, of course: a modified "ask but don't tell" policy. What people do "in private" has never been the problem, as I am sure Cardinal Law agrees.

For weeks following the initial charges in Boston, no news broadcast lost an opportunity to address "the crisis in the priesthood." From regularly scheduled news broadcasts, to personality news shows, to daytime call-in talk shows, everyone, Catholic and non-Catholic, churchgoer and nonchurchgoer, had an opinion. This should not surprise: Indeed, the rubric of scandal is *about* giving us this opinion, it helps "engineer . . . consent" (phrase originated by Edward Bernay, in Chomsky, 1989, p. 16). It would be quite easy to dismiss much of the media wash as crank and ill informed. The constant use of "pedophile" when, in fact, "ephebophile" was meant only demonstrates how seriously uninformed, not to say malicious, was much of the public discussion. Since those early days, homosexuality has been such a standard feature of the debate that it now seems central to it. Occasionally one recalls that sexual orientation is *not* the issue. Scapegoats are chosen for their political vulnerability and their expendability; too often they are in the wrong social place at the right time.[9] Throughout history, a divergent array of bodies have been set apart as bearers of social ill will; generally, they had one thing in common—some real or perceived sexual extravagance or deviance—that demarcated their transgressive status. The symbolic uses of such persons (lepers, Moors, Hottentots, Jews, the French, blacks, unwed welfare mothers, homosexuals) serve many purposes of civic policing and social management.[10] Scapegoating remains constant, even while the subject shifts. As previously ostracized groups find acceptance, the negative energies associated with them can remain unchanged or even condensed elsewhere in the society. The homosexual's relationship to organized religion is a good example of this splitting, showing how "traditional" morality lags behind civic law. Religious structures are more resistant to change than their civil counterparts, and in many Christian denominations homosexuality still remains widely divisive. Liberal church communities can represent the homosexual as an object of pity, useful for the good works of compassion and altruism he makes possible. On the other hand, conservative Christian groups, and the unchurched forces that sometimes align with them politically, can demonize the homosexual, under cover of religion, for political gain (Herman, 1997; Bull and Gallagher, 1996). In Roman Catholic practice, elements of both attitudes exist. Recent pronouncements by high-ranking church authorities have raised homosexuality to a public media issue second only to abortion. Indeed, Pope John Paul II's remarks from his piazza about the "offense" of homosexuality to "Christian values" (July 7, 2000) had the dizzying consequence of raising homosexuality to a higher metaphysical status than Original Sin (Hughes, 2000).

No wonder, then, that for many modern Catholics, homosexuality is one of the last remaining issues upon which sexual clarity and "groupthink" can still be attempted. In the United States, the first sign of the collapse of Roman hegemony was the widespread response, by clerics and laity alike, to *Humanae Vitae* (1968). Contrary to expectation, this long-awaited papal decree emphasized and even strengthened the church's ban against "artificial" contraception. Its regressive nature came as a shock to a liberalizing American Catholic culture. In conjunction with civic movements such as feminism and gay rights, the American laity has moved farther and farther away from Rome on most issues of a personal nature. From masturbation to abortion to premarital sex and birth control, even to vexed issues of genetic tampering, the laity no longer "buy it." A majority of American Catholics likewise diverge from Rome on the morality of homosexuality, adopting a "live and let live" attitude, so long as the issue remains "private."[11] However, in social practice, especially around marriage and adoption, even liberal Catholics take a more conservative approach, one more in line with Rome. A historically odd alliance thus emerges: mainline Catholics and fundamentalist Baptists find themselves in accord on homosexuality while diverging on practically everything else.

Ecclesiastical battles pitched over the homosexual body increased in intensity throughout the late 1980s, even as, and arguably because, homosexuals achieved a degree of social acceptance in civil society. The 1986 "Letter to the Bishops of the Catholic Church on the Pastoral Care of Homosexual Persons," issued by the Vatican, took pains to repeat something that had once gone without saying; in the words of the Vatican-approved text, homosexuality was "inordinately disordered." Through the decade that followed, Vatican directive and intervention directly focused upon homosexuality. The malign pastorality of "Letter to the Bishops of the Catholic Church" ejected Dignity, a Catholic/gay educational group, from church property, while priests accustomed to ministry to Dignity were forbidden to do so. In 1991, the Vatican took sides in local U.S. politics against housing rights for homosexuals. Over the years increasing pressure was put upon sympathetic priests and nuns; outspoken prelates were silenced. A decade of direct attack culminated in July 1999 when the Vatican foreclosed the ministry of Father Robert Nugent and Sister Jeannine Gramick to homosexuals and barred the two religious from working with New Ways Ministry (an "educational outreach" for gay and lesbian Catholics). The pope's statement about the offense of homosexuals to Christian values, in July 2000, was surely remarkable, but years of political and doctrinal bullying had prepared the way for it.[12]

Considering the American context, it is probable that Vatican energy during these years was aimed more at homosexual clergy than at the laity, whose sexual transgressions, after all, kept the priest in business. The Vatican was far more interested in stemming what it perceived to be a decline of clerical prestige in the United States, which evidenced itself as a chronic shortage of vocations to the all-male, celibate clergy (Ingebretsen, 1999). Beginning in the early 1960s, Gallup polls and church rosters reflected a steady erosion of Roman authority. Discontent with doctrine and disagreement with draconian church practice was deflected onto the priest, who then, as now, took the fall for Rome's intransigence. Growing lay cynicism about the church's goals and methods also severely undermined the priest's public authority. The Vatican read these facts differently, however. In the casual but nonetheless firm gender norms governing such things, Father—no longer a "real player" in the American commercial ethos— was therefore not much of a "man" at all. In the image of the old Bing Crosby film *The Bells of St. Mary,* Father no longer knew best. The perceived increase and visibility of homosexual clergy provided the Vatican with its excuse and method. As Mark Jordan's fine work in *Invention of Sodomy* (1997) indicates, neither the excuse nor the method for installing a pogrom were new. The first step was the elimination of the more obvious "women" in the ranks—homosexuals— and the second was again to reemphasize the gendered charism of the priesthood. In 1994, in *Ordinatio Sacerdotalis,* John Paul II reaffirmed the traditional ban against the ordination of "real" women, a move that accompanied the symbolic actions taken to "butch up" the presbyterate by eliminating homosexual men from its ranks.

Across civic and ecclesiastical lines through the past three decades contempt for the "homosexual" must be understood as less a crisis of biology than a failure of gender. Social weakness, rather than moral sin, explains the force and apparent unanimity behind targeting homosexual priests. Bishop D'Arcy's (2002) statement advising against the ordination of "homosexuals and excessively effeminate men" is to the point; the crisis is not so much gay priests as the perceived social weakness of the vocation they are to embody. The Marines are not alone in looking for a few (real) men. Given the typical reticence of church officials about the church's internal politics, the energy and the Gothic rhetoric is very revealing of how deeply the church experiences the collapse of authority as trauma. Garry Wills (2000) observes that many think John Paul II's "real legacy to his church is a gay priesthood" (p. 100). It is precisely this perception that strikes curial officials as apocalyptic—a mode that customarily warrants high-octane speech and public drama. Media is happy to oblige, exploiting the scene further by framing it in the traditional cartoon binaries of Gothic: triggers of civic fear—in this case pedophilic priests— prey upon sentimentalized victims and the whole is ratcheted up the full range of their effect.

Even Rome understands the trauma to be less about individual priestly lapses than about the threat to a larger system of clerical life; this accounts for the quick shift of focus from transgressing individuals to a blanket condemnation of homosexual clergy. Social historians such as Michel Foucault and R. I. Moore show how ecclesiastical authority developed and was sustained via a mechanism of sexual surveillance (Foucault, 1978; Moore, 1987). Church historians concur. For example, in *Sex, Priests, and Power: Anatomy of a Crisis*, Richard Sipe (1995) writes that in the "celibate/sexual" axis of Catholic authority, "[p]ower was consolidated in sexual terms."[13] The docility and self-distrust that resulted from this constant scrutiny—whether in its medieval-Catholic or post-Reformation Protestant variants—had two principal components. First, a rhetoric of sin, anchored to sex and aligned with gender, was aimed at the laity. In practice sexual abstinence was implicitly encouraged for all, priest as well as laity (indeed, in some instances, abstinence was even de facto legislated for married persons); however, not until the twelfth century at the Lateran Councils was celibacy mandated for clergy. Second, the primary agent of this mechanism was the priest, although his own position, vis-à-vis the rules he enforced, was seriously compromised by a conflict of interest. That is, although he shared with the laity an injunction against sexual activity, his place as "confessor" gave him dramatic power over the sexual intimacies of others. Thus, what amounted to a priest's almost complete power over the laity's internal, as well as external, lives, sharply contrasted with the priest's near total lack of agency over the daily conditions—emotional or material—of his own.

The realization, however, that priests also do not "buy" the sexual ideology they are to enforce—particularly requirements for celibacy—is an "open secret" as old as Chaucer. Garry Wills cites Cardinal Seper, speaking to a 1971 synod of bishops and expressing doubt about the observance of celibacy among priests (2002, p. 186). Addressing the contradictory and often banal content of sexual doctrine more generally, Wills (2000) asks, "Is it any wonder, given such 'doctrine' on sex, that priests themselves do not take it seriously?" (p. 189). Indeed, historically they haven't. If continual anecdotal and written record is to be accepted, Catholic laity on the whole seem indifferent to the sexual lives of their clergy, finding numerous ways to explain the priest's girlfriend, "housekeeper," or other apparent intimate. Often, such a relation is presumed even when in fact the priest is perfectly celibate. Numerous reasons might account for this seeming indifference, although given the power imbalance between lay and priest, one in particular deserves note. Sexual surveillance can work in reverse, from bottom up, as it were. Given the laity's accustomed lack of authority over their own lives in matters of church practice and belief, the bit of leverage obtained over the priest by virtue of sexual gossip could be turned to their own advantage. Scandal, as we see, has *its* private analogue in gossip. Nonetheless, there are clear limits to the laity's indifference, and these limits are broadly ideological. Heterosexual relations are more generally acknowledged than homosexual ones, for instance. Further, the "revelation" that some priests engage in sexual activity that is statutorily illegal renders the whole subject of sex more problematic than ever.[14]

The mercurial, white-hot attention of scandal fixates, in its accustomed prurient way, on sexual narrative rather than upon ideology. Scapegoating the lustful, sick, or perverse priest means that his guilt, expiation, and eventual expulsion from the social scene can be managed by means of narrative patterns familiar to detective and horror thrillers. Such a conflation makes for interesting reading (i.e., familiar to patterns of audience reception), but it leaves untouched a system of governance that finds inventive ways to remain hidden. For this reason Amnesty International addresses the structured authority by which violence is produced in hierarchical systems of authority. Similarly, the rigid structures of obedience in which priests live must be called to account, partly at least, for their behavior. Richard Sipe (1995) appropriately writes, "we must recognize that forces and systems beyond psychopathology influence and maintain this sad condition" (p. 23).

Scandal, however, rarely is interested in much beyond psychopathology. Pathologizing monsters in public dramas burden individuals with faults that sometimes should be located elsewhere. Naming and locating the monster sets into play mechanisms that distract attention from systems which can never be questioned. For example, child-killing mothers such as Susan Smith or Andrea Yates must be excoriated at full public pitch, while the sentimental pieties of motherhood—as well as the financial and gendered inequalities that sustain the role—remain sacrosanct. Similarly, it is more dramatic to target vow-breaking priests than to address the system of internal preferment by which these priests learn the codes of power, abuse, and secrecy by which they act. This disconnect, in part, explains the Gothic nature of public melodramas; they can be dramatic, overblown, even vicious, to the degree that few changes can occur in the mundane realities they breathlessly expose.

Finally, it is important to emphasize that staking the sexual priest during the past fifteen years has not been univocal in its politics or its motives. From the perspective of those "outside" of Catholic ideology, the priest stands in *for* the system itself, and so can be a convenient whipping boy. From within, disaffected Catholics—who may harbor residual guilt about "falling away"—now have an excuse, however lame, to justify their action. Similarly, the belated efforts by church authorities—more than a few homosexual themselves—to blame the homosexual priest and to expel "notorious" priests are, I think, disingenuous. On the surface, these actions seem contrite; however, the contrary is the case. The elderly priests expelled (sometimes for actions decades old), often with no legal or economic recourse, function as sacrificial tokens. Their bodies are offered to appease passions and commercial desires that are in any case a standard feature of sexual narrative. More important, however, their excision from the Body Ecclesial protects their more powerful superiors who are thereby kept from admitting legal culpability or resolution. Consider, for a moment, what would happen if just one of these expelled priests would speak up, either to tell his side of the story or to take legal counteraction. As noted earlier, narrative is a complex form, woven of many different threads, among which factuality is only one. The monster narrative is a particularly dense rendering of the logic, and in Gothic formularies of outrage, the monster cannot have voice lest the intended effects of such inflated rhetoric be lost. From the point of view of the hierarchy, any priest accused of inappropriate action dare not be brought into court of law, for fear of what he (or they) might say. (One priest, who was about to be dismissed in 1989, threatened to do exactly this if he were released from ministry; he was later quietly transferred.) The summary evacuation of priests—some on the slimmest of grounds and with very little legal care—is less an effort to reform the system than a besieged effort to preserve it *intacta*. Bad faith follows upon bad faith; deviant sex (again) is merely another pragmatic way of deflecting responsibility from a system of interlocking preferment and reprisal.

Stigmatizing of priests distracts attention from what a critic writing for Amnesty International terms "the crimes of obedience"— structures by which institutionally vulnerable persons (priests, for example, among others) find themselves trapped into behavior involving illegality, duplicity, and, sometimes, outright pain. Although Amnesty International addresses military and governmental systems, parallels exist with ecclesiastical and other corporate structures. For example, a priest might well be guilty of wrongdoing in many of the cases currently in the news. One can argue, however, that in some respects the priest is like the hapless Anderson employee who is caught up in the Enron chain of duplicity. (It is also probable that the cleric cover-up case, following as it did upon a similar Enron case, provided a reservoir of untapped social energy which exploited the succeeding scandal [Dionne, 2002].[15]) The parallel is exact. In each case the subordinate's body expiates corporate fault while the institution itself is released from legal compensation. Such behavior is not new, of course; the Nazis who ran the death camps of Germany kept their hands clean by having Jewish *Sonderkommandos* enforce camp procedures and carry out genocidal laws on their fellows. Although status and power were, at least temporarily, the reward for their compliance, few, if any, *Sonderkommandos* survived either to explain or to defend their actions. Death was the final reward for their silence and complicity. Here, too, the old priest, dismissed out of hand, finds his historical analogue.

CALLED TO ORDERS

Priests who violate their vows do exist. Nonetheless, the fright narrative of the pedophile priest—with its adaptation of nineteenth-century, Gothic villains and sentimental set pieces, spiced with 1930s scare talk about roving sex predators—does not materially address the problem (Sonenschein, 1998b). Priests who "act out" immoderate power in the context of intimate relations are, I argue, produced by the system, not an exception to it. Weak priests, disordered priests, libidinous priests: using conventional Gothic logic to drive a panic repudiation conceals the various internal means of coercion—psychological, institutional, and financial—by which a veneer of pastorality covers and excuses a rigidly hierarchical system. The mechanics of this system, and the sexual ideology upon which it is based, are thereby kept unquestioned. In other words, even at the best of times, Father's "pastorality" is only one aspect of an administrative position that, historically, is disciplinary rather than pastoral. The complexities of that role must be considered next.

Systems, unchecked, overtake the best intentions of those who create them; conversely, systems hide the distortions they create. Such a dynamic of governance sets in play the current scandal. Sexual regulation ("the celibate-sexual system" [Sipe, 1995, p. 4]) is, perhaps by historical accident, central to the institutionalization of Catholic faith. An institutional structure that is, as Philip Jenkins (1996) sums up, "[s]ecretive, byzantine, bureaucratic, patriarchal" (p. 106) reproduces secrecy, scrutiny, and surveillance as its public face. Consequently, a rhetoric of the soul and an inner life of truth gives way to a mocking parody, a slavish external conformity. The cult of obedience—both its trial and its reward—symptomatically produces priests who "act out" in a variety of related ways. Stories of sexual encounter and misuse of power are shocking, all the more so because they are deemed unusual, atypical, out of the norm. On the other hand, even the most casual churchgoer (here not limited to Catholics) has anecdotal evidence of clerical behavior—violent and tyrannical action, drunken inappropriateness and displays—that might be called emotional or spiritual, or surely doctrinal, abuse.

The clamor over unprofessional clerical sexual behavior now being announced worldwide must be considered as only one aspect of a more fundamental crisis of intimacies. The priest assumes power in a gender-driven system of preferment. In order to keep it, the priest must, in effect, pass on the inequalities by which he himself is held in place. Sipe (1995) argues, "Maintenance of the SYSTEM develops, fosters, and protects sexual abuse and violence" (p. 4). What are the mechanics of this authority? What are the consequences of an economy that rewards institutional submissiveness with an astonishing array of social power, symbolic as well as actual? A surprising and perhaps uncomfortable moment of recognition occurs when, reading about hierarchy cover-up or clerical misbehavior, one finds violence tacitly talked around that in any other context would be roundly condemned. Anecdotal reports of clerical interaction closely resemble the interaction of torturer and victim. Indeed, sometimes the language used and the action described by Amnesty International are identical to reports of priests and persons to whom they "minister."

Ecclesiastical governance has implicit parallels with its military counterpart, and sometimes—in title, rank, and function, for example—there are areas of explicit overlap. Both rely upon a strict obedience that hinges as much upon a desire for approval as it does from exterior sanction. Over time, such a complex entanglement will produce a structural immobility—a compulsion toward bureaucratic timidity or doctrinal conformity. Both systems produce "rank-and-file" functionaries who can be so eager to do well by superiors that by gradual degrees they can become agents of explicit harm. Both structures subsume personal intimacy to the formal requirements of obedience, yet to the contrary the systems also *require* intimacy in order to function. That is, in each, for its effectiveness authority depends upon the disjunction and inequality of the persons involved. Writing about the dynamics of torture in *The Body in Pain,* Elaine Scarry (1985) argues that "[the prisoner's] pain will be perverted into the fraudulent assertion of power"(p. 45).[16] Although many might recoil at the comparison, a similar dynamic is at work in the pastoral encounter. It is not so much the case that pastoring is *perverted* into power; rather, pastorality is the face of power presented by the system. Demonstrating power *over* someone else is, ironically speaking, the only "power" the priest has. That itself is the distorting problem.

It is curious that scholarship on human rights and torture takes little account of places where extrajudicial violence of the sort outlined here is often found. The United Nations, for example, frames human security as a secular right and issue; from this point of view, the agency of religious bodies in the infringement of "rights" is never considered (Gaete, 1999). That religions have been the victim of institutionalized repression and violence in every age is no surprise to mainstream liberality. What is surprising—and deeply offensive to the liberal mind—is that religious systems themselves are often deeply implicated in violence and extrajudicial coercion, in and among their members. For example, a mode of governance that has been compared to the Taliban's spiritual totalitarianism exists within contemporary Roman Catholicism.[17] The effects of such a fundamentalism of authority are profound, whether one considers those subject to it—the laity—or those bound to it in authority—the priest. Each, in different ways, is distorted by its demands.[18]

Let me consider these points for a moment. It is clear that most priests, including myself, would never see themselves as state agents of pain. That on occasion we make pastoral decisions that cause discomfort—even, sometimes, actual pain—is not, we think, torture. Nor, we argue, do we ever make such decisions for the sake of extorting confessions or coercing individuals against their will, or otherwise obtaining information that can be used against these persons. We are merely policing the doctrine that it is our "job" to enforce. Even at this basic level, then, any ministerial encounter must negotiate not only the personal needs of the counselee but the web of institutional constraint as well. Within this system the priest also has "needs," although these are rarely articulated as such. Nonetheless, any pastoral agent—priest or other "local" authority—finds himself coerced in subtle but precise ways to make decisions that will exclude, cause pain, discriminate, and even ultimately demean persons. Failure to follow the rules and to make such decisions will leave the agent himself vulnerable to reprisal. The violence I am addressing rarely gets to the point of *physical* contact. Mostly hidden, covered by convention and a rhetoric of regret and necessity, such violence can be excused as ideological—that is, required as a matter of faith or morals. The priest may regret that such and such person or persons are demeaned by being refused the sacraments or other goods of the church. These or other possibly worse actions are taken "for their own good"—and besides, the action is not unjust, etc., but in keeping with tradition, local custom, etc. The action and its violence are explained away, made to seem normative and unexceptional in the daily practice of religion. To borrow from Hannah Arendt, when violence is present, authority is already lost. When a priest must show his power as part of a pastoral encounter, already the exchange is a murky one, despite whatever rhetoric of moral uplift, doctrinal disciplining, or moral rehabilitation might cover such a display.

I pose a question and suggest a scene that might seem preposterous and, indeed, unthinkable to sentimental piety. What are the conditions in church governance in which behaviors are produced that significantly resemble the torture forbidden by 1984 UN decree? Why are such behaviors sanctioned? L. Nicole (1987) argues that "[t]orture is often hidden behind the conditions inherent to war and security operations. . . ." (p. 319).[19] Although it might be jarring to think about the church in these terms, there are ancient parallels, and alliances, between ecclesiastical structures, rhetoric and usage, and their military equivalents. If the priest is the "Miles Christi"—the soldier of

Christ—there are far-reaching consequences to the structural rigidity and the pervasive patterns of enforced silence he must face. This violence is done, first of all, to the priest, who finds himself entangled in a web of denial and self-interest that cannot be publicly enunciated, except at risk of his livelihood. Even the honorific circumlocution—"vocation"—has material consequence; it removes the priest from consideration as an "employee" to whom certain legal or financial justice would apply.[20] Honor, here, robs him of financial equity. This and other sorts of impoverishment are passed on to the "counselee"—who, from a different perspective, is also entangled in a web of doubleness, also trapped within inhumane abstractions.

The average cleric (or layperson in authority) who attempts to make sense of his (or her) participation in this cycle has limited recourse. Groundbreaking work by Stanley Milgram (1974) investigated the ways by which average, "good" people came to terms with their participation in distress-causing actions; strategic denial, evasion, even outright duplicity were common responses.[21] Distressingly, violence begets further violence; its effects are inevitably passed on, whether in observable misbehavior or, more covertly, in the gradual weakening of the priest's moral compass. Milgram concluded his research on a pessimistic note: "A substantial proportion of people do what they are told to do, irrespective of the content of the act and without limitations of conscience, so long as they perceive that the command comes from a legitimate authority" (1974, p. 189). Milgram's pioneering work has been replicated and confirmed in the study of torture as a legitimized tool of statecraft. A growing consensus exists that torturers are not born, but made: "where abuse is made legitimate, a certain proportion of people can become violent and destructive toward others" (Milgram, 1974, p. 189). How does one make a torturer? "The potential torturers among us" are many, de Zulueta (1996, p. 88) writes. "[Reenactment of past traumatic experiences] is also recognized as a major cause of violent behavior" (p. 93).

Similar analysis could be conducted within ecclesiastical structures, where in like manner responsibility for pain-causing actions is disguised by its commonness or explained away as done in "obedience." In the first instance, violence of speech or draconian action is, as the apology goes, not "personally" intended. Rather, it is the result of regrettable but necessary managerial decisions—doctrinal procedure and sacramental gatekeeping, who can or cannot receive communion, baptism, who may or may not be married, etc. At other times, however, pain and distress are dispensed overtly as ideological correctives, in order to change behavior. Such coercion is explained as an enforcement of doctrinal purity—who can or cannot hold meetings on church ground, who can or cannot speak, who can or cannot be married publicly, etc. It is never the priest's fault. Either way, responsibility for distress, if locatable at all, begins to look very much like the mechanism for torture forbidden by international law. Even underscoring that the distress is emotional or spiritual, and not exactly the torture described by the UN, such distress is, as Robert Goss (1993) writes, only "more sophisticated forms of violence" (p. 8). In the current Roman revival, the expression "confession of faith," and the various disciplinary efforts underway to enforce doctrinal orthodoxy upon prelate, clergy, and laity, can result in a confession very different from private piety. Under these conditions pastoral intimacies can become intimacies of a terrible kind.

The social status enjoyed by the priesthood and the rhetorical buttressing sustaining it ("vocation," for example, rather than "employee") would seem to place the priest far distant from the abject torturer denounced by Amnesty International—even though the systems that produce, on the one hand, the desensitization to pain required to make a torturer, and, on the other, the "crimes of obedience" that ensure its production, are similar. The priest, we say, is nothing at all like the person described in Amnesty International's "Reports on Torture Worldwide"—persons who inflict pain, routinely, for a living, upon those in their charge. To the contrary, as the media has been tirelessly announcing in recent months, quite often priests are these kinds of persons. Arguably there is truth to media claims. The National Conference of Catholic Bishops meeting in Dallas in June 2002 to address the problem of child-abusing clerics began with an extraordinary session in which victims of priests denounced the priests and then laid the responsibility for the offending actions upon the bishops themselves.

There are other situations, of course, of which we have anecdotal as well as official record, where priests inflict severe pain and suffering—mental, spiritual, and occasionally physical. Indeed, what limited research exists shows that institutionally and personally priests are subject to the compulsions that are known to produce torturers: they are unusually dependent upon authority; for a variety of reasons many lack self-esteem and as a result can be obsessively obedient. De Zulueta (1996) writes, "[F]or the insecure person whose self-esteem is low, the other can often be experienced in terms of a dehumanized object that can be used to bolster up his fragile self" (p. 94). To use an analogy that is not far-fetched, like captive persons who depend upon the good will of their tormentors, priests aim at all costs to please. They must. That is a major part of their *job* under obedience. Thus, although it is easy to make media fodder of them as lusty, weak, or sick, these are not *anomalies* in an otherwise sexless, strong, and psychologically whole clergy. To the contrary, they are more-or-less perfect products of a managerial system in which obedience is a cult and through which self-abnegation is rewarded by the mystique of honor and status.

Used often and without precision, "abuse" can lose its meaning. In daily exchange, the word sometimes refers to direct acts of physical violence. However, the word rightly refers to a broad spectrum of inappropriate actions that can characterize clerical behavior. For instance, we hear the stories of the priest who is insulting and demeaning in the confessional; the priest who is an emotional or intellectual bully; the priest whose interrogational style reduces candidates for baptism, reconciliation, or marriage to tears. All of these are forms of spiritual abuse. All of these inept pastoral encounters reflect a complex renegotiation of power. Indeed, emotionally or spiritually abusive priests are probably more common than sexually abusing ones; nonetheless, one wonders why intolerable behavior in rectory, office, confessional, or the pulpit is not recognized for what it is. With regard to the priest, I want to argue, along the lines of the feminist Susan Brownmiller, that priests who victimize their charges (in specifically sexual ways) do so less for reasons of sexual gratification than for reasons more complicated altogether (Brownmiller, 1975). Caught in a loop of emotional violence and tyranny themselves, some priests can only continue it. Abuse in the confessional, in meeting, in pastoral association, in wedding planning, in counseling—these surely differ in degree and rhetorical power (as well as criminality) from sexual abuse. Nonetheless, I would argue that all such actions present a seamless chain of authoritarian power, a statistically inevitable consequence of the emotional, intellectual, spiritual, sometimes sexual coercion enacted upon the priest himself. That is, the cognitive dissonance and personal exploitation experienced by priests, the explicit silencing of most areas of their lives, will, in turn, be passed on to those who approach them in ministry. Intimate encounters, in the confessional, in the counseling room, in the moment of vulnerability, become the vehicle, like sex, through which power, or in this case, lack of it, expresses itself.

Diminished expectations begin quite early. In my first year in the seminary, for instance, the novices were given tasks that the superior termed a "dry stick opus," the dry stick work. This was a metaphor for some apparently senseless task, such as watering a dry stick. No matter how idiotic the novice might consider the task, obedience required, indeed, compelled, unquestioned allegiance. Once, I was asked by a superior to transfer five communion hosts from one chapel to another. I went and found five hosts already in place, and so went about my business. The superior later called me in and asked why I hadn't done as he required. I explained that "it had already been done." The superior replied that it was not my responsibility to interpret or to evaluate; I had failed my vow of obedience. As a punishment he demanded that I repeat, multiple times, and with differing inflections each time, "Ingebretsen is a weak novice." Obedience was not only held up as a moral obligation; as in this case, my obedience was delivered and confirmed by simple intimidation of a pious novice. The session, though a minor example, filled me with shame and confusion. I later realized I had been set up to experience exactly such abjection, and I still recall it, and others of greater moment, with anger. Such stories, in small and large ways, characterize the process called, tellingly enough, "formation."

The priesthood no longer enjoys the social influence it once did, which brought with it a quasi-formal authority, even in secular life. Lack of vocations is usually what prompts this discussion. Arguably the diminishment of priestly religious authority results from more than one cause. One, however, is obvious, and that is simple gender panic. Bishop D'Arcy's warning against the ordination of "homosexuals and extremely effeminate men" is precisely to the point; pastoring has somehow become detached from power. Put another way, the pastor's dress (frock?) is showing and his authority—explicitly gendered even by title—is thereby frayed. What seems at first to be an unlikely comparison is historically exact, since the church's "hold" on priests is not dissimilar from marriage's "hold" on women. Both are systems dependent upon and driven by gender. The vows taken by clergy are clear parallels to marriage vows; someone else directs a priest's sexuality, money, and, under certain conditions, even covers his legal responsibility. Indeed, the gendered economy of marriage and a similarly gendered church mechanism manages its persons in similar ways. In church and in marriage, feudal economics and simple low-grade financial blackmail keep persons (priests and wives) subject who rarely are trained to do anything for which they might be employed, were they to cease being a priest or married.

Amnesty International repeatedly notes the conditions under which otherwise "good" persons become, over time, desensitized to their own pain and who have, as a consequence, fewer inhibitions about passing it on to others. Social reward, and its promise, is crucial to this process. At the same time the *socializing* environment is equally important: how, for example, individuals are daily manipulated away from their own pain; how they can be isolated from it by structure of life and rhetorical deflection; how crimes of obedience can produce, and justify, other crimes; finally, the social capital that rewards a person who manages the arduous task of being properly "formed." The inflated social authority still accorded to the priest in many places partly explains why some can seem power hungry, or at least power drunk. Nor is it accidental that many of the reports of abusive clerical behavior are decades old, when substantial social power was simply accorded the priest as his due. What can one conclude? Any such "vocation" where honor and status are the chief awards, offered in place of economic security, exploits both agent and laity. Other contradictions trouble the role: it is an authority with no center, whose functioning demands an intimacy with no equality. It is bureaucratic in the widest sense of the word, and its clerics are clerks in the worst sense of that word. Even under the best of conditions, they find themselves chained and blinkered. Powerless over the external conditions of their lives, they are likewise forced to dissemble their deepest selves. In some instances (even some is too many), the material, economic, and emotional powerlessness experienced by priests triggers exploitation, in which an assortment of casual and persistent personal diminishments are passed on to weaker persons with whom they have contact. Too often, as in patriarchy more generally, the recipients of the violence are women and children—ironically, the people who are most likely to be found in church. Sadly, then, the present crisis of intimate relations in the Catholic clergy, although not limited to that denomination, demonstrates the long-term consequences of the conflict of interest that is inherently part of ministry. Those who are powerless in their own lives are in no position to adjudicate the powerlessness of others. The sad conclusion may be that few priests, already working from a position of diminished agency, can ably or responsibly care for others.

NOTES

1. Even if the rite is distantly related to church practice, its use has civic and political consequences. In *Scandal: The Culture of Mistrust in American Politics* (1991), Suzanne Garment explores some of the ways that the practice of scandal, in the United States, made possible a political genre in which ritual cadence, repetition, and a habit of thinking by narrative eclipsed the actual facts.

2. The recent flurry of denouncements against gay clergy is, as Jordan (1997) makes evident, not a new idea either. Jordan cites Peter Damian's eleventh-century *Liber Gomorrhianus* that they (to be fair, like monks who were "experienced" with a woman) should "be deposed from ecclesiastical office" (p. 58).

3. David Sonenschein (1998b, p. 29), for example, refers to the "pedophila *of* popular culture"; Susan Bordo (1998) argues a similar point. In the film *American Beauty,* for instance, the lead actor's intense interest in the underage cheerleader goes unnoticed and therefore unstigmatized, as Sonenschein remarks in another context, probably for reasons of the pervasive way in which youth is (and youths are) eroticized in American culture.

4. The parallel moral fantasy crisis repeatedly enacted around "family values" can be brought into focus by reading the statistics for child victimization. According to the National Clearinghouse on Child Abuse and Neglect Information <http://nccanch.acf.hhs.gov>:

> Almost two-thirds of child victims (63 percent) suffered neglect (including medical neglect); 19 percent were physically abused; 10 percent were sexually abused; and 8 percent were psychologically maltreated. . . . More than 80 percent of victims (84 percent) were abused by a parent or parents. Mothers acting alone were responsible for 47 percent of neglect victims and 32 percent of physical abuse victims. Nonrelatives, fathers acting alone, and other relatives were responsible for 29 percent, 22 percent, and 19 percent, respectively, of sexual abuse victims.

For a sobering examination of the statistically frequent physical violence that is normative in the United States, see Felicity de Zulueta, "The Torturers" (1986).

5. The metaphors and images, chronological framing, forms, and genres of narrative are central to the way narrative *makes* meaning. This is, to sum up, my first point. The ideological burden of narrative is the way it makes possible a seamless movement from the constructed text to presumption of veracity. In short, telling (or hearing) is meaning.

6. According to Jon Meacham (2002, p. 39), "Across all faiths, the most common story is of the clergy's seducing female parishioners. There is at least one support group for such women."

7. Geoghan was repeatedly transferred from parish to parish for three decades; he was transferred from Massachusetts, New York, and finally to California, and his past was never brought up at any of the transfers (Ferdinand, 2002).

8. " 'This does not imply a final judgment on people with homosexuality,' added Dr. Navarro-Valls, a Spanish layman who is a psychiatrist by training. 'But you cannot be in this field' " (Henneberger, 2002).

9. To refer to my earlier point, media scandals organize themselves upon the principle that nothing is more demonstrably "true" than sexual narrative; in its exhaustive variations and repetitions it makes up what I call the daily dose of approved social titillation available to a moralistic culture, who, banning certain kinds of "real" pornography as morally bankrupt, can nonetheless indulge themselves in sex-saturated narratives ranging from documentary to ads (see Roof, 1996; Plummer, 1995).

10. Undressed in public, scrutinized by an intensely politicized moral gaze, the social closet inhabited by the homosexual often enough disguises other sorts of "looks." For example, although it was less easy to make scapegoats of homosexuals in the late 1970s than it had been in the 1950s, the homosexual nonetheless provided an area of some political consensus. In order to do so, however, and to facilitate its use in scenes of civil trauma, public homosexuality had to be anchored by association with other fear triggers, notably, child sex and multiple murder. Accordingly, Americans witnessed a vociferous campaign decrying homosexuals as sexual predators and condemning homosexuality, linked with AIDS, as a kind of serial killing. Jenkins (1996) argues that the serial killing cycle of representation in the mid-1980s was a sideways attempt to implicate homosexuality and to discredit it politically.

11. According to Meacham (2002), a narrow majority oppose the legalization of same-sex marriage.

12. In summation, then, anchoring the public morality play, either civil or ecclesiastical, homosexuality can be used by liberals and conservatives. Over the past two decades, from either direction along the political spectrum, the homosexual provided a convenient focus for ecclesiastical and civil discontent. To the liberal, the spiritually deprived, voiceless homosexual person in the pews epitomizes all that is wrong with the totalitarian, homophobic, and homosocial world of the institutional church. On the other hand, to the conservative traditionalist the homosexual—especially as portrayed in a media "lifestyle"—dramatizes all that is wrong with the secular, immoral world and the collapse of "traditional values."

13. Sipe's (1990) twenty-five-year study of celibacy, sexuality, and the clergy estimates that at any given time 50 percent of priests, irrespective of orientation, are sexually active (Meacham, 2002).

14. The media consistently collapses ephebophelia into pedophilia, which is, clinically, very different. Neither of these can be statistically linked to homosexual orientation, although the discussion too easily subsumes gender deviance within its purview. Philip Jenkins (1996) shows that statistically ministers of other faiths are equally represented. He explained that the

clergy of most major denominations were to some extent tainted by [Catholic clergy sex abuse cases] of the late 1980s. The most-quoted survey of sexual problems among Protestant clergy states that some 10 percent are involved in sexual misconduct of some kind, and "about two or three percent" are pedophiles, a rate equal or higher than that suggested for Catholic priests. (p. 50)

15. Dionne (2002) surveys a widespread distrust with public institutions, including "corporate executives, brokerage firms, pharmaceutical companies, [and] the oil industry" (p. A19).

16. Mark Jordan makes an interesting point in *Silence of Sodom* (2000):

Sodomy was and homosexuality is important in Catholic moral theology because it has been intimately connected to the exercise of power in the construction of priestly lives. It was one of the sites where moral regulation could be exercised purely, with a minimum of resistance. In this inner realm of churchly power, regulation could be exercised for regulation's sake. (p. 82)

17. The United Nations defines torture in very specific terms:

For the purposes of this Convention, the term "torture" means any act by which severe pain or suffering, whether physical or mental, is intentionally inflicted on a person for such purposes as obtaining from him or a third person information or a confession, punishing him for an act he or a third person has committed or is suspected of having committed, or intimidating or coercing him or a third person, or for any reason based on discrimination of any kind, when such pain or suffering is inflicted by or at the instigation of or with the consent or acquiescence of a public official or other person acting in an official capacity. (Article 1, *UN Convention Against Torture,* 1984)

18. See Dr. David Brown, psychologist assisting in the vetting process for the diocese of Altoona-Johnstown, remarking about Michael Rose's *Goodbye, Good Men*: "These people are pathologically homophobic, and the goal of local conservative Catholics is to have the bishop terminate my work. . . . They are the local Catholic Taliban" (Evans, 2002).

19. A recent poll reported in *The Washington Post* found most Catholics to be "loyal" to the church but saw it in a moment of crisis (Cooperman, 2002). The surprising thing, of course, about polls like this (others note similar responses) is that few seem to notice that the church has been operating in crisis mode since at least the late 1970s. In the last quarter of the twentieth century what has been called the "Roman Restoration" attempted to staunch the trauma caused to settled belief and patterns of church practice by the Vatican II "open window" (and, indeed, by two reasonably short-lived pontificates). One consequence of this panic mode was a distillation of management styles that have always been present, if less obviously so. That is, pressure for "confessional" purity produces behaviors and activities within lines of authority that not only mimic torture; indeed, I argue that these actions *intend* effects—submission, "confession," obedience—that are the standard excuses offered for the justification of torture.

20. During medieval times the church was popularly referred to as the "Church Militant"; under this governing metaphor the priest, by extension, is the "Miles

Christi," the soldier of Christ. More generally, however, even the laity can be sub-sumed under this rubric; witness the popular evangelical hymn "Onward Christian Soldiers." At a different register, and confirming the persuasive power of these ver-nacular expressions, many religious orders are organized according to a hierarchy that is explicitly military; "ranking" authority is titled "general" or "superior gen-eral" or "father general" (or, in the case of women, Superior General or Mother Gen-eral). More directly, ordination to ecclesiastical office within a wide range of Chris-tian confessional practice is technically considered "Holy Orders."

21. See "Expelling Errant Priests" (2002, p. B6): "Canon law states that depart-ing members do not have a right to any support or assets."

REFERENCES

Berry, Jason (1992). *Lead us not into temptation: Catholic priests and the sexual abuse of childen.* New York: Doubleday.

Bordo, Susan (1998). True obsessions: Being unfaithful to "Lolita." *Chronicle of Higher Education,* July 24, pp. B7-B8.

Brownmiller, Susan (1975). *Against our will.* London: Secker and Warburg.

Bull, Chris and Gallagher, John (1996). *Perfect enemies: The religious right, the gay movement, and the politics of the 1990s.* New York: Crown Publishers, Inc.

Burkett, Elinor and Bruni, Frank (1993). *A gospel of shame: Children, sexual abuse, and the Catholic Church.* New York: HarperCollins.

Cassels, Peter (2002). Hundreds protest NY priest's anti-gay remarks from pulpit. *Bay Windows,* May 2.

Chomsky, Noam (1989). *Necessary illusions: Thought control in democratic soci-eties.* Boston: South End Press.

Cohen, Daniel A. (1993). *Pillars of salt, monuments of grace: New England crime literature and the origins of American popular culture, 1674-1860.* New York: Oxford University Press.

Cooperman, Alan (2002). For Catholics, crisis of trust allayed by faith; View of hi-erarchy dimmed, but many back local clergy. *The Washington Post,* March 17, p. A1.

Cooperman, Alan and Sun, Lena H. (2002). Hundreds of priests removed since '60s; Survey shows scope wider than disclosed. *The Washington Post,* June 9, p. A1.

D'Arcy, Bishop John M. (2002). Discerning unfit candidates for priesthood. *The Fort Wayne News-Sentinel,* April 12.

de Zulueta, Felicity (1996). The torturers. In Duncan Forrest (Ed.), *A glimpse of hell: Reports on torture worldwide* (pp. 87-103). New York: New York Univer-sity Press.

Dionne, E.J., Jr. (2002). In Dallas, a first step. *The Washington Post,* June 19, p. A19.

Evans, Susan (2002). Diocese too liberal, book says. Johnstown (PA) *Tribune Dem-ocrat,* May 5.

Expelling errant priests (2002). *The Washington Post,* June 23, p. B6.

Ferdinand, Pamela (2002). Suit says archdiocese knew of priest's abuse, parishes not told, lawyer alleges. *The Washington Post,* April 9, p. A1.

Fishman, Mark (1980). *Manufacturing the news.* Austin: University of Texas Press.

Foucault, Michel (1978). *The history of sexuality,* Robert Hurley (trans.) New York: Pantheon Books.

Gaete, Rolando (1999). Rites of passage into the global village. In Eve Darian-Smith and Peter Fiztpatrick (Eds.), *Laws of the postcolonial* (pp. 233-245). Ann Arbor: University of Michigan Press.

Garment, Suzanne (1991). *Scandal: The culture of mistrust in American politics.* New York: Times Books.

Goss, Robert (1993). *Jesus acted up: A gay and lesbian manifesto.* San Francisco: Harper.

Greeley, Andrew M. (1981). *The cardinal sins.* New York: Warner Books.

Greeley, Andrew M. (1993). *Fall from grace.* New York: Putnam Books.

Halttunen, Karen (1998). *Murder most foul: The killer and the American gothic imagination.* Cambridge, MA: Harvard University Press.

Henneberger, Melinda (2002). Vatican weighs reaction to accusations of molesting by clergy. *The New York Times,* March 3.

Herman, Didi (1997). *The anti-gay agenda: Orthodox vision and the Christian right.* Chicago: The University of Chicago Press.

Hughes, Candice (2000). Pope denounces gay pride parade. *AP Online,* July 7.

Hunt, Lynn Avery (Ed.) (1993). *The invention of pornography: Obscenity and the origins of modernity, 1500-1880.* New York: Zone Books.

Ingebretsen, Edward J. (1999). "One of the guys" or "one of the gals"?: Gender confusion and the problem of authority in the Roman clergy. *Theology and Sexuality* 10(March): 71-87.

Jenkins, Philip (1996). *Pedophiles and priests: Anatomy of a contemporary crisis.* New York: Oxford University Press.

Jordan, Mark D. (1997). *The invention of sodomy in Christian theology.* Chicago: The University of Chicago Press.

Jordan, Mark D. (2000). *The silence of Sodom: Homosexuality in modern Catholicism.* Chicago: The University of Chicago Press.

Lule, Jack (2001). *Daily news, eternal stories: The mythological role of journalism.* New York: The Guilford Press.

Lull, James and Hinerman, Stephen (1997). The search for scandal. In James Lull and Stephen Hinerman (Eds.), *Media scandals: Morality and desire in the popular culture marketplace* (pp. 1-33). New York: Columbia University Press.

Manoff, Robert Karl and Schudson, Michael (Eds.) (1986). *Reading the news: A Pantheon guide to popular culture.* New York: Random House.

McCullough, Colleen (1977). *The thorn birds.* New York: Aron Books.

Meacham, Jon (2002). A case for change. *Newsweek,* May 6, p. 23.

Milgram, Stanley (1974). *Obedience to authority: An experimental view.* New York: Harper and Row.

Moore, R.I. (1987). *The formation of a persecuting society: Power and deviance in Western Europe, 950-1250.* Oxford, UK: Blackwell.

Neale, Stephen (1989). Genre and narrative. In Bob Ashley (Ed.), *The study of popular fiction: A source book* (pp. 87-91). Philadelphia: University of Pennsylvania Press.

Neuman, W. Russell, Just, Marion R., and Crigler, Ann N. (Eds.) (1992). *Common knowledge: News and the construction of political meaning.* Chicago: The University of Chicago Press.

Nicole, L. (1987). Torture: The need for a dialogue with its victims and its perpetrators. *Journal of Peace Research,* 24(3): 319.

Plummer, Ken (1995). *Telling sexual stories: Power, change, and social worlds.* New York: Routledge.

Ratzinger, Cardinal Joseph (Congregation of Defense of Faith) (1986). Letter to the bishops of the Catholic church on the pastoral care of homosexual persons. In Jeannine Gramick and Pat Furey (Eds.) (1988), *The Vatican and homosexuality: Reactions to the "Letter to the bishops of the Catholic church on the pastoral care of homosexual persons"* (pp. 1-10). New York: Crossroad.

Roof, Judith (1996). *Come as you are: Sexuality and narrative.* New York: Columbia University Press.

Rosin, Hannah (2002). In Wichita parish, priest and family ponder trust. *The Washington Post,* June 14, p. A14.

Rush, Florence ([1957] 1980). *The best-kept secret: Sexual abuse of children.* Englewood Cliffs, NJ: Prentice-Hall.

Sage, Victor (1988). *Horror fiction in the Protestant tradition.* London: Macmillan.

Scarry, Elaine (1985). *The body in pain: The making and unmaking of the world.* New York: Oxford University Press.

Sipe, Richard (1990). *A secret world: Sexuality and the search for celibacy.* New York: Brunner/Mazel.

Sipe, Richard (1995). *Sex, priests, and power: Anatomy of a crisis.* New York: Brunner/Mazel.

Smith, Rhonda (2002). Bishop to keep gay, "effeminate" men from priesthood. *The Washington Blade,* 33(16) (April 19): 24.

Sonenschein, David (1998a). *Pedophiles on parade,* Volume 1, *The monster in the media.* San Antonio, TX: Author.

Sonenschein, David (1998b). *Pedophiles on parade,* Volume 2, *The popular imagery of moral hysteria.* San Antonio, TX: Author.

Spacks, Patricia Ann Meyers (1985). *Gossip.* New York: A.A. Knopf.

Time limit concern in priest cases (2002). *Gazette.Net,* March 9. Available at <http://www.gazettenet.com/03092002/News/12289.htm>.

Weeks, Jeffrey (1985). *Sexuality and its discontents.* London: Routledge and Kegan Paul.

Whittington, Lewis (2002). Holy gay purge. *Philadelphia Citypaper.net,* May 2. Available at <http://citypaper.net/articles/2002-05-02/slant.shtml>.

Wills, Gary (2000). *Papal sin: Structure of Deceit.* New York: Doubleday.

PART IV:
A RESPONSE
FROM MARK JORDAN

Chapter 16

After *Silence*

Mark D. Jordan

Silence of Sodom (Jordan, 2000) was written as a faulty prologue. It carried the hope that its questions would be rephrased and then replaced by more expert and more varied voices. You have been listening to some of those voices here. *Silence* spoke about a few of the ways denied male desire instructs Catholic power. This book raises the next round of questions—about the place left for female desire (if any is); about money, activism, journalism; about our relation to other Christian communities; about the future. I want to join in asking the improved questions, but first I notice that we talk about them in public circumstances that have also changed, though not improved.

The fate of every book is prefigured by its publication date. *Silence of Sodom* was published three months after Donald Cozzens's *Changing Face of the Priesthood* (2000) and in the same week as Garry Wills's *Papal Sin* (2000). Early on my book was grouped with these others in a trio of reforming tracts. I was flattered but also worried that the neat trio would mislead readers about differences among us. Cozzens wrote as a seminary insider about a range of challenges to the Catholic priesthood. Homosexuality was for him only one of the challenges and not the most prominent. Speaking as a straight-identified man, Cozzens approached clerical homosexuality from outside, "carefully and respectfully," as a challenge posed by a group of Others. The same is true of Wills, who analyzed the growing percentage of gay men in the priesthood and the current exegesis of biblical passages about "homosexuality" under his general claim that lying is the besetting sin of the modern papal system. By contrast, *Silence* addressed male-male desire as its central topic and from within that group of Others. I did suggest that the systems of silence built around male-male desire were decisive in maintaining all clerical power, as I dreamed of thinking around those systems into a more articulate and freer Catholic queerness. Still, I hardly imagined myself to be providing a survey of the troubles of the Catholic priesthood, much less a sweeping diagnosis of churchly ills. So while I was gratified to be grouped with Cozzens and Wills, I assumed that their more comprehensive books would rightly eclipse *Silence* in public conversation.

Yet books have their fates. Sometimes the fate is a news story. When *Silence* first appeared, journalistic reviews were published here and there, with opposed judgments by the *Los Angeles Times* and the Web site of the self-proclaimed "Catholic League." (An author more clever than I could have written *Silence* just from material posted on the League's Web site.) Still, the book was turned down for review more often than not. A publicist reported that editors found it "too hard." How could I disagree? The book was indeed "hard." Its argument twisted back and forth as it wriggled past the machines for enforcing churchly silence. Then, too, its range of reference was idiosyncratic. I had given myself the pleasure of citing unusual Catholic authors in order to make a point about voices excluded by the parochialism of official theology. I also wanted to share deviant joys in Catholic reading, to construct a counter-canon of shockingly Catholic texts. So the reader finds, right alongside the Congregation for the Doctrine of the Faith, such unlikely religious authorities as the archaesthete J. K. Huysmans, the Nietzschean fabulist Pierre Klossowski, and Chicago's gay detective novelist Mark Zubro. Hardly the sort of stuff to fly off the shelves in supermarket checkout lanes. In fact, I felt a little guilty for abusing my publisher's trust and resolved to do what I could to sell out the small first printing, as if I were the main agent of this particular fate.

Early in January 2002, the *Boston Globe* (2002) began to report its investigations into Cardinal Law's handling of priests accused or convicted of sexually abusing minors. To be frank, I couldn't see much that was new in them or in the trial of John Geoghan. Well-publicized U.S. cases stretch back to 1985, and since then there has been a steady flow of the painful exposés. So where was the news? Or, rather, so much for my sense of what makes news. The *Globe* stories became *the* story, and the story took over nightly television specials, panels of talking heads, and the covers of every major weekly. The story also revived my "hard" book. "I've had your book on my desk for a long

time, but I could never get around to it," one religion reporter said.
"Now it's required reading!" Or, rather, it's a book one wished one
had already read, since there was no time for reading now. On a TV
show, I was asked, "Do you feel vindicated by the scandal?" I answered with an emphatic "No!" I had written a book about the silence
of clerical sexuality, not a book about pedophilia (as Lebacqz in
Chapter 13 rightly emphasizes before showing us where to find
them). More important, how could anyone feel vindicated by this sor-
did spectacle?

The "pedophilia scandal" or "Catholic crisis" is news because it
became news. What changed in the spring of 2002 were not the acts
of abuse and cover-up but their status as open secrets. In some sense,
we had already heard them. If I didn't know the details of events
around Boston, I still knew the story. I suspect that the same is true for
most writers in this collection. If you live in or near Catholic institutions in America and you pay any attention, you learn soon enough
much more than you want to know about sexual abuse by clerics—
and not just of boys (as Tolbert insists in Chapter 10). So the surprise
in 2002 was not that there were sexually abusive priests or that their
superiors covered for them but that the mainstream press screamed
about it loudly enough that the Catholic hierarchy finally had to
respond out loud.

The open secret became the news, but an open secret in the news
can still keep its secrets. The shrillness both of press coverage and official response has made it harder for us to talk seriously about clerical sexuality. The more sensationalist coverage and the bureaucratic
spluttering in response are what I call "hysterical" speech, speech designed to prevent discussion. The scandal is, indeed, from the bureaucracy's point of view, just another occasion for wheeling out the silence machines. Broadcast journalists collude unwittingly when they
distort or exhaust any language that we might use to talk about clerical desires. We talk about the topics of *Silence* in changed circumstances. In particular, our appeals to our own experiences are now in-
stantly scripted as the testimony of "victim" or "abuser," "protester"
or "defender."

To say that it is harder to talk seriously than it was even three years
ago is not to suggest that we stop trying. We need rather to talk more
cunningly, with sharp ears for the ways in which our speaking can be
distorted by media coverage or official gesticulations. "I send you

forth as sheep into the middle of wolves; so be as cunning as snakes and as innocent as doves" (Matthew 10:16). We cannot wait for broadcasters to discover nuance or curial officers to acquire habits of truth. Most important, we cannot wait on the arrival of a pristine church. I cannot imagine what social and economic changes would be required for the churchly machines of silence to be throttled back, much less shut down. Glenn (Chapter 14) imagines a "new Luther" nailing up "ninety-five theses of gender and sexual justice on the doors of all the cathedrals." A heartening image, but we have done so much nailing in the past forty years—and without any backing from the German princes. We Catholics have already lived through one failed reform, which had the backing of a pope and many powerful bishops, not to speak of brilliant theologians. I mean, of course, Vatican II. What then would a successful reform take? Not another council, which is likely to produce at the moment just the opposite of what we want. With a stacked episcopacy and growing curial claims to infallibility and direct supervision, any council during the next few decades is liable to be something stranger and more damaging even than Vatican I.

We cannot wait for the silence machines to be turned off before we talk. We have to learn to talk around them—which means both improvising ways of speech that resist them and getting out of reach of the police powers that run them. The preceding chapters have shown ways for doing both. Let me explore a few more. I begin from personal claims of identity, then move through academic theology to end with preaching and prayer. The sequence is an attempt to connect the stammering of personal queerness with the proclamation of Christian faith.

SPEAKING IDENTITIES

Friends and enemies alike have noted that *Silence of Sodom* is a personal book. Angry and sad, some say. Angry and bitter, complain others. The Catholic League called it "a primer of anti-Catholicism," while *First Things* found it more convenient to smear me in an anonymous note than to report any of the book's contents.

The book *is* personal, of course. If it is reticent about most of its author's experiences, it is, of course, thoroughly autobiographical. The book tries to understand why the child of liberal Unitarians, as yet unbaptized, intent on becoming a priest, though he had hardly met any outside of books—why he talked his way into an adult retreat while still a young adolescent. How did he discover in the churches of the Mexican highlands a religion of unashamed male beauty, of shared festival, of redeemed physical suffering? What role did he seek in it for himself? *Silence* tries to think through something of my own conversion without discussing it directly. It describes both the operation of grace through queer desire and the absorption, the betrayal of that desire into the speeches and dispositions of church bureaucracy. *Silence* generalizes from the personal testimony many of us feel the need to write or speak—a testimony of old loves that couldn't be spoken, of old pains that haunt what we say now.

Here is a more particular testimony. When I was thirteen, my mother moved into a house not far from the Basilica of Our Lady of Zapopan in central Mexico. Next door, there was a seminary for a missionary order of men. The high walls of the seminary contained what seemed to me a charmed and safe world: a garden where young men studied, practiced music, laughed over meals, and performed a liturgy alternately solemn and buoyant. One "brother" befriended me after he stopped by to ask my mother for a donation. He wore an old-style cassock with a long rosary tied at his waist. Some months later, when I was already a regular visitor to the seminary, he and some of his friends dressed me up in his cassock. Then, as my mother was about to move us from that house, he gave me the rosary from around his waist. I still keep it on my prayer bench.

Writing that paragraph, I am aware how it can be deliberately misrepresented as a way to explain or silence anything else I might try to say. So let me make clear that "nothing happened" between that seminarian and myself. Or everything happened, but it required no genital contact. My abbreviated memory is not a story of sexual abuse, broken vows, or even sins of the flesh, and yet I learned from it so much of what I needed to know about the space made for male-male desire within Catholic clerical institutions. Boisvert (Chapter 1) speaks of his boyhood devotion to Dominic Savio and the need to understand that devotion as part of a "subversively queer Catholic hagiography." I add only that our saints live sometimes just over the wall, right next door.

At thirteen, I learned something through my passions about the queerness of Catholicism, but I couldn't learn everything. Only later, for example, did I understand how my passions were solicited and then mortified by church bureaucracies. Queer passions are inflamed and then pounded out into a long submission, an "obedience" to abusive forms of male authority. Many readers have considered the most scandalous pages of *Silence* my description of clerical camp, especially in the Eucharistic liturgy. I thought that the most scandalous pages were the description of a certain sort of "orthodoxy" or "fidelity" as erotically deformed masochism, as the chronic suffocation of the capacity to take pleasure in anything but petty autocracy (Ingebretsen, Chapter 15, "the collusion of power, pain, and abjection"; Kelly, Chapter 11, "indulged child" as "petty autocrat"). Roman authority depends on homoerotic passions that have been pushed down so long that they begin to crave abusive hypocrisy, and so I quoted *The Leatherman's Handbook* as a reliable guide to certain features of "conservative Catholicism." I didn't mean to denigrate joyful play between men that mocks standardized forms of male power. I did want to say that adolescent crushes become something much uglier, much more damaging, when they are flattened by a system that trumpets "celibate" submission of men to men.

I was drawn to Catholicism not through the parish or the parochial school, but through religious orders. Indeed, I moved on from that high-walled missionary house to friaries, Jesuit retreat houses, and— as a kind of culmination—the Trappist Abbey of Gethsemani, a smudged paperback of *Seven-Story Mountain* in my pack. My desire to be baptized Catholic was indistinguishable from my powerful attraction to the religious life. So I was drawn to the Roman Church as much through my sexual orientation as through any other natural disposition. "Grace perfects nature," St. Thomas repeats. My sense of vocation to vowed life gave me my first gay identity. Whatever else grace was healing in me, it was leading me to believe that Catholicism meant the radical holiness of same-sex communities apart from "the world."

As a convert, I was of course a queer sort of Catholic in a second sense. American Catholicism often seems a federation of tribal religions, and I didn't belong to any of them. There are those who conclude that I was never really or fully Catholic; I mean, look what a heretic I've turned out to be. In fact, and predictably, my second-class citizenship within the "perfect society" of the Catholic Church once spurred me to be overly zealous in the pursuit of Catholic correctness.

Now I think that it may also have opened a saving gap in my embrace of any Catholic identity. Because Catholicism was not my tribal religion, because it was not bound up for me with family history or original social identity, I came to it as something different from my first self. I am always able to remember myself apart from my Catholicism. Through the gap of memory I can notice the ambiguities or "liminality" in the gift of my queer/Catholic identity (Johnson, Chapter 5, on Anglican identity). I can glimpse some of the double binds in which both my original queerness and my original Catholicism were designed to catch me. Because, of course, the gift of queer/Catholic identity was ambiguous in just the way the male-male desire is ambiguous within Catholic clerical institutions. Passion must be reconfigured as obedience. The identity is publicly silenced before it is ever assigned: "You can be queer with us, but you must also be silent with us. Here, slip into this cloak. Put on these delicate manacles."

Being a queer convert is hardly the only way to open gaps in the identities that are handed out within Catholicism. To be a gay priest in a stridently homophobic, feverishly homoerotic church creates deep fractures within (Mellott, Chapter 2, on "doubling"; Goss, Chapter 7, on "[fe]masculinity"). For Catholic women, and even more for Catholic lesbians, the contradictions in their multiply silenced and yet indispensable "place" may provide more than enough room for questioning and rebellion. Indeed, I suspect that the coherent performance of any contemporary Catholic gender—which is to say, of any Catholic identity, because each is gendered—is simply impossible. Every performance, done long enough and watched well enough, will generate enlightening contradictions.

To talk of Catholicism and queerness as performed identities might seem to contradict both divine election and psychological reality. I am not saying that I chose Catholicism or homoerotic orientation. I hope that my becoming Catholic was an acceptance of the divine gift of Christian faith, and I believe that my desire for men lies much deeper in me than my choosing reaches (Cartier, Chapter 8, on the ambiguities of choice with regard to identity). Still, the ways I have to articulate or perform being Catholic and being queer are not merely grace or psychological fate. If I didn't simply choose a queer/Catholic identity, the identity I ended up with was both personally and socially tailored. It's like a language: I didn't invent English and can't quite think apart from some reference to it as my mother language, but the English I "compose" here is in my voice. In the same way, I can—I should—distinguish between my call through Catholicism to God and the Catholic identity I have been given to perform. I should also distinguish my erotic configuration from the identity I have as an American gay man of a certain race, class, and age.

Basic lessons in queer theory. I rehearse them only to be able to say that I have come to be grateful for the very double binds built into the queer/Catholic identity I received in adolescence. I am grateful for the tensions and silences because they have made it impossible for me to mistake either present Catholicism or contemporary gayness for "the truth" about myself. This can be doubled with a more positive motive for gratitude: Putting on queer Catholicism as a teenager, I put on a tense identity that linked my erotic desire both with artistic or intellectual life and with the pursuit of holiness. If the built-in tensions propelled me to seek further, they never failed to remind me that what I was seeking was some complex sacrament of self, art, learning, and God.

Identities, whether religious or erotic, give us characters to play and scripts to speak. They also tell us who not to be and what not to say. Queer Catholic identities are rich enough, tense enough, to incite us to question the character and contradict the script. When they do not drive us to despair. One reason we keep telling our queer Catholic lives is to provide one another with antidotes to despair—even if the telling also supplies media sensations or official hypocrisies.

SPEAKING THEOLOGY

Most of us writing in this volume have been trained for shorter or longer times in Catholic theology. Our efforts to speak ourselves come out not only in narratives or reflections on identity but also in attempts to articulate a more adequate theology—which is, necessarily, a theology more responsive to the truths that God discloses in our queer lives. These efforts are part of the astonishing development of lesbian and gay Christian theologies in the past fifty years. Particular works by Catholics or former Catholics have been milestones in that larger development; think of the influence of Mary Daly, John McNeill, or John Boswell. Conversely, almost every work of queer Catholic theology depends on the scholarship or conceptual energy of Protestant and Anglican writings. (Queer theology is delightfully and reflexively ecumenical.) Still, it can be important to remember what distinguishes lesbian and gay theology done by Catholics from that done by other Christians.

The usual way is to begin with the distinctive sources and methods of Catholic theology. I think we would do better to look at the distinctive institutional conditions under which most Catholic theology is practiced. The institutional setting of Catholic theology gives a special but thoroughly distorted importance to questions of male-male sexuality, especially in the groups most obligated to study theology— I mean, the clergy. More important, Catholic theology in the past hundred years has more often than not been practiced under tight surveillance. Catholic theologians have been obliged to reproduce an increasingly detailed set of results and to do so with the approved apparatus. They could experiment only while watching out for the church police. Many of the most important works of twentieth-century Catholic theology were first "published" to a locked desk drawer or in private circulation among friends. To say this differently, the most exciting contemporary works on method in Catholic theology should be read as utopian fiction. They describe a method that Catholic theologians *could* follow if they were able to think in peace.

It cannot be a surprise then that the most important works of queer Catholic theology have been done by those on the margins of Catholic institutions—by priests and religious who had been dismissed or soon would be, by lay people who were not dependent on official approval for their publications or their pensions. Writers on the margins have called many times for a liberated practice of theology that would take account of the graces given to LGBT people. Indeed, many in this volume have long been calling for new theology (and then making their own contributions to it). Perhaps we could be clearer that we expect response from the margins as well. Where now, inside Catholic institutions, can this sort of theological reconstruction take place? Where is it permitted to develop theologies that think seriously about churchly homosexuality and other fundamental questions of power?

Answers to those questions are provisional and local. Some religious communities still manage to protect their members from edicts of silence. Some Catholic schools still offer space for dissenting voices engaged in fundamental reconstruction. Some bishops have shown both prudence and humanity in implementing the new policies for granting the *mandatum,* that is, for licensing teachers of Catholic theology or religion. Still, the space for serious Catholic theology on the inside is shrinking. Many American Catholic theologians stay on in Catholic institutions only by virtue of the civil system of tenure. But tenured faculty resign or retire, and new appointments are made more carefully—that is, more cautiously.

The best Catholic thinking about sexuality and church power is likely to be found during the next decades outside officially Catholic institutions. The Catholic mind is in diaspora and has been for some time. The exodus from religious orders and the diocesan priesthood that began in the 1960s (to go no further back) was also an intellectual exodus, a pilgrimage into new institutions, Catholic and non-Catholic. The pilgrimage continues. It will so long as the central church bureaucracies abuse Catholic tradition. There is no more powerful enemy of the Catholic intellectual inheritance than the Vatican offices. The effective centralization of church power since the nineteenth century really does threaten to erase the very idea of tradition, whether in theology, liturgy, the sacraments, or ecclesiology. It is trite to say that no intellectual tradition can flourish without internal debate, especially about its inheritance and its self-conception. Still, it is worth saying again that the latest controls on public dissent are prohibitions against taking our own tradition seriously. A tradition is not an inert object that you own in order to manipulate. It is a practice that you take up with thoughtful care, a set of templates that you complete by improvised enactment. Having a tradition is not a fact but a daily deed.

Bureaucracies can't tolerate the ambiguities of living tradition. So they reduce it to property, or rather to a sort of cake icing useful for decorating current policies with venerable legitimacy. The flourishing of Catholic tradition is thus coming to depend on non-Catholic institutions, or, rather, on Catholic institutions reconceived as precisely those institutions in which Catholic tradition can be kept alive. This will require as well a new imagination of what the Catholic church is. If theology is for the church (and it is), then our theology must situate itself toward a different kind of church—a Catholic church in diaspora because its central structures have succumbed to the temptations of policed silence. Is this scattering really new? The assembly of Jesus the Messiah has always been in diaspora. Diaspora is the original and final form of the church, the mark of its burning desire for an eschaton.

Many of us face such basic questions about church membership because we are both "homosexuals" and "heretics." The two go together, and not just because heretics are always accused of sexual deviance. When you refuse official Catholic condemnations of same-sex love, you are also and of course rejecting a pronouncement of the (self-styled) Magisterium. You further threaten the silence around the homoerotic constructions of clerical power. Since church officials have chosen to stake contemporary Catholicism entirely on clerical authority, questions about Catholic identity are interchangeably questions about the core authority. Assertions of queer/Catholic identity are doubly threatening, are explosive paradoxes.

One of the official complaints against Jeannine Gramick and Robert Nugent during the summer of 1999 was that they were causing confusion among the faithful. The charge was patently untrue in the sense it was intended, given how loyal the two had been in setting forth official teaching. Perhaps it was true according to the deeper bureaucratic logic of identity control. It does confuse the policing of Catholic identity to have holy ministries that respect unsilenced homosexuals. It contradicts the basic conceit of that police power.

SPEAKING THE GOSPEL

A question not often addressed in queer Catholic narratives or theologies is the simple question: Where and with whom do I celebrate the sacraments and listen to the proclamation of the Gospel? Who is my community of prayer?

The mass remains for me the supreme event of exclusion and loss. It is the event at which my loves and relations are not named—or else named to be condemned. There are parishes where lesbian and gay couples are welcomed as members more or less explicitly, but their distinctive lives will figure in the words of the liturgy only rarely and incidentally. No matter how tacitly homoerotic the setting, costume, and celebrants of a mass, queer people will be lucky to be named in the intercessory prayers—and then as Others. We are not allowed to celebrate a coming out or a nuptial mass, and we will not regularly be cited from the pulpit as examples of Christian relationship. So I find it hard to go to mass even at a parish where there are many lesbian and gay members (Ingebretsen, Chapter 3, on the leverage of sacramental access and our spiritual "anorexia"). And then I grieve my estrangement from the table of my first communion.

I grieve as well the loss of so many vocations. To speak in human terms: For an organization desperately short of talent, the Catholic Church has been astonishingly dismissive of talent that it does attract. Among my students, I see so many holy women who are evidently called by God to be priests—and precisely not in the diminished, bureaucratic form of priesthood. I see as well deeply committed LGBT Catholics who decide, quite understandably, that they will follow Jesus into a Christian community that is ready to accept them whole as full members.

The squandering of vocations is reflected in a squandering of truths. When the pope's spokesman suggested to a reporter in March 2002 that homosexual men could not be validly ordained, he was not only refusing divine vocations, he was casting out the words we Catholics have to talk about calling and ministry (Henneberger, 2002). In his clumsy "scapegoating" (Schlager, Chapter 12), Navarro-Valls was willing to reduce sacramental theology to spiteful silliness. So too with proposed regulations that would prohibit the admission of gay men to seminaries. The regulations are offensive enough, but most of all they are spitefully silly. A ban on admitting gay men to Catholic seminaries is unenforceable, disastrously counterproductive, and theologically incoherent. It cannot be enforced both because there is no test for gayness and because any test would have to be administered by those who are already priests—many of whom are gay. So a policy against gay admissions to seminary will become an affirmative action program for more accomplished liars on both sides of the admissions table. If the policy could be enforced, it would prove disastrous. The decline in numbers of American priests is already depriving Catholic communities of full sacramental life. Taking out all the gay seminarians (and priests) would shut down the American church, which is not running so well as it is.

The policy is nonsense—outrageous, but also spitefully silly. It is spiteful silliness where serious theological teaching should be. Certain bureaucrats are using the occasion of the "pedophilia scandal" to expand the homophobic regime they have been building since the 1980s (Glenn, Chapter 14). They are willing to manipulate the words of teaching in order to advance the strategy. But shouldn't we then apply the category of spiteful silliness more broadly to official "teaching"? Aren't we obliged to do so? Catholic bureaucracies are obsessed with control to such an extent that they are losing the credibility required to preach the Gospel or administer the sacraments. Credibility is not here a journalistic buzzword. I am not using it to refer to how the pope or the American bishops fare in overnight opinion polls. When I say that bureaucratic obsession damages the Catholic church's credibility to preach and to celebrate sacraments, I mean that it makes it increasingly difficult to hear the Gospel through the church structures or to believe that the sacraments are anything more than means of extorting obedience.

Does this analysis also implicate queer Catholic theology to the extent that we allow its terms to be dictated by bureaucratic obsessions? If our only business is to criticize official pronouncements or oppressions, to narrate our griefs or recite our martyrologies, then we are not very good theologians. We should continue to use the press as deftly as Kelly (Chapter 11) or Colbert (Chapter 4) do to shame bishops and prove the need for reform, but we must ask God to do even more through us. John the evangelist is called John the Divine—that is, John the Theologian—because he could write his life with Jesus so sublimely. (I say "he" according to traditional conceptions of gospel authorship.) Queer Catholic theologians—or, rather, aspirants to that beautiful title—ought to try to write how Jesus transfigures their lives too. We may have to tell who it is that will shortly betray Jesus, but our main task is to tell what it is to live alongside the Word in flesh.

We should do this work of Catholic theology where and as we can, teaching those who want to learn from us, celebrating Eucharist with those who will receive us, exercising our calls to ministry among those who acknowledge the calls. If we are expelled from convents or cloisters, refused priestly ordination or religious vows, fired or never hired in Catholic schools, silenced in the liturgy, denied the right to meet on church property, then we go elsewhere to continue our work. Hunt reminds us that many women have already shaken the Roman dust from their sandals before moving on, and Getz (Chapter 9) sharpens the point by noting that someone as theologically astute as Mary Daly was among the first. Ingebretsen (Chapter 3) makes the same point from the other side: How can we argue that we will stay "to work for change from within" if staying robs us of the spiritual capacity for change—especially in theology.

This caution resonates with a more frightening exhortation: "You follow me, and let the dead bury their dead" (Matthew 8:22). The voice that speaks the exhortation is the voice that leads us out of the gagged silence of tombs. We take with us our baptism, the truths we receive through tradition, our memories of liturgy, our practice of sacrament, and our devotion to holiness in living flesh. Wherever we arrive, we will be within the tradition that we carry. Could this be the best "Catholic Stonewall" (Goss, Chapter 7)?

REFERENCES

Cozzens, Donald (2000). *The changing face of the priesthood: A reflection on the priest's crisis of soul.* Collegeville, MN: Liturgical Press.

Henneberger, Melinda (2002). Vatican weighs reaction to accusations of molesting by clergy. *The New York Times,* March 3.

Investigative Staff of the *Boston Globe* (2002). *Betrayal: The crisis in the Catholic Church.* Boston: Little, Brown.

Wills, Garry (2000). *Papal sin: Structures of deceit.* New York: Doubleday.

Index

Order a copy of this book with this form or online at:
http://www.haworthpress.com/store/product.asp?sku=5331

GAY CATHOLIC PRIESTS AND CLERICAL SEXUAL MISCONDUCT
Breaking the Silence

_____ in hardbound at $39.95 (ISBN-10: 1-56023-536-5)

_____ in softbound at $24.95 (ISBN-10: 1-56023-537-3)

Or order online and use special offer code HEC25 in the shopping cart.

COST OF BOOKS_____

POSTAGE & HANDLING_____
(US: $4.00 for first book & $1.50 for each additional book)
(Outside US: $5.00 for first book & $2.00 for each additional book)

SUBTOTAL_____

IN CANADA: ADD 7% GST_____

STATE TAX_____
(NJ, NY, OH, MN, CA, IL, IN, PA, & SD residents, add appropriate local sales tax)

FINAL TOTAL_____
(If paying in Canadian funds, convert using the current exchange rate, UNESCO coupons welcome)

☐ **BILL ME LATER:** (Bill-me option is good on US/Canada/Mexico orders only; not good to jobbers, wholesalers, or subscription agencies.)

☐ Check here if billing address is different from shipping address and attach purchase order and billing address information.

Signature_____

☐ **PAYMENT ENCLOSED: $**_____

☐ **PLEASE CHARGE TO MY CREDIT CARD.**

☐ Visa ☐ MasterCard ☐ AmEx ☐ Discover
☐ Diner's Club ☐ Eurocard ☐ JCB

Account # _____

Exp. Date_____

Signature_____

Prices in US dollars and subject to change without notice.

NAME_____

INSTITUTION_____

ADDRESS_____

CITY_____

STATE/ZIP_____

COUNTRY_____ COUNTY (NY residents only)_____

TEL_____ FAX_____

E-MAIL_____

May we use your e-mail address for confirmations and other types of information? ☐ Yes ☐ No
We appreciate receiving your e-mail address and fax number. Haworth would like to e-mail or fax special discount offers to you, as a preferred customer. **We will never share, rent, or exchange your e-mail address or fax number.** We regard such actions as an invasion of your privacy.

Order From Your Local Bookstore or Directly From
The Haworth Press, Inc.
10 Alice Street, Binghamton, New York 13904-1580 • USA
TELEPHONE: 1-800-HAWORTH (1-800-429-6784) / Outside US/Canada: (607) 722-5857
FAX: 1-800-895-0582 / Outside US/Canada: (607) 771-0012
E-mail to: orders@haworthpress.com

For orders outside US and Canada, you may wish to order through your local
sales representative, distributor, or bookseller.
For information, see http://haworthpress.com/distributors

(Discounts are available for individual orders in US and Canada only, not booksellers/distributors.)

PLEASE PHOTOCOPY THIS FORM FOR YOUR PERSONAL USE.
http://www.HaworthPress.com   BOF04